# The Future of

# TERRORISM

In Memory of Iryne Muriel Kushner
1920-1989

# The Future of

# TERRORISM:

## Violence in the New Millennium

# HARVEY W. KUSHNER

### Editor

SAGE Publications
*International Educational and Professional Publisher*
Thousand Oaks   London   New Delhi

*For information:*

SAGE Publications, Inc.
2455 Teller Road
Thousand Oaks, California 91320
E-mail: order@sagepub.com

SAGE Publications Ltd.
6 Bonhill Street
London EC2A 4PU
United Kingdom

SAGE Publications India Pvt. Ltd.
M-32 Market
Greater Kailash I
New Delhi 110 048 India

Printed in the United States of America

*Library of Congress Cataloging-in-Publication Data*

Main entry under title:

The future of terrorism: Violence in the new millenium/
  Harvey W. Kushner, editor
      p.  cm.
    Includes bibliographical references and index.
    ISBN 0-7619-0868-4 (cloth: alk. paper).—ISBN 0-7619-0869-2 (pbk.: alk. paper)
    1. Terrorism—United States—Forecasting.  2. Twenty-first century—
Forecasts.  I. Kushner, Harvey W.
    HV6432.F87  1998                                                        97-21184
    363.3'2'0973—dc21

98  99  00  01  02  03  04  10  9  8  7  6  5  4  3  2

| | |
|---|---|
| *Acquiring Editor:* | C. Terry Hendrix |
| *Editorial Assistant:* | Dale Mary Grenfell |
| *Production Editor:* | Michele Lingre |
| *Production Assistant:* | Karen Wiley |
| *Typesetter:* | Marion Warren |
| *Indexer:* | Molly Hall |
| *Cover Designer:* | Candice Harman |
| *Print Buyer:* | Anna Chin |

# Contents

# Preface

Nowadays, a considerable number of books devoted to terrorism spend an inordinate amount of time discussing how difficult it is to define the concept. Guess what? Readers are usually left more confused than before they started. The authors who contributed to this book did not become bogged down in a morass of verbiage in trying to craft the universal definition of terrorism. They chose instead to discuss terrorism without detailed discussions about the problem with the problem definition.

In addition, Herculean efforts at formulating definitions, as well as mumbling about freedom fighters and terrorists, betray an insensitivity to the consequences of terrorism. Committing random violence, killing innocent people, and creating a frightful atmosphere are the actions of criminals, not freedom fighters. Was George Washington really a terrorist? Is Yasir Arafat really a freedom fighter? I leave the formulation of answers to these questions to all those capable of cutting the Gordian knot. For those interested in exploring the potential for terrorism in America, I invite you to consider the contents of these never-before-published chapters.

# Acknowledgments

My sincerest appreciation goes to all the authors who took time out from their busy schedules to participate in this project. Each in his own way helped make the editing of this book enjoyable, as did Bernadine Siuda of Kroll Associates and Laura Jaffa and Tamar Tesler of the Middle East Forum's Investigative Project on Religious Extremism. Particular thanks to my good friend, research associate, and media partner, Brian Levin. His ideas, comments, and suggestions on terrorism and extremism were very helpful. Moorhead Kennedy, Tom Mijares, Dave Perkins, and Doug Kash also deserve credit for their sustained interest in this project. Tom Oberle's friendship, along with his unwavering commitment to fighting terrorism, is appreciated. The late Kenneth Hollister Straus's generosity, as well as his extraordinary interest in stopping terrorism, is forever with me. Ken's support and encouragement contributed to my research and, in turn, to this book.

My graduate research assistant at Long Island University, Lisa Sherrin Margolin, helped research all those obscure facts about some terrorist group or individual that merited verification. Her efforts are truly appreciated. My secretary, Marylouise Radano, could be counted on to get it done; I am amazed at her uncanny ability to find the proverbial needle in the haystack. C. Terry Hendrix, my acquisitions editor at Sage, deserves my thanks for making all this happen. In addition, special thanks to my copy editor, Linda Poderski, for her valuable guidance, especially for being a second set of eyes. Others at Sage, especially Dale Mary Grenfell and Michèle Lingre, were also ready to lend a helping hand and make things happen. Finally, I thank my spouse, Sara, and my daughter, Merry Hope, who with encouragement and love made this work possible. And thanks to our two feline companions, Patches and Candy, for agreeing to stay off the computer keyboard long enough for me to make my deadlines.

# PART 1
---

# THE THREAT
# FROM OUTSIDE

The bombing of the World Trade Center should not have surprised anyone paying attention to international events, says Harvey W. Kushner. In Chapter 1, "The New Terrorism," Kushner discusses the events that made it possible for a new breed of foreign terrorists to bomb the World Trade Center on February 26, 1993. According to Kushner, the new breed of foreign terrorists is potentially more potent than the state-sponsored terrorists who targeted Americans prior to the toppling of the shah of Iran and the collapse of the Soviet Union. The new terrorists are harder to combat as well. In the past, Kushner says, it was easy to contain terrorists who organized themselves into corporate-type organizations with discernible power structures. The new terrorists, he warns, are much harder to infiltrate because they are fluid and not organized in any systematic way.

In Chapter 2, "Armed Prophets and Extremists: Islamic Fundamentalism," Robert J. Kelly discusses why Islamic fundamentalism, which Kushner identifies as the major component of the new terrorism, constitutes a terrorist threat to the United States. It is because the armed prophets and extremists view the United States as the custodian of Western values. With prominence and leadership, Kelly reasons, comes the inevitable price of hatred. For this author, however, the future is not all that bleak if the United States rethinks its commitments.

Rounding out Part 1, on the threat from outside, is Chapter 3, Steven Emerson's "Terrorism in America: The Threat of Militant Islamic Fundamentalism." Emerson documents how militant Islamic leaders have duped the media into thinking they were human rights activists of sorts. According to Emerson, these leaders have used the United States as a safe haven to carry out activities they would be prohibited from carrying out in their homelands. Currently, these Islamic leaders are torn, writes Emerson, between two conflicting emotions: (a) the need to keep the United States safe to organize a *jihad*, a holy war, and (b) the need to carry out a jihad against the United States. Emerson concludes that terrorism is likely to occur within the United States whenever the rage of the fundamentalists exceeds self-restraint.

# 1

# The New Terrorism

## HARVEY W. KUSHNER

On Friday, February 26, 1993, at 12:18 p.m., a massive explosion occurred in the garage area beneath the Vista Hotel, located at the World Trade Center complex in New York City. By the afternoon of the next day, it had become clear to law enforcement officials that the explosion was the result of a bomb, rather than an accident such as a gas leak. Until this despicable act of cowardliness took the lives of six innocent people and injured nearly 1,000 others, textbooks devoted to the study of terrorism downplayed the possibility of international terrorism coming to the United States.

In *Perspectives on Terrorism,* Harold Vetter and Gary Perlstein (1991) argue that the continental United States should remain relatively "free from much of the violence that seems to be endemic to other parts of the world" (p. 50). Jonathan White (1991) agrees; terrorism, writes White in *Terrorism: An Introduction,* "is something that happens in other places" (p. 163).

Clearly, these textbook writers of the early 1990s missed predicting that international terrorism would strike right here inside the United States. Should these academicians have been reading tea leaves? Journalists like Steven Emerson (Emerson & Dell Sesto, 1991) and Jeff Kamen (Kupperman & Kamen, 1989) were not; they were busy documenting the terrorist threat to the United States. So, too, were many of the documents published by the U.S. Department of State (1992, 1993, 1994) and the FBI's Terrorist Research and Analytical Center (1995). Because the study of terrorism involves the study of changing global politics and violence, most scholars believe that journalists, government bureaucrats, and law enforcement officials have trouble being objective, albeit scientific, about their observations. Are academicians immune from doing the same? Clearly, they are not. Actually, textbook writers like Vetter, Perlstein, and White should have followed the lead of investigative reporters like Emerson and Kamen, as well as the writings of the U.S. Department of State and the FBI, and paid closer attention to some political and social occurrences that spelled trouble for the United States. Now, we look at all those events that made it possible for a new breed of foreign terrorist to bomb the World Trade Center and plot to bomb other landmarks in New York City.

## Out With the Old

### The Soviet Union and Terrorism

In the 1960s and 1970s, many Middle Eastern terrorist groups sent their followers to the Soviet Union for training in low-intensity warfare, which is a rather benign-sounding name for terrorism. Actually, the Soviets viewed terrorism as compatible with their efforts to support wars of national liberation even though they knew that violence against civilian populations was inconsistent with traditional Marxist-Leninist thinking on class struggle. The Soviets hoped that Palestinian terrorism against Israel would enhance their position within the Arab world and erode that of Israel's staunchest supporter, the United States.

Patrice Lumumba University in Moscow was where Palestinians would go to learn terrorist tactics. Their curriculum included liberal doses of Marxist ideology interspersed with demonstrations on how to handle Kalashnikov assault rifles and make bombs. Some of the more promising students were recruited for more elaborate training by the Russian secret police, the KGB.

Lumumba graduates would often return home to assume leadership roles in many of the Palestinian terrorist groups that sponsored their stay at the university. Some learned their lessons so well that they opened their own terror academies. Soon, organizations as diverse as the Irish Republican Army (IRA), the Red Army Faction (RAF), and the Basque Nation and Freedom (Euskadi Ta Askatasuna [ETA]) had members enrolled in these upstart terrorist schools.

For nearly a decade, Soviet-trained and -supported terrorism operated without impunity in the Middle East and, to a lesser extent, in Europe. The Soviets, as Roberta Goren (1984) notes, viewed terrorism as "indirect aggression" and a useful instrument of political subversion. According to Goren, the Soviet Union was quick to support terrorist activities that could systematically "undermine a society with the ultimate goal of causing the collapse of law and order and the loss of confidence in the state" (p. 14). Terrorism, write Ray Cline and Yonah Alexander in *Terrorism: The Soviet Connection* (1984), was simply another way to aid the Soviets in their efforts to destabilize the West.

As events in the Middle East or Europe would threaten to affect public opinion, or worse, U.S. intervention, Soviet leaders would rein in their client terrorists. The Soviets always kept their terrorists on the proverbial "short leash." Moreover, the Soviets never granted anything without strings attached, much less unconditional support for terrorists. In fact, conditional support of the Palestinian cause created considerable resentment against the Soviets within the very Palestinian terrorist groups they aided and abetted.

Some actions of the more radical Middle Eastern terrorist groups eventually caused the Soviets to become less enthusiastic about the potential destabilizing benefits of low-intensity warfare. This especially was true whenever the Soviets were on the receiving end of a terrorist operation. The hijacking of a Soviet airplane in October 1970 even caused the Soviets to vote for the punishment of hijackers. After a Soviet diplomat was murdered in Lebanon in 1985, the Soviets had had enough and proceeded to vote, in the United Nations, for a strongly worded condemnation of terrorism. Actually, the Soviets, according to Walter Laqueur (1987), always opposed terrorist hijackings and attacks against diplomats. By the late 1970s, Soviet sponsorship of terrorism had lessened, but these Middle Eastern terrorist groups had a life of their own. The evil genie that was terrorism was out of the bottle, and there was no getting it back inside.

Nearly three decades after the Soviet Union trained its first batch of Palestinian terrorists, it began to sense its own vulnerability to terrorism. In 1989, under the watch of Mikhail Gorbachev, the Soviets, in what Galia Golan (1990) called a major shift in policy, began to implement a counterterrorism policy. By the next decade, the former Soviet Union and the United States actually took steps toward resolving terrorist issues with the formation of a joint task force to prevent international terrorism. Still, until its collapse, a somewhat less enthusiastic, notwithstanding more vulnerable, Soviet Union played the "terrorist" card and made money and weapons available to terrorists by way of its client states.

The collapse of the Soviet Union in 1991 finally deprived Palestinian terrorist groups of a significant source of money, weapons, and safe havens. German reunification also had an impact; it ended East Germany's role as an important supplier of money, weapons, and sanctuary for terrorists to hide after their operations. Aid from Albania, Bulgaria, Czechoslovakia, Hungary, Poland, and Rumania also dried up with the collapse of the Soviet-sponsored Warsaw Treaty of Friendship, Cooperation, and Mutual Assistance, better known as the Warsaw Pact. Even former Soviet client states Syria and Libya, which at times were independent sources of money and weaponry, refrained from overt support of terrorism. Instead, Damascus and Tripoli embarked on a series of covert actions in support of Palestinian terrorists because they could no longer get backing in any confrontation with the United States from a Soviet Bloc that no longer exists.

### The Persian Gulf War

The Persian Gulf War saw a dramatic increase in international terrorist incidents. Yet, it took only 1 year for the U.S. Department of State to record one of the largest 1-year decreases in these occurrences since the United States began keeping such records. Attributing this decline to the destruction of Iraqi terrorist networks is as problematic as trying to explain the decrease on an increase of low-level terrorist events brought about by the Gulf War itself. Those interested in pursuing the numbers game can consult the State Department's yearly publication *Patterns of Global Terrorism* for the specific years in question. Those interested in the impact of the war on the changing face of terrorism itself are asked to consider Yasir Arafat's tactical mistake of siding with Iraq before and during the Persian Gulf War in 1991.

Long before the Gulf War, Arafat, the man with the stubby face and checkerboard *kaffiyeh* who personified terrorism itself, knew he could not run his Palestine Liberation Organization (PLO) with the whimsical support of Libya's Moammar Gadhafi or the cash-and-carry conditional backing of the former Soviet Union. He set out to create alternative sources of funding that would give the PLO the stability it needed to carry on a protracted terrorist campaign. According to the British journalist James Adams (1986), a significant portion of this funding came in the form of protection money from the conservative and vulnerable oil states.

At the time of the Gulf War, PLO assets were about $2 billion, with Saudi Arabia and the other oil-rich Persian Gulf states providing a large chunk of the PLO's annual operating budget of several million dollars. Khaled Abu Toameh (1993) estimates that the Saudis alone contributed almost $86 million a year to the PLO. The Kuwaitis were said to have contributed another $50 million. Arafat's support of Saddam Hussein would shut down this extraordinary flow of oil money from Kuwait and Saudi Arabia. With the generous subsidies from the Persian Gulf sheiks and Saudi princes a thing of the past, the PLO found itself in the middle of its worst financial crisis since its inception in April 1964. PLO Chairman Arafat, some said, trusted no one but himself on financial matters, and he alone would authorize and sign checks for large expenditures. At PLO headquarters in Tunis, as well as throughout PLO offices around the world, staff salaries were reduced and lifestyles were strictly curtailed. Arafat was forced to sell off some of the PLO's valuable real estate holdings and to close down its newspapers. Just at about the time the oil money stopped flowing and Arafat himself was strapped for money, the United Nations Relief and Works Agency (UNRWA) cut much-needed financial aid to Palestinian refugees in the occupied territories. In addition, the *amwal al-sumud,* or "steadfastness funds," that Palestinians "outside" sent Palestinians living "inside" under Israeli occupation, all but dried up when Saudi Arabia and Kuwait expelled Palestinians after the Gulf War. Palestinians working in these countries would routinely have 5% of their salaries automatically deducted from their paychecks to contribute to these steadfastness funds. Rumor had it that the money that did make it to the territories was pocketed by some prominent local Palestinians. More serious than the PLO's financial woes was a political crisis made worse when oil money went to Arafat's sworn opposition in the occupied territories, the shadowy terrorist group Hamas.

### The Islamic Resistance Movement

*Hamas,* the Arabic acronym for Islamic Resistance Movement, which means "zeal," is a militant mass movement with solid support among the millions of Palestinians living in the West Bank, Gaza Strip, and East Jerusalem. Leadership is divided between those inside the territories and those operating outside, mainly in Damascus, Syria. Hamas was formed by Sheik Ahmed Yassin during the *intifada,* or uprising, against Israeli occupation of the territories in 1987 to stop stone-throwing Palestinian youths from joining the PLO. Hamas, which traces its roots to the Muslim Brotherhood founded in Egypt during the 1920s by Hassan al-Banna, fights what it sees as the secularization of Islam by spreading its virulent fundamentalist beliefs within the area's mosques. Hamas has also taken to running its own educational systems, hospitals, and other services so that the money it raises is fungible. In this way, mosques, schools, and hospitals are its weapons as much as bombs; and Arafat, as much as Israel, is its target. The goals of Hamas are to destroy the peace process, Israel, and a PLO it views as corrupted by the West.

In addition to some very real differences over Islamic values, Hamas viewed the PLO's financial investments as a liability rather than an asset in the war against the infidel. Hamas leaders saw the PLO leadership generally, and Arafat specifically, as reluctant to jeopardize their sizable fortune in support of the uprising against Israel. They accused Arafat and the PLO of running an *intifada* on a "shoestring." Some Islamic radicals even went so far as to point a finger at Arafat for going outside the faith to marry Suha Tawil. This blond, Sorbonne-educated, 28-year-old was viewed as another example of Arafat's Western ways. The fact that she converted to Islam did not matter to her Islamic detractors.

Israel, in contrast, thought that pressure from a nascent religious movement like Hamas could be a useful tool in depleting the PLO's influence in the region. Some say this is why the Israelis supported the upstart Hamas in their campaign against Arafat in the occupied territories. The Israelis quickly withdrew their support when they realized the xenophobic Hamas was beyond their control.

### The Peace Process

Despite an occasional breakaway group, the PLO has long been acknowledged as the official voice of the Palestinian people, with Arafat as its spokesman. Arafat has always been careful to surround himself in the PLO with friends from al-Fatah, the military wing of the PLO that Arafat and seven confederates founded in 1962, so that leadership changes have been minimal. In recent years, however, Arafat has lost some of his top military, intelligence, and security aides. Specifically, a joint force of Israeli commandos and agents from Mossad, Israel's intelligence service, assassinated Khalil al-Wazir (Abu Jihad), the head of the PLO terrorist operations against Israel, in Tunis in April 1988. In January 1991, the rival Abu Nidal Organization (ANO), in a campaign of inter-Palestinian fratricide stemming from Saddam Hussein's invasion of Kuwait, assassinated Arafat's deputy in charge of PLO intelligence and a key figure in al-Fatah, Salah Khalef (Abu Iyad) and Hayil Abd al-Hamid, al-Fatah's security chief. According to some estimates, several hundred moderate PLO leaders and supporters have been assassinated by order of Sadri al-Banna, better known to the world by his nom de guerre of Abu Nidal. Arafat's remaining associates openly criticized his rule for the first time in nearly 25 years, and PLO militants dropped out or turned to the fanatical Hamas.

Fifteen months after he lost his trusted deputy in charge of intelligence and security chief to ANO henchmen, Arafat suffered a serious head injury in an airplane crash in the Libyan desert in April 1992. While recovering, Arafat had time to ponder the loss of his comrades, as well as his own future. He was said to have told some close friends that the loss of his associates to assassins' bullets, coupled with his own mortality, moved him to seek peace with Israel.

Since the beginning of Arafat's historic Middle Eastern peace talks in October 1991, which marked the first time Israel and the Palestinians had attended a conference together, and the signing of the 1993 Gaza-Jericho peace accord, Palestinian terrorist groups and radical Middle Eastern governments have rattled their sabers. These "rejectionists" threaten to use any means available, including violence, to impede the peace process. The threat posed to the United States, which has taken a lead in this peace initiative, is ever present. Until now, Hamas has confined its terrorist activities to targets within Israel. There is no guarantee, however, that the United States will not be targeted in the future. In any event, or for whatever the reason behind the signing of the peace accord, Arafat and the PLO have moved away from committing violence to bring about political change. Abdel-Rahman Abdel-Raout Arafat al-Qudwa Al-Husseini, known to the world as Yasir Arafat, has begun to shed his image as the world's most recognizable terrorist. Only time will tell whether he will wear the mantle of a statesman and, in turn, earn the title of "freedom fighter." Clearly, his actions have no doubt changed the face of terrorism.

## In With the New

### Militant Islam

The new terrorism began long before Arafat's miscalculation or the collapse of the Soviet Union. It can be traced, in part, to the start of the Iranian Revolution of 1979. Almost immediately after the Ayatollah Ruhollah Khomeini toppled Mohammad Reza Pahlavi, the modern shah, Iran embarked on a systematic campaign of supporting militant Islamic fundamentalist movements throughout the Muslim world. Central to the battle was destroying the United States. For Iran, the United States was the source of all imperialism; its influence is satanic and must be destroyed.

The first regime to follow Iran's lead came nearly a decade later, when a military coup destroyed Sudan's inept democracy. The mastermind behind Sudan's Islamic counterreformation was the thin, rather ascetic looking, Sorbonne-educated Sheik Hassan Abdallah al-Turabi. The charismatic Turabi is committed to ending the bitter historic enmity that has separated Sunni and Shiite sects since the 7th century. Turabi might just move the Muslim world a bit closer toward a much-feared militant Islamic monolith.

In April 1991, Sheik Turabi took the first step toward his goal of Islamic reconciliation by hosting a 4-day meeting of Islamic politicians and intellectuals in the Sudanese capital of Khartoum. Among the participants were such notables as Gulbuddin Hekmatyar, the radical militant leader of Afghanistan's fundamentalist Hezb-i-Islami faction; Ibrahim Shukri, a chief of the Muslim Brotherhood of Egypt; Abassi Madani, then one of the two leaders of Algeria's ascendant Islamic Salvation Front (FIS); and, of course, high-ranking representatives of the Shiite Islamic Republic of Iran. Also in attendance at this star-studded event were terrorist leaders such as the notorious Dr. George Habash of the Popular Front for the Liberation of Palestine (PFLP) and Nayif Hawatmeh of the Democratic Front for the Liberation of Palestine (DFLP).

The group ultimately endorsed a six-point manifesto containing Machiavellian prescripts for advancing extremist Islamic regimes throughout the Muslim world. Read in its entirety, the manifesto's underlying message was that, in Islam's war against the West and the struggle to build Islamic states at home, the ends justify the means. This document, Judith Miller (1994) writes, represents the first time that an Islamic state defined a new world order with a strategy for achieving it. Moreover, writes Miller, the conference made progress toward Turabi's long-stated goal of overcoming the rift between Sunni Muslim states, such as Sudan, and Shiite states, such as Iran.

Few serious observers of militant Islam would argue that the Khartoum conference represented the end of animosity between Sunni and Shiite and the beginning of reconciliation between divergent Islamic sects, much less a conspiracy led by Iran and Sudan. These two Islamic states have parted ways on too many occasions, such as was the case during the gulf crisis when Khartoum refused to follow Tehran's lead in isolating Iraq and in turning against the PLO, to consider them part of some Islamic terrorist plot. Moreover, recent reports indicate a further widening since Iran has been less than generous with financial aid to Sudan for capital building projects. Iran has even made the bankrupt Sudan pay market prices for Iranian crude. Fewer still think the "Red Menace" of the Cold War era has been replaced by a monolithic "Green Peril," green being the color of Islam. Most knowledgeable observers of the Islamic world, including John Esposito (1992) and Judith Miller (1996), know that militant Islam is as diverse as the Arabs themselves and the countries in which it is taking hold. But despite their differences, Iran and Sudan are, and are likely to remain, anti-Israel, anti-West, and decidedly anti-America.

### Boot Camps for Terror

In August 1993, Sudan joined Iran on the U.S. State Department's short list of state sponsors of terrorism. "We are on the terrorist list because the United States is anti-Islamic," proclaimed an angry Turabi. What was not said is that an Iranian-trained adjunct to the Sudanese military, the quasi-military body known as the Popular Defense Forces (PDF), maintains a series of terrorist camps throughout Sudan (U.S. Department of State, 1994). Turabi claims these 30-odd terrorist training camps throughout the Sudan countryside are nothing more than a network of militia camps ("Sudan: Terrorist Haven," 1997, p. 1). The Iranians place so much importance on these PDF-run terrorist camps that their ambassador in Khartoum is the infamous Majid Kamal, known for his role in the takeover of the U.S. Embassy in Tehran and the development of the Hezbollah terrorist group in Lebanon.

Sudanese terrorist camps serve as convenient transit points, training centers, and safe havens for Iranian-backed terrorist groups such as the Palestinian Islamic Jihad (PIJ), the Lebanese Hezbollah (Party of God), the Islamic Resistance Movement (Hamas), and Egypt's al-Gama'at al-Islamiyya (Islamic Group, or IG). Potential terrorists enter these camps with an unshakable faith in militant Islamic fundamentalism. Their beliefs are reinforced by Islamic instructors who learned bomb making and other terrorist tactics while fighting alongside the *mujahideen*, freedom fighters, in Afghanistan.

When the Soviets invaded Afghanistan in 1979 to prop up an embattled communist government, thousands of young warriors of Islam from as far away as Algeria, Egypt, Saudi Arabia, and the United States answered the call to fight a *jihad*, or holy war, at the side of their Afghan brothers. Stirred on by the preachings of incendiary clerics, they streamed to Peshawar, Pakistan, for weapons training and indoctrination. The U.S. Central Intelligence Agency (CIA), eager to humble the Soviets in what turned out to be the last superpower tussle, invested billions in weaponry and training to turn these young warriors of Islam into a cadre of freedom fighters capable of driving out the Soviets. Those who survived the decade-long war helped turn Afghanistan into a veritable boot camp for terrorists. Carrying a Kalashnikov in Afghanistan is as common as wearing a watch in the United States.

In the hills near Kunduz operates one of these boot camps for the grooming of these new terrorists. Six more are in the Jalalabad region, and two more are south of the Afghan capital, Kabul (Cable News Network [CNN], 1994). Of the country's nine terrorist camps, six are run by Gulbuddin Hekmatyar's militant Islamic group Hezb-i-Islami.

Veterans of these Afghan classrooms have taken their jihad not only abroad to Sudanese terrorist camps but also to Algeria, Azerbaijan, Bangladesh, Bosnia, Burma, Egypt, India, Morocco, Pakistan, Tajikistan, Tunisia, Uzbekistan, Yemen, and the streets of New York. Remember, it was Afghanistan where Mir Aimal Kansi, indicted for the murder of two Americans in Langley, Virginia, in 1993, fled. Kansi worked for a Virginia courier company that serviced the CIA. And Kansi's hometown, Oueda, Pakistan, was a CIA command post during the Afghan War. Rumor has it that Kansi was a CIA informant during the war and now is under protection among followers of the rabidly anti-Western Hekmatyar. It was also Afghanistan where the men—Mahmud Abouhalima, Ahmad Ajaj, Nidal Ayyad, and Mohammad Salameh—convicted and sentenced to 240 years in prison in March 1994 for the bombing of the World Trade Center learned strategy and tactics and the alleged "mastermind" of the trade center bombing, Ramzi Ahmed Yousef, fought.

## A New Terrorism

The capture in 1994 of Carlos the Jackal, born Illich Ramírez Sánchez, signaled the changing of the guard. Carlos, the product of a Marxist lawyer father and socialite mother, was at one time the world's most wanted terrorist. For the Sudanese who handed him over to the

French, Carlos was a burned-out Marxist-Leninist of no use to anyone, even the most radical of states that sponsor terrorism. The capture of others like Carlos would soon follow. In 1995, German authorities extradited Johannes Weinrich, alleged accomplice of Carlos, from Yemen. Weinrich, 48, is accused of carrying out the 1983 bombing of a French cultural center in Berlin that killed 1 person and wounded 22. Also that year, Margot Christa Frohlich, 53, another alleged accomplice of the Jackal, was arrested in Italy for the 1982 terrorist attack on a Paris office of an Arabic newspaper in which two people were killed.

The new terrorists who attend these Afghan and Sudanese terror academies are not at any disadvantage. Actually, their militant Islamic instructors have more field experience than the Soviet trainers of the past. These veterans of the Afghan battlefield are experts in guerrilla warfare, antiaircraft weapons, and rocket-propelled grenades (RPGs). They are adept at firing the U.S.-made FIM92A, better known as the Stinger surface-to-air missile, supplied by the hundreds to the Afghans by the CIA in the 1980s. In 1996, one of these sophisticated CIA-supplied weapons was confiscated from the home of a former Afghan fighter in Pakistan's Balochistan province. The CIA is even reputed to be trying to buy back these Stinger antiaircraft missiles for many millions of dollars more than their initial cost. Dale Andradé (1997a, p. 3) reports that, in 1993 alone, the CIA spent an estimated $55 million on buybacks. Andradé goes on to cite a General Accounting Office (GAO) report released in 1994 that 40 Stingers out of 6,373 may have found their way onto the terrorist marketplace when they were not returned to the depot after U.S. forces came home from Operation Desert Storm.

The new students of terror come to these training academies directly from a life of poverty and repression. They are not from the same Palestinian families able to send their children to the university: Yasir Arafat (of the PLO) graduated with a civil engineering degree from King Faud University in Egypt; George Habash (of the PFLP) received a medical degree from the American University of Beirut; and Sadri al-Banna, better known as Abu Nidal, studied engineering for 2 years at the University of Cairo.

The new students of terror enter the Sudanese and Afghan terrorist camps with a strong belief in Islam as the way out of their social situation. Their militant fundamentalism is reinforced by trainers who focus on the verses of the Koran and the *Hadiths* (the sayings of the Prophet Muhammad) that form the basis of Islamic law and idealize the glory of dying for Allah. They graduate with a religious zeal that makes them more implacable foes than their graying, often flamboyant, Soviet-trained counterparts.

The new students of terror are harder to combat as well. Why? Because they are able to carry out their terror with a wide variety of readily available and less sophisticated devices. The new terrorist is adept in the use of handguns and knives and splashing lye on the bare legs of mini-skirted female tourists vacationing in the Middle East. Look for what the former FBI assistant director in charge of the New York City office during the World Trade Center investigation, James Fox, called a "witches' brew" of nitrate fertilizer and fuel oil, in addition to plastic explosives such as Semtex, developed in the former Czechoslovakia.

Less sophisticated also means less organized than their secular predecessors of the 1960s and 1970s, and consequently more difficult to spot, track, and intercept. In the past, Patrice Lumumba University in Moscow and other universities inside the Soviet Bloc were not only centers for recruiting and training terrorists but also places to ex-change terrorist rhetoric and to organize terrorist cells. These ter-rorist groups organized themselves very much like the Mafia or even like a large corporation—that is, pyramidally and linearly with a discernible descending or ascending power structure.

Knowing the structure of the terrorist group made fighting terrorism easier. Law enforcement and intelligence agencies could contain terrorist organizations such as the PLO by infiltrating them at either the top or the bottom. It is much harder for today's law enforcement agencies to infiltrate groups that are fluid and not organized in any systematic way. Xavier Raufer, France's leading terrorism expert, highlights the problem by comparing the new terrorists to the changing constellations in the universe: "At any given time, you can take a picture of the worldwide Islamic terrorist infrastructure—but two hours later, the entire constellation will ap-pear radically different" (Emerson, 1995, p. 161).

The new students of terrorism are easily inspired by their spiritual leaders. The involvement of the blind cleric Sheik Omar Abdel Rahman in a terrorist campaign of bombings and assassina-tions intended to destroy the United Nations Building and other New

York landmarks; kill hundreds, if not thousands, of people; and force the United States to abandon its support for Israel and Egypt illustrates the power a spiritual leader can have on the actions of his or her followers. So does the story, possibly apocryphal, often attributed to Sheik Rahman, of a young man seeking his spiritual leader's advice on what to do about the opening of a video rental store in Egypt. The cleric, it is said, advised the young man of two courses of action: "Either put an end to it with your own hand or know in your heart that it is evil." The young man asked, "What shall I do?" "The decision must be yours," answered the cleric. The young man blew up the video store. So much for the power of suggestion.

Inspiration may also explain, in part, the spate of suicide bombings that visited Israel in 1996. In a nine-day span, four separate suicide bombers in Israel killed 59 people, including 2 Americans. These suicide bombers may have been inspired to commit the ultimate sacrifice by the prodding of their spiritual handlers. Suicide bombers leave for their missions directly from their mosques after completing many days of chanting the relevant scriptures aloud with their spiritual handlers. A favorite verse reads: "Think not of those who are slain in Allah's way as dead. No, they live on and find sustenance in the presence of their Lord." The bombers' frenzied mantras are said to create a strong, as well as pleasurable, belief that they will soon sit with Allah. So strong is their belief that the bomber is able to walk among the enemy without exhibiting the slightest anxiety. On February 25, 1996, Israeli television reported that a suicide bomber dressed in an Israeli army uniform mingled with solders at a bus stop and hitchhiking post in coastal Ashkelon before setting off an explosion, killing himself and two Israeli soldiers. Witnesses to other bombings have told the authorities they never suspected the bomber on the bus was a suicidal terrorist on a mission.

It would be naive to think of these suicidal terrorists as merely fanatics. *Fanatic*, like *terrorist*, is a pejorative term that, according to Maxwell Taylor and Helen Ryan, "applie[s] to the state of mind of those who are wholeheartedly committed to a set of beliefs and condemned for it" (1988, p. 92). It would be equally foolish to dismiss the impact of incendiary Islamic clerics, like Sheik Rahman, on the minds of impressionable youngsters, just as it would be to categorize these suicide bombers' actions as just acts of *taqlid*, or blind following, of a spiritual leader (e.g., see Kushner, 1996). One should be aware, however, of the role that inspiration plays in helping precipitate the actions of those who would commit acts of terrorism.

Interspersed within this spate of bombings was another example of how inspiration can lead to a potentially new and more dangerous form of terrorism: *freelance terrorism*. This surfaced when an Israeli was killed after a car driven by Ahmed Hamideh crashed into a crowded north Jerusalem bus stop. Bill Hutman, writing for the *Jerusalem Post* (1996), reported that Hamideh, an Arab American visiting Israel, told his friends the night before to watch for him on television the next day. Police added that Hamideh, who had recently become fanatically religious, was not a known member of any terrorist group.

## Conclusion

Loosely affiliated groups of these new terrorists walk the streets of Islamabad, Pakistan, where Ramzi Ahmed Yousef, found guilty for plotting against U.S. airlines in East Asia in 1995 and suspected of masterminding the World Trade Center bombing, was arrested and extradited to the United States. Members of Sheik Rahman's group, al-Gama'at al-Islamiyya, congregate in the suburbs of Cairo and train in the terrorist camps in Jalalabad, Afghanistan. These new students of terror travel freely throughout the Muslim world. The World Trade Center bombing and the aborted plot to bomb other landmarks in New York City tell us that they are here with a well-documented penchant for taking care of business. So, too, does Ahmed Hamideh's act of terrorism in the streets of Jerusalem. The possibility does exist that freelancers like Hamideh may see fit to act out their hostility inside the United States.

On February 23, 1997, a 69-year-old Palestinian from the West Bank, Ali Hassan Abu Kamal, fired a semiautomatic handgun into a crowd on the Empire State Building's 86th-floor observation deck. One person was killed and six others were injured before the gunman shot himself to death. Police found a letter, handwritten in English, in the gunman's pocket; it explicitly stated that he chose New York City to attack the "den" of Zionists who had carried out the anti-Palestinian agenda of the United States, France, and Great Britain

("My Restless Aspiration," 1997). The specter of freelance terrorism, like that practiced by Ahmed Hamideh in Jerusalem, may have reached the United States. To be sure, the consequences are chilling.

These loosely affiliated groups of terrorists are difficult to identify and do not easily conform to the rigid categorizations used by Western law enforcement organizations. Members of these groups may not consider themselves to be citizens of any particular country, but instead seek common political, social, or personal objectives that transcend nation-state boundaries. The Terrorist Research and Analytical Center of the FBI (1994) labels these groups and their criminal or terrorist actions "international radical terrorism" (IRT). The World Trade Center bombing and the plot to destroy other New York City landmarks is an excellent example of IRT. Persons indicted for, or identified with, these events include Egyptians, Iraqis, Jordanians, Palestinians, Sudanese, a Puerto Rican, and other U.S. citizens. Their membership is, for the most part, fluid, with the leadership or chain of command not as readily identifiable as it was for the Palestinian groups of the past. The new terrorists could potentially avoid detection until they had carried out a terrorist act, like the Arab American freelancer, Ahmed Hamideh. Freelancers may prove even more dangerous to the United States than the state-sponsored terrorists of the last two decades.

Although an international terrorist act in the United States is a rare occurrence and terrorist groups remain reluctant to strike here, their contingency plans for a possible action continue to progress. The support infrastructures are being upgraded, and group members are receiving training in terrorist boot camps throughout Sudan and Afghanistan.

International terrorist group members from more traditional terrorist groups like the Abu Nidal Organization (ANO) also reside in the United States. On July 26, 1994, for example, the U.S. government got Tawfig Musa of Milwaukee, Wisconsin; Saif Nijmeh of St. Louis, Missouri; and his brother Luie Nijmeh, also from St. Louis, to plead guilty to violating one felony count of the Racketeer Influenced and Corrupt Organizations (RICO) Act by conspiring to participate in the ANO. The group smuggled, transferred, and transported currency, information, and intelligence to other members of terrorist organizations inside the United States and throughout the world. The Nijmeh brothers, Musa, and another ANO member, Zein Isa, had been previously indicted by a federal grand jury for substantive violation of the RICO Statute on the basis of their activities with the terrorist group. On October 21, 1994, the U.S. District Court sentenced Musa and the Nijmeh brothers to 21 months in prison. The charges against Isa were dropped because he was already serving a life sentence for murder. The imprisonment of these ANO operatives culminated an investigation that took nearly a decade, demonstrating the extent to which these and other terrorist groups have been operating in the United States.

Particularly disturbing is the fact that many of these international terrorist groups are in communication with one another in the United States. Steven J. Emerson, in his award-winning documentary *Jihad in America* (1994), captured on videotape some of the world's most notorious Islamic radicals meeting in Kansas City, Missouri, in 1989 and in Detroit, Michigan, in 1991. These terror conferences can and do result in the sharing of information and expertise. With a common enemy in the United States, these often divergent organizations may be contemplating cooperative efforts against the United States.

Data from Britain's Center for the Study of Terrorism and Political Violence indicate that terrorism increasingly is attributable to these new terrorists. Specifically, the number of state-sponsored terrorist incidents declined from 73 in 1988 to 10 in 1994. Andradé (1997b) suggests that the diminishing ranks of these state-sponsored terrorists will be "replaced by 'freelance' extremist groups supported outside national boundaries" (p. 4). It would be prudent to take this seriously. The bombing of the World Trade Center shattered the illusion that the United States is immune from the hand of these new terrorists. Their success could only embolden and inspire other groups that hold a hatred for the United States and wish to bring violence to its shores. It would be foolish not to take seriously the call for retaliation issued by supporters of the blind fundamentalist cleric when he and his followers were sentenced in January 1996 to long terms in federal prison for their acts of terrorism.

Only a few days after the sentencing, U.S. forces in Bosnia were put on high alert, following intelligence reports suggesting that militant Muslim groups intended to retaliate for the life sentence given to Rahman (Hedges, 1996). In January 1997, such retaliation may have begun. Letter bombs were sent to the Leavenworth Federal

Prison, where Mohammad Saleh and Victor Alvarez, both convicted with Rahman, are serving time for the plot to blow up the United Nations headquarters and other buildings in New York (Lyall, 1997). Speculation aside, vigilance is appropriate, given the new terrorism the United States faces in the 21st century.

# 2

# Armed Prophets and Extremists
## *Islamic Fundamentalism*

### ROBERT J. KELLY

On February 26, 1993, at 12:18 p.m., an explosive device of roughly 1,200 pounds of combustible materials was detonated on the B-2 level of the parking garage at the World Trade Center (WTC) in New York City. Although approximately 50,000 people were in the WTC complex at the time of the blast, only 6 people were killed and about 1,000 injured.

The WTC is a major symbol of U.S. wealth, power, and prestige. The choice of this target, which houses many of the country's most important corporations, was not merely opportunistic. Although the plot may have been technically flawed, it was socially and politically shrewd in making the point that the very nerve center of the U.S. economy, located in a major population center, was vulnerable to the crippling blows of a dedicated group of believers.

In the past, the United States had been relatively free of foreign terrorism, unlike American citizens and facilities abroad, which have often been targets of terrorist incidents. Actually, the fact that Americans have been and are victimized by terrorists should come as no surprise because they are everywhere in the world. Associated with their presence is the perception that the United States exercises a powerful influence on political events. Perhaps this is a burden that a nation with world leadership credentials must bear, as must its citizens. Consequently, as the world's sole remaining superpower, the United States is often held accountable by many for a variety of international problems. Whether the United States is the originator of these problems, or a biased participant in these disputes, or a less than competent party in negotiating and peace making, the issues remain unresolved in the eyes of aggrieved parties.

Before the WTC bombing, attacks by terrorist groups occurred within the United States, but that is not the public's general sense of events. As Brian Jenkins (1980) pointed out, the United States was not immune to terrorist violence through the 1960s and 1970s. Terrorism is thought to be primarily a foreign phenomenon that, from time to time, laps up on the shores of this country. Indeed, although it was sometimes a convenient venue for the continuation of foreign struggles, when compared with Lebanon, Great Britain, Germany, France, Italy, or Spain, the United States has not been terribly afflicted with foreign terror on its soil. But that fact alone is not especially reassuring or consoling.

Until 1993, attacks on Americans mostly occurred outside the United States. Through 1992, the patterns of terrorist attacks against Americans were more or less uniform, occurring most often against U.S. business people in Latin America (U.S. Department of State, 1993). The constraint not to venture into the United States proper may have been carefully calculated, or it may have reflected ambivalence toward Americans. In Ayatollah Ruhollah Khomeini's rhetorical denunciations of the "Great Satan," the United States, a political severance was made between the American people and their government. This division may no longer apply. With the WTC bombing, an important psychological threshold was crossed. In the future, are terrorists more likely to bring their struggles to the United States and involve the American people? And if so, why now? These are pressing questions. It does seem odd, however, that the United States has escaped major, externally based terrorist actions for so long, given this country's thousands of miles of open borders, porous immigration control service, easily accessible firearms, and the availability of unfettered travel.

As for those circumstances that appear to set off terrorist violence instigated and carried out by Islamic fundamentalists against U.S. citizens, we can legitimately wonder whether anything inherent in Islam promotes terrorism. There are some provocative opposing views on this question.

## Islamic Fundamentalism: Is It a Threat?

The question whether Islamic fundamentalism constitutes a terrorist threat to the United States may sound as if it were launched in the dark. But the question is asked with the knowledge of what kind of answer may be appropriate. And the answer may increase security concerns.

Serious students and observers of Middle Eastern terrorism are deeply concerned over what Harvey Kushner calls "the new terrorism." Since the 1979 toppling of the shah of Iran, an Islamic revolutionary movement has emerged in the Middle East—a movement that supports a terrorism more dangerous than the terrorism that flourished during the Cold War. According to Kushner (1994), we should be more vigilant of this new terrorism. As he puts it,

> Do not be misled by the new terrorists' lack of sophistication. Actually, the new terrorism will be even deadlier than the old. It will be harder to combat too, precisely because its practitioners are less sophisticated which means less organized than their forebearers and consequently more difficult to spot, track and intercept. It is much harder to infiltrate groups that are not organized in any systematic way. (p. 43)

The new terrorist whom Kushner describes emerged during the Islamic revival sparked by Ayatollah Khomeini's inspirational role in the Iranian Revolution. Today, in almost every Arab capital or city, followers and imitators of Khomeini, Shiite and Sunni alike, promise a more virtuous and authentically Islamic, as opposed to secular, government. And in almost every Arab state is a struggle for power between autocratic rulers and Islamic militants. The latter claim to represent the poor, the disaffected, the alienated, the illiterate, the educated but unemployable, and the "futureless" young—those whom Muslims call the "disinherited" (see Miller, 1996).

Contemporary radical Islamic movements are often classified as "fundamentalist." Fundamentalism turns out to be as old as Islam itself. In its latest form, however, it attempts to impose a militant version of the "straight path," the way enjoined by the Prophet Muhammad, according to some Muslim intellectuals and political radicals.

Much of the fundamentalist influence derives from the success of the Iranian Revolution and the social and political conditions that have prevailed in a region where modernization and democracy have been stunted by autocratic elites and age-old desert monarchies. In many Middle Eastern states, the mosque is perhaps the only place where equality, if only spiritual, exists. Every week, men, whatever their station in life, are told that the servant and the master are one in prayer. They are also told that the laws of people are not to be obeyed when they violate or oppose the teachings of the Koran. In this manner, the ayatollah's retrogressive enterprise of an Islamic Republic is reinforced.

Despite the media's roguish and grotesque profiles of the makers of the Iranian revolution, Khomeini's influence remained intact. He often appeared as a man of high medieval learning. Faith like his—faith in the faith—consolidated the fact of revolution. Islam for the ayatollah was not just religion, but culture and civilization. He emotionally rejected the West while treating the shah's regime with contempt. The shah's government, as a usurper of Islamic values, was portrayed as wicked and corrupt; its laws harmful; its ministries corrupt; its police cruel; and its officials callously oblivious to the impoverished. Khomeini attributed the plundering of the country and indifference to the people as a predictable consequence of apostasy involving Islamic precepts. He pressed the idea that those in the clerical class were the true heirs of the prophet and entitled to lead the collective community of believers. Khomeini's Islamic political recipe turned the faith into a fever.

It would seem that the political activists motivated by religion are more dangerous than their secular counterparts. But why ideologies and utopian schemes steeped in religious ideas, concepts, and language are so effective in mobilizing people has not been thoroughly studied. A provisional answer may be that because of their very simplicity and lucidity, religious beliefs are enormously appealing. At the least, fundamentalist views offer their believers a core of settled meanings. They are self-contained and provide the faithful with the means to settle their problems and disputes. More important, however, religious doctrines claim a privileged status—a divine origin or inspiration. Hence, the need to satisfy ordinary standards of validity does not apply; their mere assertion by authority figures is enough for them to be taken seriously.

*Islam* as the term is used today seems to mean one simple thing but, in fact, is part fiction, part ideological label, and part minimal designation of a religion called Islam. In no significant way is there a direct correspondence between Islam in common Western usage and the enormously varied life that goes on within the world of Islam, with its more than 1 billion people (Said, 1981). The caricatures are well known: oil suppliers, frenzied passions, bloodthirsty mobs, unshakable prejudices, terrorists. For most Americans, and for that matter, Europeans, Asians, Africans, and Latin Americans who live in the secondhand worlds of indirect experience, the tenets of Islam are delivered via television, radio, and newspapers. As a result, Islam is torn loose from its historic contexts and reduced to the preposterous image of clamoring, hysterical mobs. Consequently, Muslims are treated with suspicion and disdain.

Fundamentalism has succeeded principally through armed struggle in Iran, Afghanistan, Indonesia, and the Sudan, and obtained power through political means in Algeria. In the 1980s, Europe was the theater for terrorism; in the 1990s, it has come to the United States. Iran creates an influential climate of opinion in the Muslim world. Still, there is no global equivalent of the Comintern, no "Islamintern" or World Muslim Front.

One of the worst aspects of terrorism and fundamentalism is that they are fearful images that tend to lack discrimination and careful definition, and because of this, there seems to be little resistance to inflated claims, undocumented allegations, and the suppression of facts. Even if we allow that the media are seduced by notions of newsworthiness, spectacle, and power and that they have immense difficulties distinguishing between isolated and politically worthless acts of desperation and orchestrated acts of genocide, it is still baffling to explain how or why they say nothing or leap on the bandwagon (Kelly & Rieber, 1992; Said, 1993).

The view of Islam as essentially a terrorist tool interchangeable with its fundamentalism has caused the entire Iranian Revolution to be trivialized as an outbreak of Muslim fanaticism and extremism. Khomeini was depicted in the media as a stubborn and obstinate die-hard reactionary. Yet in 1979, Iran was a hotbed of political activity, with political parties proliferating and political discussions and debate about the structure of the government ongoing and fierce. All this activity reflected a wide range of opinion that had been smothered by the shah's secret police, the dreaded SAVAK. Still, Iranian revolutionaries were typically depicted in the media as "fanatics."

In the fundamentalist scheme—and here is its inherent appeal to the impatient political extremists—to know the Koran, or the Bible, is to know everything worth knowing: economics, politics, science, philosophy. Fundamentalism provides an intellectual thermostat. The faith pervades everything, and for the true believers, the *suras* are not the statute books of the golden ages but the mystical record of an extended upheaval spreading across the world. Fundamentalism sanctifies rage, a rage about the faith and a readiness to contemplate great convulsions. Islam may be understood as a "memorial ideology," much like Catholicism. The faithful must believe that everything of moral and ethical importance lies behind them. Could the prophet, or Jesus, have forgotten to mention something morally and ethically significant? In these belief systems, the role of the cleric is primarily to edify doctrines and dogmas and to interpret the relevance of secular events in terms of sacred ideas and truths. But some have broadened the theological role to include political advocacy and, in so doing, have exploited the prestige of the clerical status they inhabit to propagandize radical politics.

In themselves, despite the fears they may engender, such doctrines are not agendas or blueprints for terrorism. Rather, those committed to extremist solutions find in these dogmas some ideas and cling to them, adopting, interpreting, and twisting them into rationales that justify violent actions. And if the psychology of the religious fanatic were probed deeply, one would find a personality prone to violence, a pervasive sense of alienation and despair that arises from a complexity of social causes and circumstances, some of which are purely fortuitous (Ferracuti, 1990; Kellen, 1990). These appear to be the precedent factors of the terrorist impulse.

The religiously inspired terrorist is petulant, with no taste for bargained compromises or accommodations. Such attitudes betray an authoritarian streak that eventuates in fateful, indeed fatal, paranoia and self-assurance. Politically, the question that must haunt any society confronting religious fanatics prepared for terror is whether it can muster the strength and resolve to stand up to the threat. Formulating solutions will depend on how community coalitions can be generated that deflect the energies of radical groups into less destructive channels.

The writings and speeches of fundamentalist thinkers and leaders indicate that Westernization and modernization have failed to fulfill their promise. In their place, salvation by faith and tradition are preached.

Another assumption that can be teased out of the fundamentalist ideology concerns the nature of society. For the fundamentalist, society is not a bank or a limited liability company formed by individuals who are fearful and suspicious of being duped or exploited. Rather, it is based on the assumption that people cannot govern themselves and must rely on the authority of the state.

## Desert Storm and Apocalyptic Legacies

In June 1996, a huge truck bomb took 19 American lives in Dhahran, Saudi Arabia. In the early 1990s, Dhahran was a major military installation for the U.S.-led Gulf War forces that undid Iraq's invasion of Kuwait. Today's volatility, however, is, in part, a result of a mix of poverty and its frustration. Moreover, the region is a veritable demographic time bomb of young, notwithstanding restless, youth. In Saudi Arabia, for example, almost 60% of the population is under age 24.

Although Iran is frequently portrayed as the principal patron and sponsor of terrorism throughout the world, graduates of the Afghanistan War of liberation against the Soviets may pose an even more potent threat. The *mujahideen,* or holy warriors, in their war against communism, were backed by the U.S. Central Intelligence Agency (CIA) and the Saudis. The CIA and the Saudis exploited these warriors for their own limited geopolitical purposes. The mujahideen, however, who were infused by the spirit of *jihad,* or holy war, returned the favor. They carried their militant message beyond the Afghan mountains right back to the very groups that previously supported their revolutionary goals. The CIA aptly refers to this phenomenon as "blowback." The WTC bombing and the 1996 attack against U.S. military personnel in Saudi Arabia are examples. So, too, is the retribution aimed at their once Arab partners, the Saudi royal family, who authorized the beheading of four individuals who were supposedly responsible for the car bombing in Riyadh in 1995.

Since U.S. troops arrived in the Saudi kingdom during the Gulf crisis, clerics have posed challenges to the government amid widespread accusations of corruption and decadence. Moreover, religious and social criticism has grown as the price of a barrel of oil has dropped, the principal source of Saudi wealth and the most effective internal pacification of dissent, and with it the safety net of free education, easy and well-paying jobs, and cheap, albeit decent, housing.

The point may seem labored, but why the United States? Why is the United States targeted by terrorists? One obvious answer is that the United States is the unchallenged superpower, the leader and symbol of the West, and the foreign power most actively involved in the Middle East. It is thus the biggest and best target. To challenge America, to hurt and humiliate her, may bring glory and prestige.

The United States is an attractive target of terrorists for yet another reason. After, for example, the U.S. Marine barracks slaughter in Beirut, the Pan Am 103 explosion over Lockerbie, and the WTC bombing, terrorists realized they could count on the U.S. media to provide them with unlimited publicity and, perhaps more important, some form of advocacy to create a situation in which the immediate victims and their families become the arbiters of U.S. foreign policy. The role of the "Great Satan" came to the United States by inheritance and is retained by its leadership because it is the preeminent superpower and the custodian of Western values. With prominence and leadership comes the inevitable price of hatred.

## Counterterrorist Responses
## and Current Dangers

If the threat of terrorism is greater today than it has ever been, then one must ask whether the capacities to respond are adequate. Are the federal and local governments able to identify the threats and mobilize counterterrorist resources? At the 50th anniversary celebration of the United Nations in 1995, President Bill Clinton used the occasion to remind the General Assembly that terrorism was a global problem that had to be dealt with by all nations. But even after the Clinton administration successfully foiled an Iraqi assassination plot against former President George Bush, the administration has been unable to explain why ordinary Americans have been targeted by terrorism.

The terrorist plot that led to loss of life, injuries, and havoc at the WTC and the aborted plot to blow up numerous New York landmarks, including the United Nations, wears the label of ordinary crime. This crime, as compared with acts of international terrorism, still tends to be treated in the government with a different standard of seriousness. The disconnection has been telling. By all appearances, the United States still finds it cleaner to contend with trouble outside its borders than within.

The Dhahran attack that was deliberately engineered to destroy American lives may have been directed symbolically at other victims as well, perhaps the Saudis. The blast that rocked the WTC, however, was unmistakably aimed against Americans and was a signal that the "new" Middle Eastern terrorism had arrived in the United States.

Disparities in the approach to terrorism that ignore border distinctions and confound official thinking may have less to do with personal myopia among bureaucrats than with U.S. laws that tend to provide intelligence agencies and the military with more latitude to operate overseas than in the United States. Further, the freedom from scrutiny that potential terrorists enjoy in the United States makes the society more vulnerable. No doubt, any free society always has some exposure to terrorism. Indeed, Great Britain has found it almost impossible to curb IRA terrorist bombings despite the adoption of some rather draconian security measures. Notwithstanding pledges that counterterrorism policies at home will be toughened, the question remains: Can domestic inefficiency against terrorism be explained by deference to civil liberties? Several realizations and possibilities are listed in the following summary.

## Summary

First, in terms of Cold War politics, citizens within a superpower have ingrained habits of dividing the world into spheres of power and influence and processing these disturbing bits of information through an "us and them" perspective. Thus, Islam and the West are often seen as irreconcilably at odds. The assumption underlying this attitude is that they are coherent, insulated categories of cultural and political reference in which every Westerner and every Muslim is somehow completely assimilated and adjusted into his or her "civilizational" category. The fact is that neither Islam nor its alleged opposite, "the West," is all inclusive or politically homogeneous. Second, following on the first point about social diversity in both worlds, the imposing list of oppositional groups, from the Abu Nidal Organization (ANO) to the Hezbollah (Party of God), does not reflect a shared ideology. Every ideological formation may appear to be uniform, but on further inspection one will always discover exceptions, concessions, and barely disguised duplicities that tell the "real story" of a political agenda cobbled together out of disparate and contradictory elements. No master narrative or plan is shared by all fundamentalists. Ideological homogeneity is a fiction. Fundamentalists engaged in terrorism pretend they all share common objectives and values. Third and last, although fundamentalism is so turbulent, societies such as Egypt, Jordan, and Lebanon are still largely secular despite the clamoring over Islamic government. Even in Iran, ongoing life and all its complexities and interactions render it secular. Fundamentalists use Islamic idioms for purely political ends in the contest for power. More important, however, their formulas for social change and revolution are, at best, vague and not very appealing as social blueprints for a revitalized theocracy.

Terrorist attacks by small groups are indeed possible in the future and, given technological sophistication, probable. The more we see and learn, the less likely it seems that a coherent Islamic uprising of the kind confected by media and some experts is im-

minent. Whatever force fundamentalists possess feeds on governments that are kept in place because of the United States. Our
allegiances to the house of Saud, the Kuwaiti Sabahs, and so on,
which create a negative image of this country, weaken its ability to
cool down the confrontational atmosphere and engage in real
dialogue.

In the obsession with rabid fundamentalists, like Sheik Omar
Abdel Rahman, many well-known Muslim intellectuals and political
philosophers across the Arab world who dispute the dogmatism of
the orthodox have been ignored. Those who speak and write openly
and bravely certainly deserve the attention and aid of the West. For
the West and the United States, the best antiterrorist weapon eludes
simple description. It may hinge on concrete facts reported with
accuracy no matter how irritating, facts that acknowledge the
modern history of the postcolonial Middle East for what it is: a world
disfigured with war, tyranny, poverty, and populations so taunted
and ridiculed in the media that they have been plunged into anger
and despair. A clear picture of the Arab world would doubtless
diminish significantly fundamentalist terrorist threats to the United
States.

The problem of Islamic fundamentalist terrorism is not generic;
nor, strictly speaking, is it a security issue. It is a political problem
that the crisis management industry redefines as a security matter.
Security technologies can provide more "hardened" targets, but
terrorists will seek out overlooked weaknesses. Today, it is passengers in aircraft who are victimized; tomorrow, it could be schools.

Security technology is only part of the response to terrorism.
Apart from state-sponsored terrorism, which is a separate problem
but also one entailing a political solution, serious attention must be
paid to radical dissident movements in countries where the United
States has friendly relations or is involved in alliances. Our commitments must be weighed and relationships reevaluated in terms of the
possible violent consequences for the United States and its citizens.

If the question raised above—Why the United States?—is refor-
mulated—Why not the United States?—it may yield substantive
answers about the U.S. image as the world's most powerful and
affluent country. Inhabiting the superpower role means that the
discontented and embittered may hold the United States responsible for their poverty, their weakness, their ignorance, and their

irrelevance. In the tumultuous settings of international relations and images, the question of more reliable counterterrorism security should be preceded by questions concerning our political alliances and how these may make us potential targets.

# 3

# Terrorism in America
## *The Threat of Militant Islamic Fundamentalism*

STEVEN EMERSON

More than four years after the 1993 World Trade Center bombing in New York by a group of militant Islamic fundamentalists, the reverberations of the bombing were still being felt in the counterterrorism community in the United States. At first glance, the initial assumption by law enforcement was that the immediate national security threat was confined to a small band of extremist followers of a charismatic but obscure Islamic religious leader named Sheik Omar Abdel Rahman. Sheik Rahman, a militant cleric from Egypt, had arrived in the United States in 1991 and recruited a band of fanatic followers who were mobilized by his calls for *jihad*, holy war, against the West. But like the proverbial blind man who cannot determine that he is touching an elephant until he feels the entire animal, the intelligence community, too, began groping at a larger unidentified entity. It is too soon even today to know whether we are fully

33

cognizant of the beast that awaits us. In fact, since the bombing, prosecutors, intelligence agents, and law enforcement officials have discovered that militant Islamic extremists have established extensive networks throughout the United States. "Islamic militants . . . [now pose] [t]he greatest threat coming to us domestically in the United States," stated FBI counterterrorism chief John P. O'Neil in a rare open statement in 1996, "[T]hese groups now have the capability and the support infrastructure to attack us here if they choose to" (quoted in Gertz, 1996, p. A3). Although no established hierarchy has been found that centrally coordinates the activities of the myriad networks, the intelligence and law enforcement communities agree that the entire spectrum of radical groups from the Middle East has been replicated in the United States. "The groups operating in the United States," says Andrew McCarthy, the lead prosecutor in the World Trade Center bombing conspiracy trial, "include Hamas, Hezbollah, Islamic Jihad, Islamic Salvation Front, Islamic Liberation Party, Jamat Islamiya, and every other radical Islamic fundamentalist group from the Middle East. Ironically, the United States, with the exception of Sudan, Syria, and Iran, may have a greater concentration of terrorist groups than any other country in the Middle East" (A. McCarthy, Assistant United States Attorney, U.S. Department of Justice, personal communication, February 1997).

## The Threat of Radical Islam

In any discussion of the threat of radical Islam, it is imperative to point out that radical Islam is not synonymous with mainstream Islam. Those who practice radical Islam today are simply practicing their totalitarian interpretation of a religion. The vast majority of Muslims do not support in any way the politics of the extremists. Nevertheless, to deny the existence of radical Islam—as some Islamic groups have asserted recently in the United States—or to pretend it does not exist is tantamount to defending the militants as one and the same with peace-seeking moderates. Rather than protect the moderates from being tarred with the extremist brush, it only paints them further. For the militants, of course, the deliberate blurring of the distinction between militant and moderate Islam is designed to

hide under the protection of mainstream Islam. Extremist Islam is no
different from any other religious extremist movement—whether it
be that of a Jewish terrorist who shot the Israeli prime minister
because he believed he was commanded to do so by God, or the
antiabortionist assassin who believed he had the right to kill anyone
in the name of God. A religious extremist differs only in the religion
he or she invokes to commit a crime. For a variety of reasons, some
relating to the available sources of external Persian Gulf funding and
others relating to the migration of radical Islamic leaders to the
United States, most of the "mainstream" Islamic groups operating in
the United States are dedicated to carrying out a radical agenda. "The
United States, if you will, has become fundamentalist occupied territory," says Professor Khalid Duran, who has studied the rise of
radical Islamic groups for nearly 25 years, "because militant Muslims
saw the West as the best place to operate from. If you study their
activities and agenda, it is clear these organizations reflect the interests of radical Islam groups, not of Muslims living in America"
(K. Duran, personal communication, January 1997).

Thus, the leadership of the primary Islamic groups in the
United States support militant Islamic causes and groups tied to the
Middle East, such as Hamas, Islamic Jihad, the Turkish Welfare
Party, and the Muslim Brotherhood. In some cases, the U.S. organizations function as either support branches of these groups or as actual
primary worldwide headquarters for their militant subsidiaries back
in the Middle East. As a practical matter, the overt activities of these
groups include fund-raising for Hamas charities, distributing
militant Islamic propaganda, organizing opposition against federal
antiterrorist initiatives, castigating and attacking the media for exposing militant Islam in less than a favorable way, preventing Salman Rushdie from meeting at the White House, and mobilizing
support for imprisoned radical Islamic terrorists, such as Musa Abu
Marzuk or Sheik Omar Abdel Rahman.

## An Inattentive Media

Even with these public activities, radical Islamic groups do not
receive the same scrutiny in the media—and thus receive far less

attention—than their militant domestic brethren, such as the radical white militia or Ku Klux Klan, which manifest the same conspiratorial paranoia about the U.S. government and Jews. For non-Muslim observers, the fact that radical fundamentalists control major Islamic organizations is largely obscured through deception, naïveté, political correctness, or a witting suspension of disbelief by Western journalists. Indeed, many journalistic outlets, such as the *Washington Post, Christian Science Monitor,* National Public Radio, and even the *New York Times* have published or broadcast during the past several years reports in which radical Muslim groups have been falsely represented as moderate or in which the leaders of these groups have been uncritically portrayed as "human rights" activists. In particular, National Public Radio has repeatedly broadcast interviews with militant Islamic extremists but allowed them to falsely project a policy of moderation designed more for gullible Western consumers than for their own internal constituents. By falsely defining Islamic terms such as *jihad* as pacifist in nature (National Public Radio) or by legitimating militant Hamas officials as "civil rights" advocates (*New York Times*), journalists are only sowing the seeds of their own demise and laying the cornerstone for the permanent importation of radical Islamic values destined to clash head-on with the principles of the First Amendment. For the public, this misreporting constitutes an intellectual deceit and fraud that ultimately deprives the American public of the information it is entitled to know. Ultimately, the legitimation of radical Islamic groups poses a major national security threat that will only boomerang on journalists themselves. (In fact, the results are already being seen. In 1995, 1996, and 1997, major Islamic groups initiated chilling campaigns of intimidation against newspapers, magazines, encyclopedias, and even Hollywood merely for writing about Islam or about Islamic terrorists in ways deemed "offensive to Islam."

For American Muslim moderates, the harsh reality of having their organizational gravity taken over by radicals is something they have to confront all the time. "Radical Islamic groups have now taken over the mainstream Islamic institutions in the United States," says Seif Ashmawi, an Egyptian American newspaper publisher,

> and anyone who pretends otherwise is deliberately engaging in self-deception. I know because I have studied these groups for

years from the inside. Unfortunately, Americans are a naive people, refusing to believe that foreign extremists would actually lie to them. The only threat American reporters seem to talk about is the right-wing militia. But the agenda of groups like the American Muslim Council, the Muslim Arab Youth Association, and the Council on American Islamic Relations is no different from the right-wing militias. Its just that they hide under the umbrella of mainstream Islam. (S. Ashmawi, personal communication, January 1997)

Ashmawi himself has been the target of death threats for his criticism of Islamic militants in his New Jersey area, particularly that of the group supporting World Trade Center bombing leader Sheik Omar Abdel Rahman. Even Ashmawi's Muslim workers have been threatened (FBI officials and local New Jersey law enforcement, personal communication, December 1995).

## The Radical Infrastructure

The locations of the radical groups span the entire United States. Certain areas are known to have larger concentrations of Islamic radicals and are the sites of offices of Islamic militant groups that raise funds, recruit new members, disseminate propaganda, and in some cases recruit terrorists, provide military training, and even direct terrorist operations back in the Middle East. These areas include Chicago, Boston, Los Angeles, Santa Clara, New York, Washington, D.C./northern Virginia, Miami, Tampa, Dallas, Oklahoma City, North Carolina, Arizona, Kansas, and New Jersey. Even with the known location of front groups, Islamic militants pose a more difficult challenge to law enforcement than any other terrorist group operating in the United States. "What makes these groups so troublesome is that they hide under a religion, do not have a traditional linear hierarchy, speak a foreign language, and generally go about as far as they can in pushing the limits of the law without our being able to track them when and if they go over the line," says Oliver "Buck" Revell, former executive assistant director of investigations of the FBI. "Their agenda in the United States is to not only build their infrastructure and raise funds but also to be in a position to ultimately move against the United States" (O. Revell, personal communication, November 1996).

Until the bombing of the World Trade Center on February 26, 1993, the United States was considered largely immune from attacks by foreign terrorist groups. Although "only" six people were killed in the Trade Center blast, documents seized from the homes of the perpetrators and wiretapped conversations show that the intention was to kill upward of 50,000 to 70,000 civilians and to try toppling one of the trade towers onto the other. Forensic bombing specialists provided expert testimony that had the amount of explosive firepower been increased by various amounts and had the vehicular bomb been placed a few yards closer to a central pylon supporting the skeleton of the building, the tower could have been weakened to the point of collapsing.

Despite a series of nearly immediate arrests of a group of main perpetrators, an associated group of extremists embarked on an even more grandiose plan—to bomb bridges, tunnels, and federal landmarks and buildings. Although the scheme was successfully interdicted by the FBI through the efforts of an Egyptian informant, the intended causalities from the second plot could have reached from 100,00 to 150,000 dead—a scale of death that would have exceeded even the number of those killed in atomic blasts on Japan in World War II. The horrific combined total of intended victims for both plots led Judge Michael Mukassey to the sobering conclusion that had the United States suffered such levels of civilian casualties, the number would have been more dead or wounded than any other domestically based event since the Civil War.

Did the trial put a dent in the terrorist infrastructure of radical Islamic fundamentalists in the United States? Not really, according to Andrew McCarthy, chief World Trade Center prosecutor:

> We should not delude ourselves into believing that the Jihad group lead by Sheik Omar has really put these guys out of business. Islamic radicals have established a vast infrastructure in the United States, and we ought not deceive ourselves that we are safe because of one set of convictions. The threat of radical Islam on American soil is growing, not receding. Whether the public can see its manifestations like they see the activities of the militant white militia is another story. (A. McCarthy, Assistant United States Attorney, U.S. Department of Justice, personal communication, February 1997)

The threat of militant Islam is distinctly visible overseas, where the United States and its pro-Western allies have been subject to deadly attacks by Islamic militants. These include the lethal car bombs against U.S. military targets in Saudi Arabia in November 1995 and June 1996, the Hamas and Islamic Jihad suicide bombs against Israeli civilians, the series of attacks against French civilians in Paris and Lyon, and the attacks by Egyptian radicals on Egyptian tourists and Christian Copts.

A series of incidents and events that transpired in the United States in 1995 and 1996 should leave no doubt that radical Islamic militants have made the United States their political and military safe-haven:

- *The arrest of Musa Abu Marzuk, the de facto chief executive officer of Hamas, at Kennedy International Airport, New York, in July 1995.* He had been secretly living intermittently in the United States for some 15 years, during which time he had set up an elaborate Hamas military, command and control, and financial infrastructure. In his possession at the time of his arrest was paperwork showing his business companies to be worth more than $10 million, which law enforcement officials believe to have been part of a massive money-laundering operation for Hamas in the United States. Equally significant was the discovery of Marzuk's personal telephone directory, which contained the telephone numbers of nearly every top Islamic and Arab terrorist leader in the world today. (Interestingly, more than 20% of the telephone numbers were those of Marzuk's contacts and senior terrorist collaborators in the United States.) A subsequent Israeli extradition request showed that Marzuk was directly involved in orchestrating terrorist attacks against Israeli civilians. A series of federal court rulings confirmed the accuracy of the intelligence and other documentary evidence acquired by the Israeli government. Contrary to claims made by apologists for Marzuk and repeated uncritically by various newspaper reporters, the evidence collected against him includes voluntary confessions in Arabic supplied by Marzuk's couriers arrested in Israel. Together with the separate documentary evidence of U.S.-based Hamas terrorists obtained by federal agents under the Foreign Intelligence Surveillance Act, the documentation proved beyond any doubt that Marzuk was in control of a terrorist apparatus responsible for killing or wounding dozens of Israeli civilians.[1]

- *The deportation of Bashir Nafi in July 1996 from the United States.* Nafi, a senior official of the Islamic Jihad terrorist organization, had been living in the United States illegally. He had come to the United States to work for the World Islamic Studies Enterprise (WISE), an self-proclaimed academic outfit attached to the University of South Florida in Tampa. In fact, WISE, according to federal documents and law enforcement officials, turned out to be a front for the Islamic Jihad terrorist group. The head of WISE, Ramadan Abdullah Shallah, was a professor at the University of South Florida in Tampa from 1991 through October 1995, when he suddenly surfaced in Damascus, Syria, to assume the head of the Islamic Jihad terrorist organization. (Beyond the issue of how a terrorist front could operate undetected for nearly 5 years, an interesting question raised was to what degree was the University of South Florida complicit in the creation of the terrorist cell? According to documents collected by federal authorities and interviews with various university officials, mounting evidence suggests that university officials closed their eyes to the warnings and indications that a terrorist cell was operating with university imprimatur.)[2]

- As a result of Shallah's appointment as head of the Islamic Jihad, the FBI, in December 1995, executed a series of search warrants in Tampa against individuals connected to WISE and other front groups for the Islamic Jihad. The resulting searches produced one of the largest treasure-troves of radical Islamic documents and raw intelligence material collected in the United States. The materials showed that WISE and its leaders—including Shallah and Professor Sami Al-Arian (who founded WISE and an affiliated "charity" called the Islamic Committee for Palestine)—were involved in running Islamic Jihad in the United States. The terrorist organization raised millions of dollars, obtained visas for terrorists to come to the United States, organized seminal gatherings of major Islamic terrorists around the world, and actually directed terrorist operations back in the Middle East.

## A Terrorist Internet

The fact that the top terrorist leaders of both Hamas and the Islamic Jihad radical groups were found to have been living in the United States should disabuse anyone of the notion that militant Islamic organizations are not using the United States for a safe haven. FBI director Louis Freeh testified for the first time on the record that Hamas raises "substantial cash funds from the United States to areas in the Mid-East where we could show Hamas receipt and even expenditure of those funds" (*International Crime*, 1996). Both Hamas and Islamic Jihad have not only raised considerable amounts of funds in the United States but also set up operational headquarters in the United States where terrorist attacks and military strategies have been orchestrated. In turn, both Islamic Jihad and Hamas have succeeded, in large part, in establishing their support infrastructure because both groups have networked together with other militant Islamic groups.

The culmination of this pan-Islamic militant partnership may have been seen in the World Trade Center bombing: Rather than being an attack dominated by the militant Islamic Jama from Egypt, evidence now shows that the bombing was the product of collaboration from five different radical Islamic organizations—the Gama Islamiya, Islamic Jihad, al-Fuqra, Sudanese National Islamic Front, and Hamas. The scope and breadth of these militant Islamic groups should demonstrate unambiguously that although they are not coordinated formally on an operational level, the militant Islamic groups network with one another in a sort of terrorist "Internet." At virtually every place on the globe today—Paris, Rome, Dallas, New York, or Manila, Peshawar, Gaza, Beirut, and Khartoum—militant Islamic groups can network with one another in receiving or providing assistance, obtaining safe haven, and generating mutual support for all their activities.

The absence of a traditional hierarchy within these terrorist groups has created a new terrorist paradigm. In 1995, in testimony before the Senate Judiciary Committee, then-acting director of the CIA, Admiral William Studeman, stated,

> [Islamic] groups are even more dangerous in some ways than the traditional groups because they do not have a well-established organizational identity and they tend to decentralize and compartment their activities. They are also capable of producing more sophisticated conventional weapons as well as chemical and biological agents. They are less restrained by state sponsors or other benefactors that are the traditional groups. These new groups appear to be disinclined to negotiate, but instead seek to take revenge on the United States and Western countries by inflicting heavy civilian casualties. The World Trade Center bombers are prime examples of this new breed of radical, transnational, Islamic terrorist. (*Omnibus Counterterrorism Act of 1995*, 1995)

In the United States and other Western countries, Hamas and other radical Islamic groups do not, of course, operate under their generic Islamic names. Rather, these movements operate front groups under innocent-sounding names patterned after other minority advocacy groups. Often self-defined as "religious" or "research," these monikers entitle the groups to nonprofit status, as well as to de facto immunity from federal surveillance that would normally be applied to secular groups espousing the same ideology. "Besides the fact that these groups operate under the cloak of religion, they also hide their ideological screeds in religion as well—making it very difficult if not nearly impossible to separate the trangressible incitement from the lawful religious citations," says Don Lavey (personal communication, February 1996), a former FBI official and one-time head of the Counterterrorism Division at Interpol. One of the most formidable challenges facing World Trade Center bombing prosecutors was the need to show that Sheik Omar's invocation of jihad was not simply a mundane religious exercise, but rather a pivotal structure in the mobilization of his cadres in launching violent attacks against U.S. targets.

Still, despite the success of the World Trade Center prosecutors, the overwhelming majority of militant Islamic actions are either not monitored or deemed to fall outside the U.S. attorney general's guidelines that prescribe the limits of Justice Department investigations into political and religious groups, even those that advocate violence. Says former FBI official Revell,

> One of our problems in tackling the area of militant Islamic radicals is that we really do not know about the problem until after it occurs. Remember, the FBI is constituted as a law enforcement organization, not as an intelligence organization. Even the collection of simple newspaper articles for inclusion into a file is prohibited unless the creation of the file has been approved in a systematic way. (personal communication, November 1996)

The safeguards against domestic abuses of spying by intelligence agencies were instituted in the mid-1970s following the disclosure of the illegal activities of the FBI and the CIA in conducting politically motivated surveillance operations, as well as "dirty tricks" designed to smear political opponents of those in office.

Together with the legal restrictions and the limitations of FBI cultural and linguistic expertise, a major void has been created in the ability of law enforcement to preempt or prevent terrorists from using the United States to plot attacks to be carried out here or overseas. In the World Trade Center case, prosecutors revealed during the trials that FBI surveillance was conducted on several major conspirators in 1992—for nearly a year before the bombing—but the conspirators still managed to carry out the terrorist attack. Similarly, an examination of Marzuk's achievements is instructive in understanding how Hamas has been able to develop a widespread network on U.S. soil without scrutiny or restrictions.

## Musa Abu Marzuk and the Growing of Hamas

Born in 1951 in the town of Rafiah in the Gaza Strip, Musa Abu Marzuk got a college degree in engineering in Cairo in 1975 and soon moved to Louisiana to get his doctorate. By the early 1980s, Marzuk became increasingly involved with a growing community of militant Muslims in the United States whose worldwide ideological fundamentalist fervor was unleashed by the Iranian Revolution, the assassination of Anwar Sadat, and the *jihad* against the Soviet occupation of Afghanistan. Together with several colleagues, Marzuk helped create an umbrella organization called the Islamic Association for Palestine (IAP); Marzuk would be elected head of the group's *Majlis al-Shura*, or consultative council that oversaw all of the group's activities. By the mid-1980s, several years before Hamas came into formal existence in December 1987, the IAP had established offices in Indiana, Arizona, Illinois, and California and published a militant magazine called *Ila Falistin*, which routinely called for the death of "infidels and Jews." Moreover, internal Hamas documents strongly suggest that the 1988 Hamas charter—a virulent anti-Semitic conspiratorial tract that incorporates elements of both Nazi dogma and the notorious turn-of-the-century Protocols of the Elders of Zion—was first written by members of the IAP in the United States in the early to mid-1980s.

As Hamas began demonstrating its special violent trademarks—stabbings and mutilations of its victims—in Israel, Gaza, and the West Bank, it was controlled and funded from the United States. Marzuk, according to the confessions of several captured Hamas terrorists, appointed the military commanders and dispatched couriers to the territories with specific instructions to carry out terror attacks and the money to do so. Although some cash would be given directly to Hamas death squad leaders, other monies—collectively totaling tens of millions of dollars—would be channeled through Islamic charities known as *zakats* that would serve as indoctrination greenhouses for Hamas operatives, provide a conduit to fund terrorism, and serve as a powerful social-religious magnet to the population. In the meantime, Marzuk was busy further establishing the Hamas network under the guise of seemingly innocent religious and research institutions and investment companies. According to federal documents, in 1989 Marzuk became the founding president of the United Association of Studies and Research (UASR), a self-described Islamic "think tank" that in reality served as a covert branch for planning Hamas operations and for disseminating Hamas propaganda. In an interview with the *Washington Post* in 1995, Ahmed bin Yousef, the current head of the Virginia-based UASR, denied any affiliation with Hamas and claimed that Marzuk was only a "businessman" who briefly served on the UASR's board of directors. In June 1991, the largest international gathering of Islamic leaders ever in the United States was held in the outskirts of Washington, D.C. Sponsored by the UASR, the extraordinary conference—which focused on the need to respond to the Western "crusades" against Iraq, the need to destroy the "Jewish state," and the threat of American-Crusader imperialism—was represented by nearly every major radical fundamentalist organization, including Islamic Jihad, Hizba Tahrir, Hezbollah, Al-Jihad, and Jamat Muslimeen. Representatives—to pick at random—at this extraordinary conference included Marzuk, Ahmed bin Yousef, Abdulrahman Alamoudi (now director of the American Muslim Council [AMC]), Sami Al-Arian (head of the Tampa-based Islamic Jihad front group known as the Islamic Committee for Palestine), Ramadan Abdullah (now head of Islamic Jihad and former head of the Tampa-based Islamic Jihad front known as the World Islamic Studies Enterprise), and many senior terrorist chieftains from overseas. The presence of so many militants made this gathering the all-time all-star terrorist conference in U.S. history. Scores of papers and resolutions were presented that condemned the United States and Jews as part of a diabolical world plot to destroy Islam; those present also decided to support one another in their respective Islamic confrontations with their non-Islamic hosts.

Among the Jordanians was the radical parliamentarian Ishaq al-Farhan, who only a few months before had given a pep talk to Naser Hidmi and the 25 other Hamas rising stars, and a few years earlier had collaborated with Yusuf al-Azm on gun running for Hamas leader Ahmed Yasin in its pre-Intifadhah armament phase. Leith Shbeilat, another Jordanian parliamentarian at the conference, was later caught with Ya'aqub Qarash maintaining a cache of weapons paid for by Iran and implicated in a plot to assassinate King Hussein. At the time this conference was held, as with other conferences as well, U.S. law enforcement and intelligence were totally unaware of its existence. These conferences would provide opportunities for the worldwide militant Islamic network to coalesce and establish new linkages. As for planning specific operations, Marzuk, according to the confession of Mohammed Saleh, an American Palestinian arrested by Israelis for smuggling funds to Hamas terrorists and confirmed independently by the statements of other Hamas operatives, told Saleh and other Hamas operatives which terrorists to meet and how much money each was to be given. On another occasion, Marzuk gave Saleh, prior to his departure from the United States, the location of the body of an Israeli soldier kidnapped and murdered by Hamas to negotiate the release of imprisoned Hamas leaders. On still another occasion, Marzuk sent Saleh to the territories in 1990 to create a military-security apparatus for Hamas and a means of coded communication for Hamas operatives to communicate to their commanders in the United States and London. Marzuk secretly visited the West Bank and Gaza in 1989 and 1990 to provide firsthand instructions to his troops on the ground. Although Hamas supporters deny that Saleh worked for Marzuk, bank records tell a different story. The records show that Marzuk deposited hundreds of thousands of dollars into Saleh's Chicago bank accounts. Ultimately, Marzuk was tripped up because his aides were caught in Israel.

## MAYA and IAP

Today, the overt activities of militant Islamic groups can still be observed by examining the actions of two of the largest Islamic groups in the United States: the Muslim Arab Youth Association (MAYA) and the Islamic Association for Palestine (IAP). Headquartered in Plainfield, Indiana, MAYA was formed in the 1970s by Muslim religious students from the Persian Gulf. The group was started, according to an internal publication, when a group "of Kuwaiti young Muslims became aware of the dangers of moral degradation that their Muslim brothers coming to study in North America are exposed to." MAYA conventions in recent years have featured some of the leading Islamic fundamentalists in the world, including Rashid Gannuchi, leader of the militant Tunisian Al-Nahda movement (who was sentenced to death in absentia for his role in organizing a series of lethal terrorist attacks in Tunisia and subsequently granted political asylum in Britain); Mustapha Mash'shur, the Egyptian Muslim Brotherhood Deputy Supreme Guide; Musa Abu Marzuk, a top Hamas leader who lived in the United States from 1973 through 1993: Muharram al-Arifi, of the Lebanese Muslim Brotherhood; Yousef Al-Quardawi, of the Egyptian Muslim Brotherhood based in Qatar; Ahmed al Qattan, a radical Hamas leader based in Kuwait; Sheik Ahmed Noufal, a known recruiter of Hamas terrorists in Jordan; and Ibrahim Gousheh, Hamas's official spokesperson in Jordan.

The central tenets of MAYA, like the philosophy of its parent Moslem Brotherhood, is that Western society, particularly the United States, is morally corrupt, intrinsically anti-Islamic, and full of evil. "In the heart of America, in the depths of corruption and ruin and moral depravation, an elite of Muslim youth is holding fast to the teachings of Allah," states the preface to MAYA's Constitution, printed in Arabic and distributed at its conventions. "[MAYA will] uncover conspiracies against Muslims as well as criticize actions and positions that openly contravene the Islamic Shar'riah"—the Islamic legal and religious code. A companion MAYA publication, *Guide for the Muslim Family in America,* also distributed at its conferences, does not hide its revulsion for the West: "Western civilization is based upon the separation of religion from life . . . [whereas] Islamic civilization is based upon the fundamentals opposed to those of western civilization."

Hamas's principal American support group is known as the Islamic Association for Palestine (IAP). Currently headquartered in a nondescript strip shopping mall in Richardson, Texas, the IAP has affiliate branches in more than three dozen cities and on scores of college campuses. IAP has set up an elaborate publications and video operation to promote the ideology of Hamas. More recently, the IAP has produced and distributed terrorist recruitment videos. One such production is called *Iz ad-Din al-Qassam Brigades.* It opens with dramatic shots of bearded Palestinian men, armed with Kalashnikovs, jumping out of trees and aiming their rifles. Hamas fighters are featured arming and preparing weapons, machine guns, and Molotov cocktails. Interspersed with the operational video, fighters are interviewed and boast of their heroic killings of Jews and Palestinian "collaborators." There are even chilling interviews of blindfolded Palestinians "confessing" to their "crimes" moments before their execution. At the end of the video is the line, "To order your copy, call Aqsa Vision," and the Texas telephone number of the IAP. (The Aqsa Vision office and address are the same as that of the IAP. The labels of other publicly available tapes state "IAP Aqsa Vision." Although Aqsa Vision is Hamas's audiovisual arm, it is operated under a separate corporate entity known as the American Media Group.)

The IAP publishes Hamas communiqués, such as one that urged the "killing of Jews . . . the bloodsuckers . . . and killers of prophets." Another condemned the United States as a "full participant in the conspiracy" to wipe out the Palestinians, specifically blaming the United States for participating in the Sabra and Chatilla massacres. And following the dispatch of U.S. forces to Saudi Arabia after Iraq's invasion of Kuwait in 1990, the IAP not only published Hamas communiqués threatening the United States for its "fierce Crusade, an imperialist attack . . . on the Muslim Ummah [nation]," but also passed its own resolution condemning the "American Crusades . . . for protecting economic, political interests with the Zionist entity's security and oil resources at the top."

Today, Hamas's flagship U.S. publication is *Al-Zaitanouh.* Although dedicated to promoting Hamas, the newspaper also supports other Islamic fundamentalist liberation movements, including in Kashir, the Philippines, Egypt, and Algeria. *Al-Zaitanouh* frequently celebrates successful Hamas attacks: In its October 27, 1994, issue, for example, *Al-Zaitanouh*'s headline was "In Its Greatest Operation, Hamas Takes Credit for the Bombing of an Israeli Bus in the Center of Tel-Aviv. Articles routinely warn of international

"Mossad plots" and other massive Jewish worldwide anti-Muslim conspiracies.

The IAP also publishes an English-language newsletter called the *Muslim World Monitor*. Following the convictions of four men in the World Trade Center bombing, the *Muslim World Monitor* published an editorial claiming that the guilty verdicts represented "the degree to which anti-Muslim venom had penetrated society and that the U.S. government suppressed evidence showing that the Mossad, Egyptian intelligence, and the FBI, were all involved in the bombing. Frequently, the *Muslim World Monitor* publishes articles alleging diabolical conspiracies perpetrated by Jews and other "enemies of Islam."

Together with its sister publication *Al-Zaitanouh*, the *Muslim World Monitor* reaches tens of thousands of readers, constituting the largest indigenously published Muslim newspapers in the United States. One article in the *Muslim World Monitor*—to pick at random— contended that Jews ritually slaughter non-Jews during the holiday of Purim, thus explaining the actions of the Jewish terrorist Baruch Goldstein in his massacre in Hebron in 1994.

## Funding Terrorism Inside the United States

One of the first efforts the Clinton administration made to stop the flow of terrorist funds in the United States was the imposition, in January 1995, of an executive order freezing the assets of 14 Middle Eastern terrorist groups. These included 2 radical Jewish fundamentalist groups and 12 Arab and radical Islamic groups, including Hamas and Islamic Jihad. The executive order followed a major policy review ordered by Secretary of State Warren Christopher on the heels of a Hamas suicide bombing in Jerusalem that killed 18 civilians in October 1994. In his address at Georgetown University on October 24, 1994, Christopher outlined the need to crack down on terrorist funding in the United States for Hamas:

> The international community must reject the terrorism of Hamas, Hezbollah, and other extremists. Strong condemnation of terror, especially from Israel's Arab partners, is an essential starting point. But condemnation is not enough. A real penalty must be imposed. We must join together to turn off all foreign sources of

funding for terrorism, both public and private. Front organizations based abroad that are linked to terrorism must be shut
down. And the perpetrators and organizers of terror must be
punished.

Following initiation of the executive order, FBI investigators
and agents found upward of $15 million in suspected terrorist assets
held under terrorist front groups throughout the United States. They
made recommendations to the Justice Department to seize the assets
(FBI, State Department, and Treasury Department, personal communications, June 1995 through March 1996). For reasons that are
still officially unknown, however, the Justice Department elected not
to seize the assets. Some Justice Department officials (and Clinton
administration officials, personal communications, January 1996 and
March 1996) explained privately that seizure of the terrorist assets
would have compromised "sources and methods"—implying that
seizing these funds would have interrupted ongoing intelligence
operations. Others in the FBI speculated that the refusal to seize the
terrorists' assets had more to do with the growing political clout of
U.S. Islamic groups and their ability to influence the actions of
the White House. Whatever the real story, the undeniable fact
remains that the terrorist fund-raising, financial apparatus, and
political organizations of radical Islamic groups remain fully intact
within the United States. Moreover, by early 1997, radical Islamic
"charities" and "front groups" had proliferated throughout the
United States with unimpeded growth. Paralleling that growth was
another disturbing development: White House acceptance of radical
Islamic charities and front groups posing as "mainstream" Islamic
groups.
    The degree to which these Islamic charities have been able to
deceive the American public in portraying themselves as mainstream
and legitimate was readily apparent following the April 1995 Oklahoma City bombing when several radical Islamic groups, one directly connected to the World Trade Center bombing and another tied to
suicide attacks in Israel, were lauded in the American press and by
local public officials for their financial contributions to a relief fund
set up to aid Oklahoma bombing victims. In 1996, First Lady Hillary
Clinton hosted several receptions in the White House for radical
Islamic groups, including the Council on American Islamic Relations
and the American Muslim Council. The entry of these groups into
the White House elicited the concern of many FBI agents and

and counterterrorist officials who saw in these visits the hemorrhaging of the Clinton counterterrorism doctrine.[3]

## CAIR and AMC

The first group the Clinton administration invited into the White House, in early 1996, was the Council on American Islamic Relation (CAIR). Established in 1994 by funds from radical Persian Gulf donors, CAIR says its agenda is to protect "Muslim civil rights." In fact, it has openly and covertly championed the most violent international terrorists in the world today. These include Musa Abu Marzuk, the Palestinian Hamas commander arrested in New York in 1995; and Sheik Omar Abdel Rahman, convicted for the World Trade Center bombing.

CAIR's officials (listed as members of CAIR's board of advisors and board of directors) include one Islamic official who was listed by the Justice Department as a potential unindicted coconspirator in the World Trade Center bombing and other officers who have attacked the United States and promoted blatant anti-Semitism. In addition, CAIR has organized or sponsored the visits of radical fundamentalists in the United States, including those that have called for killing Jews and attacking the United States. CAIR's own newsletter touted the meetings in Washington it arranged for visiting Jordanian Islamic Action Front official Bassam al-Amoush. What CAIR did not reveal was that in another of al-Amoush's visits to the United States—this one in December 1994—al-Amoush openly called for the killing of Jews at a radical Islamic gathering in downtown Chicago. In Jordan, al-Amoush has openly attacked the United States.[4]

Federal records show that CAIR was created by the Hamas front group in Texas, the IAP. Until he became the founding head of CAIR, Nihad Awad served as a top official of the association, whose Dallas-based offices, according to telephone records released in the World Trade Center bombing trials, were in contact with convicted conspirators behind the bombing.

In 1994, Awad declared at a university symposium in Florida, "I am in support of Hamas. . . . I know that this movement as an Islamic movement has not been objectively reported in the United States." Accordingly, both Awad and Ibrahim Hooper, CAIR's communication director, have repeatedly attacked as "anti-Muslim" journalists and others who have written about the terrorism committed by Hamas and other radical Islamic terrorist groups. Hooper has openly defended Hamas, the Sudanese National Islamic Front, and other violent anti-American terrorist groups by claiming that articles that are critical of these violent organizations or that expose their American connections are "smears against Islam." CAIR has also initiated street protests against news organizations that have written about the history of militant Islam—going to the point of lambasting anyone who refers to "fundamentalist Islam" or to the concept of a "holy war" (jihad) in Islam as guilty of "defaming Muslims."

The other group repeatedly wined and dined at the White House is the American Muslim Council (AMC): First Lady Hillary Clinton allowed the AMC in 1996 to organize a reception for itself at the White House, even selecting all the participants. In addition, the AMC has provided talking points for the First Lady for her syndicated column and speeches.[5] Seif Ashmawi, publisher of the *Voice of Peace* in New Jersey, has publicly protested the White House's embrace of the AMC as "legitimizing radicals and supporters of international terrorism." Ashmawi, who testified in 1996 before the U.S. Senate Foreign Relations Committee on the AMC and other radical groups operating in the United States, believes that the "White House has been manipulated into believing that the AMC and other such self-anointed radical groups represent genuine American Muslim voices when in fact they represent supporters of extremism and violence."[6]

Although the AMC claims it is against "violence and terrorism," its publications, conferences, and internal materials tell a different story. The AMC has repeatedly championed and supported Hamas and its leaders, routinely declaring Hamas "is not a terrorist group," and claiming that U.S. efforts to clamp down on terrorist funding in the United States are "anti-Islam." Following the 1995 arrest of Hamas terrorist commander Musa Abu Marzuk, Alamoudi became Marzuk's primary defender. "I know the man, he is a moderate man on many issues," Alamoudi was quoted in the *Washington Post*, adding, "This [arrest] is an insult to the Muslim community" (Thomas & Hall, 1995, p. A31). Soon, Alamoudi began organizing Marzuk's defense fund. In 1997, Alamoudi stated on Arab television, "I have known Musa Abu Marzuk before, and I really consider him to be from among the best people in the Islamic movement, Hamas. . . . I work together with him."[7]

The AMC has collaborated closely with known Hamas and Islamic Jihad front groups, such as the Virginia-based United Association for Studies and Research (UASR) and the Florida-based World and Islam Studies Enterprise (the latter has now shut down and is under federal investigation for serving as a terrorist command and control center in the United States). Records show that Alamoudi has actively participated in or sponsored militant Islamic conferences featuring some of the leaders of the most violent Middle Eastern terrorist groups and their front organizations in the United States. One such radical gathering, at which Alamoudi was a speaker along with known terrorists from the Middle East, was held in Virginia in 1991.

Alamoudi has closely worked with the UASR, not only distributing UASR materials but also cosponsoring conferences. One such conference, cosponsored by the AMC and the UASR, at which Congressman Robert Torricelli was the guest speaker, was held in October 1993. Beyond support for Hamas, the AMC has provided office space to the Algerian Islamic Salvation Front; organized press conferences for visiting officials of the Sudanese National Islamic Front (an organization defined as "terrorist" by the U.S. State Department); lauded the electoral victory of the radical Islamic Turkish Refah Party, known for its open anti-Semitism and anti-Americanism; championed the radical Iranian-trained anti-American *mujahideen*, holy warriors, in Bosnia; portrayed President Clinton's meeting with Salman Rushdie as an insult to Muslims comparable to the Holocaust against the Jews; and attacked the media for exposing militant Islam's repression of women and their human rights.

## Conclusion

In December 1996, the full strength of the radical Islamic groups could be seen once again, this time at their unprecedented five annual conferences held in four cities: Toledo, Ohio; Sumerset, New Jersey; Los Angeles, California; and Chicago, Illinois. The groups that sponsored the conferences included the Muslim Arab Youth Association, the Islamic Assembly of North America, and the Islamic Association of Palestine. At every conference gathering, at which 25,000 Muslims collectively showed up, radical Islamic literature and incendiary anti-Semitic and anti-Western materials were freely distributed. The notorious anti-Semitic turn-of-the-century forgery from Czarist Russia, *The Protocols of the Elders of Zion*, for example, was given out in all five conferences; other documents attacked the United States, the West, and promoted Islamic terrorist groups.

At the most radical gathering of the annual Islamic conferences, organized by the IAP, known Islamic militants from the Middle East gave incendiary speeches and talks exhorting their listeners to exterminate Jews and other "enemies of Islam." A well-known American Islamic leader, who had met only recently with senior officials of the Clinton administration, told his audience that if they were outside the United States, they could all pray, "May Allah destroy America" and that if they were inside the United States, they had to refrain from violence because Islam on its own would take over the United States. For one Middle Eastern visitor to the IAP convention, it was "like attending a radical Islamic conference in Gaza. The only difference was that some of the sessions were in English" (participant at Islamic Association for Palestine Conference, Rosemont, Illinois, personal communication, January 1997).

In the end, Islamic radicals have used the United States primarily as a safe haven to carry out activities they would be prohibited from carrying out in their homelands. On the one hand, these groups are fully cognizant of the fact that should they draw too much unwanted and negative attention to their activities in the United States, it might jeopardize their status and relative immunity from overt scrutiny and freedom to operate unimpeded. On the other hand, the very premise of the Islamic groups' ideological identity is a hatred toward the United States, the West, and other "declared enemies of Islam." This delicate balance between the two conflicting emotions—torn between the need to keep the United States safe to organize jihad and the need to carry out jihad against the United States—is the principal determinant of when Islamic terrorism is carried out. When the rage of the fundamentalists exceeds the self-restraint, that is when terrorism is likely to be carried out in the United States.

## Notes

1. The last court ruling against Marzuk—following a series of negative judgments against him—was issued by U.S. District Judge Kimba Wood on October 9, 1996. Judge Wood ruled that "the Arabic statement in Abu Ahmad's [Abu Ahmad is the name of Marzuk's terrorist courier whom Marzuk dispatched from Chicago to Israel to orchestrate and fund terrorist attacks] own hand that was given by him to some other inmates furnishes strong support" for earlier court rulings affirming the admissibility and authenticity of the evidence against Marzuk.

2. Author interview with Professor Hiba Hechiche, University of South Florida in Tampa (personal communication, January 1996); author interview with two senior university administrators who insisted on retaining anonymity (personal communications, 1996); author review of public documents released by USF (personal communication, January 1996); and author interview with FBI officials (personal communication, March 1996); who provided warnings to the university in 1994. In addition, the author's television documentary *Jihad in America* (1994) exposed the USF-terrorist connection when the film was broadcast on PBS in November 1994 but university officials ignored the evidence. The following year, in May 1996, reporter Michael Fechtor wrote a series of impeccably documented stories detailing the USF connection to the Islamic Jihad; once again, the university ignored the reports. In 1991 and 1992, the university ignored a series of caveats from professors on campus who specifically warned that foreign but unidentified money was being poured into a university offshoot with radical Islamic connections.

3. Author interviews with Revell (personal communication, April 1996); Peter Probst of the Pentagon's Office Special Operations and Low Intensity Conflict (personal communication, May 1996); Gene Gately, formerly of the CIA (personal communication, May 1996); former Counter-Terrorism State Department Coordinator Ambassador Jerry Bremer (personal communication, February 1996); and a dozen other active FBI and Justice Department officials (personal communications, September 1995 through June 1996) who asked for anonymity.

4. The details and facts on CAIR and al-Amoush are taken from hundreds of U.S. government and internal CAIR documents, audio- and videotapes of radical Islamic conferences, Foreign Broadcast Information Service reports, interviews with U.S. law enforcement and intelligence officials, and other Islamic materials obtained from sources within the Islamic community.

5. The information for the section dealing with the American Muslim Council comes from documents obtained from law enforcement officials, video- and audiotapes of Islamic radical conferences, documents and literature produced by the American Muslim Council, materials obtained from the White House, and interviews with numerous law enforcement and AMC officials.

6. Author interview with Seif Ashmawi (personal communication, March 1996). Also, see comments of Ashmawi at the press conference of Congressman Charles Shumer on the existence of radical Islamic groups throughout the United States (Shumer, 1996). For Ashmawi's congressional testimony see, *Existence of Radical Islamic Groups* (1996).

7. Middle East television interview with Abdulrahman Alamoudi of the American Muslim Council. Alamoudi: "Yes, I am honored to be a member of the committee that is defending Musa Abu Marzuk in America. That is a mark of distinction on my chest. . . . I have known Musa Abu Marzuk before, and I really consider him to be from among the best people in the Islamic movement Hamas, eh . . . in the Palestinian movement in general, and *I work together with him*" (personal communication, March 22, 1997).

# PART 2

# THE THREAT FROM WITHIN

There are days in your lifetime when you remember where you were when an event happened. Such was the case when President John F. Kennedy was assassinated. On April 19, 1995, at 9:02 a.m., Americans relived that same darkness when in a matter of seconds downtown Oklahoma City had been rearranged to resemble Beirut or Belfast—places that had always seemed worlds away. Unlike the foreign terrorists responsible for the bombing of the World Trade Center, the suspects in the Oklahoma City bombing were homegrown. Unfortunately, the conditions that might have precipitated the bombing of the Alfred P. Murrah Federal Building lead the authors in this section to predict more of the same.

In Chapter 4, "Terrorism, Hate Crime, and Antigovernment Violence: A Review of the Research," Mark S. Hamm paints a frightful picture of the state of research pertaining to domestic terrorism, as well as the possibility of more terror in the years to come. With regard to correcting the former, he calls for a clearinghouse for identifying and cataloging massive amounts of academic literature on domestic terrorism and for making these data available to scholars in a timely manner. As for the future of terrorism, Hamm sees a continued potential for antigovernment violence. He notes that the growing number of high-profile international terrorists behind bars in the United States may move some to engage in acts of terrorism to free them. In addition to the vulnerability of the Federal Bureau of Prisons, Hamm sees American right-wing antigovernment violence increasing against judges and other law enforcement officials. For this author, the upcoming millennium, as well as special days in the mythology of the terroristic subculture, pose the greatest threat to society.

In Chapter 5, "The Patriot Movement: Past, Present, and Future," Brian Levin demonstrates how the American Patriot antigovernment movement represents the greatest threat of domestic terrorism to the United States at the end of the 20th century. Levin describes how these antigovernment extremists are tied together through informal means as diverse as the Internet and Patriot publications and expos and paramilitary trainings. Their trail, says Levin, is hard to follow because they either act alone or band together in small, autonomous, "leaderless resistance" cells. Their targets are media outlets, financial institutions, abortion clinics, gay establishments, and civil rights groups, all of which, Levin writes, are culled from an expanding list of perceived enemies.

Brent L. Smith and Kelly R. Damphousse, in Chapter 6, "Two Decades of Terror: Characteristics, Trends, and Prospects

for the Future of Terrorism in America" further our understanding of the nature of domestic terrorist groups. Smith and
Damphousse, as Hamm and Levin before them, also identify
the violent fringes of the extreme Right to be the greatest threat
to the public's safety. They argue that the Right, unlike the Left
of earlier decades, has chosen to maintain an aboveground
presence through its Christian Identity outlets and to go underground to accomplish acts of terrorism through small,
"leaderless resistance" cells. Smith and Damphousse, like the
other authors in this part of the book, see the approaching
millennium as symbolic and crucial for both extremists and
federal law enforcement.

# 4

# Terrorism, Hate Crime, and Antigovernment Violence
## *A Review of the Research*

### Mark S. Hamm

Throughout history, wild hatred has driven people to extremes of violence—against others because of their race, ethnicity, religion, lifestyle, physical disability, or political beliefs. From the Nordic Vikings of the Middle Ages, to the Ku Klux Klan of the American Civil War era, to Hitler's storm troopers of 20th-century Germany, political fanatics have committed atrocities that defy the imagination. Unfortunately, they continue to this day in the ravages of "ethnic cleansing" and mass rapes in Bosnia and in Skinhead attacks against foreigners, Jews, persons with disabilities, and leftists across

AUTHOR'S NOTE: This chapter was presented at a March 1996 planning meeting on terrorism and hate crime research to the Committee on Law and Justice of the National Research Council's Commission on Behavioral and Social Science Education. The author's research for this chapter has benefited from the support of Jeffrey Ian Ross and the Harry Frank Guggenheim Foundation.

the European continent. Such crimes are routinely carried out on a north-south axis as well: from the mass killings in Rwanda and Somalia to the peasant rebellion in Chechnya. To be sure, they occur around the world with amazing regularity. In recent years, hundreds of fatal political crimes have occurred in (at least) Algeria, Armenia, England, France, India, Iraq, Japan, Lebanon, Mexico, Pakistan, Spain, and Turkey.

Here in the United States, most Americans look on this sort of crime as a long-forgotten chapter of their national past (e.g., the lynching of more than 2,000 black males by the Ku Klux Klan following the Civil War) or as something that occurs far from home. There is good reason for such a view: Terrorism *has not* been part of the recent American experience. This is no doubt because, with the exception of what amounted to state-organized genocide against some three million Native Americans during the 1800s, terrorism has never been used by the U.S. government as a formal instrument of social control—as it has been used, of course, with such alacrity and terrible consequences in Nazi Germany, the Soviet Union, Cambodia, Iraq, Uganda, and South Africa in the 1900s.

Americans are a pragmatic people. They view terrorism as inconsequential because it does not affect them directly. Terrorism is always something that happens "overseas." Then came the Oklahoma City bombing of April 19, 1995. In one imperceptible instant, 163 men, women, and children inside the Alfred P. Murrah Federal Building were killed with a fertilizer bomb planted by a young man with connections to the American far Right. Not only was the Oklahoma City bombing the most egregious act of political violence ever waged on U.S. soil, but some have speculated that it may have been the greatest single act of nonstate domestic terrorism in world history.

## Domestic Terrorism and Social Science

The Oklahoma City bombing, then, gives U.S. social scientists an unprecedented reason to stop and ponder the state of research on that category of crime known as *domestic terrorism*. Below, I attempt to show—with as little pessimism as possible—that the data necessary to conduct this research are in a sad state of affairs.

### Definitions

Although it is a global phenomenon that is becoming increasingly more violent, domestic terrorism is still a crime in search of a sociological definition. Unlike other areas of criminology that have a precise definition of the criminal event (e.g., aggravated assault, robbery, murder, drug trafficking), there is no social scientific consensus on the meaning of domestic terrorism. In fact, the crime is so freighted with complexity that it seems to defy every rule of typology building. Alex Schmid (1983) identified more than 100 official and academic definitions of political terrorism published internationally since World War II. These definitions range from one-sentence federal policies to ambitious 20-page scholarly articles. In the United States, *domestic terrorism* is defined by the federal government as "a violent act or an act dangerous to human life in violation of the criminal laws, to intimidate or coerce a government, the civilian population, or any segment thereof, in the furtherance of political or social objectives" (U.S. Department of Justice, 1993, p. 25).

Central to this definition is the role of the group. For the FBI to classify an incident as an act of domestic terrorism, the crime must be the result of decisions made by individuals with the conspiratorial support of others (Smith, 1994). For example, the crimes committed by the Unabomber would not be considered domestic terrorism because the suspect appears to have acted alone. The man convicted in the Oklahoma City bombing, in contrast, is believed to have had such conspiratorial support.

### Official Data

Armed with this definition, the federal government hands over responsibility for enumerating incidents of domestic terrorism to the FBI. The FBI record is published in annual reports of the bureau's Terrorist Research and Analytical Center. Beginning in 1980, the report was called the *FBI Analysis of Terrorist Incidents in the United States*. In 1984, the title was changed to *FBI Analysis of Terrorist Incidents and Terrorist-Related Activities in the United States*. The 1986 report reverted to the pre-1984 title. Since 1987, it has been called simply *Terrorism in the United States* (all published by the U.S. Department of Justice, 1980-1993, 1993 being the year for which data are most currently available). Social science is data driven; hence, any researcher interested in domestic terrorism must start with an inspection of these figures. Simply stated, the FBI has not provided researchers with much to go on. The bureau did not even publish its definition of the crime until 1980, exactly a half-century after definitions of robbery, murder, and aggravated assault first appeared in the Uniform Crime Reports (UCRs). Since then, the collection of FBI data on terrorist incidents in the United States has had four phases.

### Phase I: 1980-1987

Phase I began in 1980 and ended in 1987. In many ways, Phase I produced the best numbers on domestic terrorism ever published by the FBI. Figures for that period are shown in Table 4.1.

In this first 8-year phase, the FBI counted 153 incidents resulting in 12 homicides and 35 injuries. As would be the case in subsequent years, the vast majority of these cases involved a bombing attack against either a commercial business, a U.S. military installation, or a federal building. Who were responsible for these crimes? That question was not answered until Phase II.

### Phase II: 1988

For 1988, the *Terrorism* figures were as follows:

| Year | Incidents of Terrorism | Killed | Injured |
|------|------------------------|--------|---------|
| 1988 | 9 | 0 | 0 |

In addition to these data, for the first time the FBI released information on terrorist incidents by group dating back to 1984:

**Terrorist Incidents by Group: 1984-1988**

| Anti-Castro | Jewish | Left-Wing | Puerto Rican | Right-Wing |
|-------------|--------|-----------|--------------|------------|
| 1 | 7 | 13 | 35 | 5 |

The outstanding feature of these data is that they are mathematically inconsistent with the Phase I reports. A total of 63 incidents were recorded for the period 1984 to 1988, yet only 61 incidents are attributed to anti-Castro, Jewish, left-wing, Puerto Rican, or right-wing elements. (Although it is reasonable to assume that [a] the identity of the groups responsible for the two residual incidents was

**TABLE 4.1** Terrorist Incidents Known to the FBI: 1980-1987

| Year | Incidents of Terrorism | Killed | Injured |
|------|------------------------|--------|---------|
| 1980 | 16 | 0 | 4 |
| 1981 | 26 | 1 | 1 |
| 1982 | 37 | 5 | 26 |
| 1983 | 20 | 6 | 4 |
| 1984 | 13 | 0 | 0 |
| 1985 | 7 | 2 | 10 |
| 1986 | 25 | 1 | 19 |
| 1987 | 9 | 0 | 0 |

unknown or [b] the FBI did not officially recognize two crimes as terrorist incidents until 1988 and reclassified them, such explanations do not appear in the report.)

*Phase III: 1989-1991*

Phase III began in 1989 with the optimistic news that incidents of domestic terrorism had fallen to an all-time low:

| Year | Incidents of Terrorism | Killed | Injured |
|------|------------------------|--------|---------|
| 1989 | 4 | 0 | 0 |

Yet with the 1989 report came another measure of confusion:

**Terrorist Incidents by Group: 1985-1989**

| Anti-Castro | Jewish | Left-Wing | Puerto Rican | Right-Wing | Special |
|-------------|--------|-----------|--------------|------------|---------|
| 1 | 6 | 1 | 33 | 5 | 7 |

You can see both a surplus number of incidents by group and another group classification added to the report. The figures suggest no new incidents attributed to anti-Castro, Jewish, left-wing, Puerto Rican, or right-wing groups. And although there were only four new incidents for the year, seven incidents were attributed to special interest groups primarily interested in the environment. The figures suggest that the FBI had begun recording special interest incidents as early as 1985, yet they were not upgraded to terrorism status until four years later. The problem for social scientists was the lack of an explanation of this in the 1989 edition of *Terrorism in the United States*.

These data carried two other implications for social scientists. First, the majority of cases were unavailing from the standpoint of examining terrorism in the continental United States. More than 60% of incidents were attributed to the Pedro Albizu Campos Revolutionary Force or the Ejercito Popular Boricua-Macheteros, the Machete Wielders, Puerto Rican groups dedicated to the removal of all U.S. presence from Puerto Rico, and were committed on the island of Puerto Rico.

Second, it was clear that anti-Castro terrorism was going nowhere, Jewish terrorism was failing, and left-wing terrorism was on its way to becoming extinct. That left as stable only right-wing terrorism, along with the new category of special interest terrorism.

The following data were reported for 1990 and 1991:

| Year | Incidents of Terrorism | Killed | Injured |
|------|------------------------|--------|---------|
| 1990 | 7 | 0 | 0 |
| 1991 | 5 | 0 | 0 |

**Terrorist Incidents by Group: 1986-1990 (1990 report)**

| Anti-Castro | Jewish | Puerto Rican | Right-Wing | Special |
|-------------|--------|--------------|------------|---------|
| 1 | 2 | 36 | 5 | 3 |

**Terrorist Incidents by Group: 1987-1991 (1991 report)**

| Anti-Castro | Jewish | Puerto Rican | Right-Wing | Special |
|-------------|--------|--------------|------------|---------|
| 1 | — | 23 | — | 10 |

As can be seen, by 1991 the category of "Left-Wing" terrorism had been removed from the report (although it would be reinserted in 1992 and 1993), incidents of right-wing terrorism had fallen to zero, Puerto Rican terrorism had declined sharply, and special interest terrorism had achieved a major status in the threat of homegrown American extremism.

### Phase IV: 1992-1993

Two significant changes in reporting procedures occurred in 1992. Here are the figures for that year:

| Year | Incidents of Terrorism |
|------|------------------------|
| 1992 | 4 |

Notice that the categories "Killed" and "Injured" were deleted from the report, thus prohibiting any trend analysis of those variables. But a second change introduced in Phase IV brought even more problems. In 1992, the FBI published the group data in a 10-year increment. Here are those data:

*Terrorist Incidents by Group: 1982-1991*

| Anti-Castro | Jewish | Left-Wing | Puerto Rican | Right-Wing | Special |
|---|---|---|---|---|---|
| 12 | 16 | 23 | 77 | 6 | 31 |

Not only was no attempt made to explain and reconcile the numerical differences reported in Phase IV with previous reports, but the following year the FBI once again changed the period of reporting from a 10-year increment back to a 5-year frame. Here, then, are the most recent official statistics on terrorism in the United States:

| Year | Incidents of Terrorism |
|---|---|
| 1993 | 12 |

*Terrorist Incidents by Group: 1989-1993*

| Left-Wing | Puerto Rican | Right-Wing | Special | International |
|---|---|---|---|---|
| 0 | 13 | 0 | 17 | 2 |

These figures signaled a new era in U.S. terrorism and a strange new beginning in FBI reporting. In a strictly numerical sense, special interest groups now ranked at the top of the list. Nine of the 12 incidents recorded for 1993 were attributed to a 2-day spree of attacks against clothing stores in Chicago by the Animal Liberation Front (ALF). These attacks are reflected in the 1989-1993 trend data reported above. Two other incidents were attributed to the new category of "International" groups, both of which are also reported in the trend numbers. These included the February, 26, 1993, bombing on the B-2 level of the parking garage at the World Trade Center in New York City. Because of the recent changes in reporting procedures, however, there was no way to capture the full magnitude of the incident. That is, gone was the mechanism to quantify and set in its proper context the fact that six people were killed in the blast and more than 1,000 were injured.

Yet the 1993 report contains an even more curious development. In the text of the report, two more incidents are identified for

1993, bringing the total to 13, not 12, as shown in the 1993 incident table. These included the American Front Skinhead (AFS) pipe bombing of the National Association for the Advancement of Colored People (NAACP) headquarters in Tacoma, Washington, on July 20, 1993, and the AFS bombing of a homosexual bar in Seattle two days later. Notice the lack of incidents under the category of "Right-Wing" terrorism for the years 1989 to 1993. Either by mistake or by design, the FBI had failed to enter these two cases into its trend data. Thus, nearly 17% of total incidents are missing from the most recent official statistics on terrorism in the United States.

### Summary

Social scientists interested in U.S. domestic terrorism are confronted with a unique set of obstacles. Because Americans have had little experience with terrorism, a variety of bureaucratic, legal, and learned contradictions surround the issue. Indeed, not only does the research community lack consensus over the definition of domestic terrorism, but there are actually no laws against domestic terrorism; that is, no federal (or state) statutes outlaw terrorism on U.S. soil. Hence, when terrorists are arrested, they must be charged with other crimes. The perpetrator of the Oklahoma City bombing, for example, was charged, under Title 18 of U.S. Code, Section 844, with "malicious danger and destroying by means of an explosive a federal building" (Hamm, 1997).

Understanding domestic terrorism is also hampered by the shortcomings of official statistics. Unlike the UCRs, which have continually improved since first appearing in 1930, official data on domestic terrorism have become less comprehensive. Whereas methods of counting index crimes have been consistent for 50 years, procedures for enumerating incidents of terrorism have undergone four major revisions in a relatively short period. These revisions have, in turn, mitigated against the use of both longitudinal and cross-sectional analyses commonly employed by social scientists. And although the terrorism data share with the UCR data the problem of being unweighted, the problem becomes more serious in the former case because of the nature of terrorism itself. Take, for instance, the World Trade Center bombing and just one of the attacks waged by the ALF in Chicago. Each was recorded as one incident for 1993. Yet the former incident left 6 dead and more than 1,000 injured, whereas the latter resulted in no death or injury.

Finally, although not all crimes are reported to the police and, therefore, do not appear in the UCRs, incidents of domestic terrorism are especially susceptible to legal and bureaucratic ambiguities, and their proportional unreported rate probably exceeds that of index crimes. The crimes of the AFS offer a good example of this. Its bombing of the NAACP headquarters and the homosexual bar were classified by the FBI as incidents of domestic terrorism in 1993. If these bombings qualified as acts "dangerous to human life in violation of the criminal laws . . . in the furtherance of political or social objectives," then would not the definition also apply to AFS attacks—with brass knuckles, knives, ball bats, and steel-toed boots—on individual blacks or homosexuals? For the FBI, they do not. They are classified and counted another way.

## Hate Crime and Social Science

The increase in Skinhead violence against racial minorities led civil rights advocates of the late 1980s to press the U.S. Congress for legislation requiring the FBI to gather and publish data on acts of prejudicial violence (Ellis, 1990; Hamm, 1993). At the time, similar policies were receiving strong support at the state level of government as 43 states passed some form of statute against institutional vandalism and 31 states enacted laws against bias or harassment, including interference with religious worship, and against cross-burning (Finn & McNeil, 1988). This political consensus introduced the term *hate crime* into the lexicon of U.S. criminal justice administration and led Congress to enact the Hate Crime Statistics Act of 1990. Under the act, hate crimes are defined as

> crimes that manifest evidence of prejudice based on race, religion, sexual orientation, or ethnicity, including where appropriate the crimes of murder, non-negligent manslaughter, forcible rape, aggravated assault, simple assault, intimidation; arson; and destruction, damage or vandalism of property. . . . Bias would be reported when the law enforcement investigation revealed suffi-

cient objective facts to lead a reasonable and prudent person to conclude that the offenders actions were motivated, in whole or in part, by bias. (FBI, 1992, u.p.)

The act led to the immediate passage of Public Law 101-275, which required the U.S. attorney general to gather statistics on hate crimes, along with numbers collected for the annual UCR. The FBI's UCR instructions stipulated that "hate crimes are not [to be considered] separate distinct offenses, but rather traditional crimes motivated by the offender's bias." Categories of bias were listed as "the victim's religion, race, ethnicity, or sexual orientation" (FBI, 1992, u.p.). Hence, the public law created a new set of data for social scientists to contemplate. But like the terrorism data, the hate crime statistics contained their own considerable biases and shortcomings.

### Definitions

Once again, crimes that manifest evidence of prejudice based on race, religion, sexual orientation, disability, political belief, and ethnicity have occurred throughout history and in nearly all human communities. Yet, similar to domestic terrorism, there is no social scientific consensus on the meaning of this type of crime. In today's Germany, it is alternatively defined by scholars and policymakers as *right-wing violence* (e.g., Heitmeyer, 1993) or *xenophobic violence* (e.g., Aronowitz, 1994a). In Belgium, the Netherlands, Norway, and Sweden, it is referred to by researchers and government officials as *racist violence* (Lööw, 1995a; Witte, 1995). In Britain and France, it is called *racial violence* (Bowling 1994; Witte, 1994). And still other countries, such as Italy, do not consider the symbolic status of victims or the motivation of perpetrators and simply treat the problem with existing criminal statutes (Hamm, 1994a).

Here in the United States, though, we suffer from an excess of definitions. For example, Skinhead attacks against African Americans, immigrants, gays, and religious institutions have been referred to with such diverse terms as *hate crime, hate-motivated crime, bias crime, bias-motivated crime, possible bias crime,* and *ethnoviolence* (Hamm 1994a). And as indicated in the previous section of this chapter, such attacks have also been officially classified as acts of domestic terrorism.

These diverse definitions derive from the fact that *hate crime* is an emotionally charged term that often feeds community divisiveness and demagoguery over the identity of the national character. As William Ellis argued in his 1990 commissioned paper for the National Research Council, "bias crime is a form of political violence" (p. 2). Because of its political underpinning, state governments and local municipalities—which are responsible for reporting data under Public Law 101-275—have also adopted various definitions in accordance with local traditions.

Although a full review of these definitions is impossible to conduct here because of space limitations, several examples are instructive of the wide range of lexical and stipulative conditions employed. In 1993, 23 states used the FBI definition of hate crime (Ball & Curry, 1995). But along with "religion, race, ethnicity, or sexual orientation," some states identified additional victim categories. Connecticut, for example, added those with "physical disabilities" to the list of possible victims. Florida added "color and ancestry" to the list, but not physical disability. Illinois added "color, creed, ancestry, and physical or mental disability." Rhode Island included the general categories of "disability" and "gender," but left out color, creed, and ancestry. And although Pennsylvania adopted most of the FBI's definition, the state did not recognize sexual orientation as a victim classification. It is possible, then, for the states to accept in full the FBI's definition of hate crime, to add victim classifications, or to delete those parts of the definition they may find inconsistent with local traditions.

Those are examples of how the states can manifest their own political and cultural profiles in the identification of victim characteristics of hate crime. The states can also manifest their profiles in the identification of specific offenses. Thirty-one states recognize cross burning as a hate crime. Twenty states do not (which is not to say that there are no laws against it; as in Italy, it is simply treated with existing criminal statutes covering harassment or vandalism). In Maryland, the disruption of a religious meeting is considered a hate crime (or "bias crime," as it is known in that state). Although Pennsylvania does not recognize sexual orientation as a victim status, it does proscribe—along with a dozen other states— paramilitary training and fomenting racial violence as part of their statute. And in addition to recognizing cross burnings and paramilitary training as hate crimes, South Carolina includes as part of its statute the wearing of masks to conceal individual identity on public property (Ellis, 1990).

As soon as one appreciates both the enormous variety of individual and social characteristics that may serve as symbolic statuses of victims and the lexical and stipulative conditions of offenses used to classify these offenses, one overriding sociological implication follows: There is extraordinary heterogeneity in hate crime (Berk, 1994), a heterogeneity that ultimately—to come full circle—shapes the very definition of the crime itself (Witte, 1995).

### Official Data

The short history of the FBI's statistical program on hate can be summarized briefly. The first data were released in 1991 and were supplied by 2,771 law enforcement agencies in 32 states. "While these initial data are limited," commented Director William S. Sessions at the time, "they give us our first assessment of the nature of crimes motivated by bias in our society" (FBI, 1991a, u.p.). A year later, reporting had improved considerably. Data for 1992 were supplied by 6,180 law enforcement agencies in 41 states and the District of Columbia. This represented a more than 150% increase in reporting by the states. Beyond that, the classifications of offenses remained stable, allowing for some preliminary, albeit cautious, comparisons. The FBI data for the first two years are shown in Table 4.2.

These figures provided the first empirical snapshot of hate crimes in the United States. They clearly indicated that intimidation was the most frequent hate crime, followed by destruction/damage/vandalism of property and simple and aggravated assault. The reports also offered the first base of information on victims. For both 1991 and 1992, hate crimes motivated by a victim's race were the most frequent (62% for 1991 and 1992), and the target was most often a black person. Crimes motivated by a victim's religion were the second most frequently reported (19% in 1991, 15% in 1992), and the target was most often a Jew. Sexual orientation was the third most frequently reported victim characteristic (9% in 1991, 11% in 1992), and most of those crimes were committed against homosexuals. Ethnicity was the least frequently reported characteristic (9% in 1991, 10% in 1992), and the most likely victim was a Hispanic.

**TABLE 4.2** Bias-Motivated (Hate) Crimes Known to the Police:
1991-1992

| Offense | 1991 | | 1992 | |
| --- | --- | --- | --- | --- |
| | Number | Percentage | Number | Percentage |
| Murder | 12 | 0.3 | 17 | 0.2 |
| Forcible rape | 7 | 0.1 | 8 | 0.1 |
| Robbery | 119 | 2.5 | 172 | 1.9 |
| Aggravated assault | 773 | 16.3 | 1,431 | 16.0 |
| Burglary | 56 | 1.2 | 69 | 0.8 |
| Larceny-theft | 22 | 0.5 | 36 | 0.4 |
| Motor vehicle theft | 0 | 0.0 | 5 | 0.1 |
| Arson | 55 | 1.2 | 47 | 0.5 |
| Simple assault | 796 | 16.7 | 1,765 | 19.8 |
| Intimidation | 1,614 | 33.9 | 3,328 | 37.3 |
| Destruction/ damage/ vandalism | 1,301 | 27.4 | 2,040 | 22.9 |
| Total | 4,755 | 100.0 | 8,918 | 100.0 |

SOURCES: FBI (1991a); FBI (1992).

In 1993, the FBI report became more comprehensive both in terms of agency reporting and in the classification of offenses. The data were supplied by 6,865 agencies in 46 states and the District of Columbia. Three new categories were added to the report: (a) the number of incidents, (b) the number of victims, and (c) the number of known offenders. The most recent statistics are provided in Table 4.3.

As can be seen, the offense patterns held steady: Intimidation was the most frequent hate crime, followed by destruction/ damage/vandalism of property and simple and aggravated assault. The new classifications also filled in some missing pieces of the hate crime puzzle. They show that incidents of hate crime often produce multiple offenses. They also show that incidents typically involve multiple victims and—especially in the areas of aggravated assault, robbery, rape, and murder—multiple offenders. The most serious hate crimes, then, are group projects, suggesting that perpetrators share a conspiratorial motive for their violence.

**TABLE 4.3**    Bias-Motivated (Hate) Crimes Known to the Police: 1993

| Offense | Incidents | Offenses | Victims | Known Offenders |
|---|---|---|---|---|
| Murder | 11 | 16 | 16 | 22 |
| Forcible rape | 13 | 15 | 15 | 17 |
| Robbery | 157 | 161 | 202 | 378 |
| Aggravated assault | 1,044 | 1,452 | 1,452 | 2,395 |
| Burglary | 84 | 88 | 104 | 38 |
| Larceny-theft | 55 | 61 | 71 | 48 |
| Motor vehicle theft | 9 | 9 | 9 | 9 |
| Arson | 53 | 53 | 61 | 36 |
| Simple assault | 1,462 | 1,754 | 1,754 | 2,491 |
| Intimidation | 2,451 | 3,056 | 3,056 | 2,126 |
| Destruction/ damage/vandalism | 2,222 | 2,294 | 2,604 | 1,011 |
| Other | 26 | 28 | 28 | 39 |
| Total | 7,587 | 8,987 | 9,372 | 8,610 |

SOURCE: FBI (1993).

The victimization figures also held steady. By far, the most frequent motive for hate crime was race (62% of total incidents), and the most frequent victim was a black person. Religion was the second leading motive (17% of total), and again the most frequent victim was a Jew. Sexual orientation was third (11%), and again homosexuals were the most frequent victim; ethnicity was last, with Hispanics the most frequent victims.

### Summary

Before passage of the Hate Crime Statistics Act, no national public data source on the extent or characteristics of hate crime existed. The goal of the act was to collect and disseminate such information. To the extent that increased comprehensiveness, increased rates of reporting, and the discovery of criminological trends are a measure of that goal, the FBI's program on hate crime statistics can be considered nothing less than a success.

## The Social Science Literature

Given both the newness and the remaining shortcomings of official statistics, social scientists have made significant contributions to the study of domestic terrorism and hate crime. During the past 10 years, social scientists have published more than 100 books, articles, chapters, monographs, and dissertations on the subjects. They have delivered perhaps twice that number of papers at academic conferences around the world. They have developed their own databases, designed numerous typologies and definitions, and advanced theories to account for all manner of political crime. In fact, as I attempt to show below, so much literature has emerged that even distinguished libraries cannot keep up with its effluence.

### University Databases: 1986-1996

Nine computerized databases contain citations on domestic terrorism and hate crime at the Indiana University (IU) Library, a university library that currently ranks 17th in the nation. To the extent that academic pedigree is correlated with the cataloging of social scientific knowledge, an inspection of these databases may answer two important questions: (a) Who is shaping the emerging and thriving academic discourse on domestic terrorism and hate crime? and (b) How well does this discourse help us understand the Oklahoma City bombing?

If answers to the first question do exist, perhaps they can be twisted out of a classification of the databases (a) in terms of the number of citations per database and (b) by identifying the primary focus of each citation as legal research, political science research, research in criminology or sociology, research in religion, or law-enforcement/social work research. This classification of the databases is presented in Table 4.4 for the years 1986 to 1996.

These figures reveal that research in criminology and the sociology of social movements currently constitutes the lion's share of academic literature on domestic terrorism and hate crime, followed by studies in law enforcement/social work, legal research, studies in political science, and religion. But this conclusion may be

**TABLE 4.4** Computerized Databases for Domestic Terrorism and Hate Crime

|  |  | Primary Focus | | | | |
|---|---|---|---|---|---|---|
| Source | Number of Citations | Legal | Political Science | Criminology/ Sociology | Religion | Law Enforcement/ Social Work |
| Political Science Abstracts | 4 | 4 | 0 | 0 | 0 | 0 |
| PAIS International | 18 | 3 | 5 | 5 | 0 | 5 |
| Sociological Abstracts | 15 | 0 | 2 | 8 | 1 | 4 |
| Social Science Index (4/94-5/95) | 6 | 2 | 0 | 2 | 0 | 1 |
| Criminology, Penology, and Police Science Abstracts (1994-1995) | 4 | 0 | 0 | 1 | 0 | 3 |
| IUCAT (Indiana University Catalog System) | 12 | 1 | 1 | 6 | 1 | 3 |
| Criminal Justice Abstracts | 17 | 1 | 0 | 11 | 2 | 1 |
| Books in Print | 12 | 0 | 0 | 9 | 1 | 2 |
| Eureka | 6 | 2 | 0 | 3 | 0 | 1 |
| Total | 94 | 13 | 8 | 45 | 5 | 20 |
| % of Total |  | 14% | 9% | 48% | 6% | 22% |

precipitous: Despite the sophistication of electronic databases, they do not, by any means, capture the full extent of research in any area of social science.

Any social scientist who has ever published his or her work—only to find it has been ignored by the *Social Science Index*—is well aware of this problem. University librarians do not routinely catalog citations on book chapters and monographs. They do not catalog citations on conference presentations or public lectures. But more important, librarians do not even begin to catalog the full range of scholarly publications in books and academic journals. Below, I offer two brief case studies to illustrate this problem because it is crucial to answering the question about the Oklahoma City bombing of a federal building.

### Terrorism: An International Journal

The first academic journal in the United States with an explicit interest in political violence was *Terrorism: An International Journal,* published by the RAND Corporation of Washington, D.C. When I stacked all the back issues of *Terrorism* on top of each other, they came up to my knees; I am 5 ft 10 in. tall. During the next four hours, I conducted a content analysis of *Terrorism* and found that since its inaugural issue in 1979, the journal has published 279 articles (excluding reprints of official documents, book reviews, symposia, and speeches).

Of these 279 articles, 159 (57%) were published between 1986 and 1995. Yet none of them (zero) were cataloged in the various databases. There is perhaps good reason for this as well: Of the 159 articles, only 22 (a mere 7%) dealt with terrorism inside U.S. borders. The overwhelming majority of articles focused on terrorism in the Middle East, Northern Ireland, Turkey, and Africa. Half of the 22 U.S. domestic terrorism articles were written from a law enforcement perspective. The remainder were written from either a criminology/sociology perspective (36%) or a political science perspective (18%). Importantly, for reasons that will soon become apparent, there were no articles on the religious antecedents of terrorism.

### Terrorism and Political Violence

The second case study involves *Terrorism and Political Violence (TPV)*. In its inaugural issue—published in January 1989—the editors declared that *TPV* was "the first truly academic multi-disciplinary journal in its field" (Wilkinson & Rapoport, 1989, p. 5). By 1995, the journal's frontmatter would list 19 editors and editorial board members, 10 of whom were affiliated with universities in the United States. But again, very few of the articles dealt with terrorism inside U.S. borders.

A total of 157 articles were published in *TPV* between 1989 and 1995 (excluding, e.g., official documents, reviews, and technical reports). Of this number, 133 (85%) focused on terrorism in Europe, Africa, and South America. I was unable to classify 12 articles, and the remaining 12 (only 8% of the total) dealt with terrorism in the United States. Seven were written by political scientists; five were written by religion scholars. Only one article, Michael Barkun's "Millenarian Groups and Law Enforcement Agencies: The Lessons of Waco" (1994a), showed up in the computerized database search.

But a broader point is to be made here: All nonstate terrorism, when it is waged against a country's citizens by other citizens of that country in order to influence the government, is domestic (Gibbs, 1989). Hence, lessons learned about domestic terrorism in one country could apply to another country. For example, since 1992, *TPV* has published six well-researched articles on right-wing violence in Germany. Knowledge about this domestic terrorism in Germany may carry important implications for understanding domestic terrorism in the United States. If so, university libraries are doing a woefully inadequate job of cataloging it.

## Social Science and the Oklahoma City Bombing

Three weeks after the bombing of the Alfred P. Murrah Federal Building, more than 700 law enforcement administrators from about 126 federal, state, and local agencies gathered in Baltimore for a conference entitled "The Impact of Hate." Among the keynote speakers was U.S. Attorney Lynne A. Battaglia, who declared that the Oklahoma City bombing was a "hate crime" and that hate crimes are terroristic: acts of "focused randomness . . . worse than random violence because they are directed against us for things that may be immutable" (quoted in Rosga, 1996, p. 1). Social scientists share this view. Perhaps because of the blending of the two concepts in official records, social scientists often use the terms *hate crime* and *domestic terrorism* interchangeably (e.g., Aronowitz, 1994b; Berk, 1994; Hamm, 1994b, 1994c; Kellett, 1995; Levin & McDevitt, 1993; Ross, 1994). If the Oklahoma City bombing was a hate crime, and if hate crimes are terroristic, then research on hate crime and domestic terrorism should help explain the Oklahoma City bombing. Because the preponderance of the literature appears to have emerged from criminology and the sociology of social movements, it is only logical to focus on those studies, supplanting them with findings from other disciplines when necessary.

## American Terrorism

In my opinion, the most informed analysis of domestic terrorism in the United States is Brent L. Smith's *Terrorism in America: Pipe Bombs and Pipe Dreams* (1994). Smith's book is important because it moves behind the import of both official reports and journalistic accounts to offer a detailed study of American terrorism based on an extensive analysis of records from federal district courts, national archives, the U.S. Sentencing Commission, and the Administrative Office of U.S. Courts. Smith explains why the FBI statistics on terrorism "are a confusing enigma" (p. 25) and proceeds to an analysis of the demographic and psychological profiles of individuals who turn to terroristic violence.

Of the 173 individuals indicted under the FBI's counterter-rorism program between 1980 and 1989, Smith (1994) found, "103 were members of or associated with a loose coalition of right-wing groups frequently referred to as being part of the Christian Identity Movement" (p. 32). Religion, then, was the common thread binding these right-wing groups together. Of these 103 individuals, 78 were affiliated with the paramilitary groups known as the Order (head-quartered near Hayden Lake, Idaho); and the Covenant, the Sword, and the Arm of the Lord (CSA), based in the Ozark Mountains of northern Arkansas (p. 14). Yet, as Smith convincingly shows, a criminal conspiracy was ongoing between the two groups.

Contrary to both popular opinion and criminological research on criminal careers (e.g., Blumstein, Cohen, Roth, & Vister, 1986), Smith found that the average age of these American terrorists was 39. The overwhelming majority of them (97%) were white males with nothing more than a G.E.D. equivalent or less. More than half were unemployed or impoverished or both at the time of their indictment, and nearly all came from rural areas of Arkansas, Idaho, Kentucky, Colorado, and Arizona (Smith, 1994, p. 47). These white men held views that were strongly anti-Communist, anti-gun control, pro-Protestant, and pro-working class. Their tactical approach to terrorism was built on a campaign of national networking via campgrounds and the emerging computer bulletin board technology. For funding, they relied on the robbery of armored trucks, which netted them more than $5 million during the 1980s. The primary targets of their violence were federal law enforcement agencies or those American citizens who advocated particularly eccentric views about race and religion (Smith, 1994, p. 37). Smith also discovered that extremist members of the Christian Identity movement, especially those who belonged to the Order and CSA, used "the directives of *The Turner Diaries* as a guide" (p. 26). (*The Turner Diaries* is best described as a fantasy-oriented science fiction novel, published in 1978 by William Pierce under the pseudonym Andrew Macdonald, that provides a blueprint for fomenting racial, ethnic, and anti-government violence.)

Smith's study is prescient for two reasons. First, numerous references to *The Turner Diaries* were found among the belongings of the two men charged in the Oklahoma City bombing. Also found was a well-thumbed copy of *Armed and Dangerous: The Rise of the Survivalist Right*, journalist James Coates's authoritative account of The Order and the CSA (Coates, 1987; Hamm, 1997). Second, Timothy McVeigh, the man convicted of the Oklahoma City bombing, had known ties to a CSA splinter group located in the Ozark Mountains, called Elohim City, a Christian Identity commune (Annin & Morganthau, 1996).

These themes actually derive from sociologist James Aho's *The Politics of Righteousness: Idaho Christian Patriotism* (1990). Aho begins with an analysis of 51 fatalities related to U.S. right-wing activity between 1980 and 1985. He found that roughly half of the killings involved individuals with Christian Identity associations and that nearly half of those involved members of the Order and CSA. In an attempt to bring structure to our understanding of the people involved in the Identity movement, Aho created a typology of "hedgehogs" (grand theorists) and "foxes" (empiricists). Hedgehogs derive their radical views from macrostructural theories of history and society and "are able to fit events as diverse as earthquakes, venereal disease, and commodity prices into an overarching theoretical scheme" (p. 17). Foxes, in contrast, are concerned with such mundane problems as school textbooks, sex education, and the availability of condoms. The emotional impetus for terrorism is created, of course, by the ideologically oriented hedgehogs.

Aho (1990) applied this typology to the social profiles of 520 "Christian Patriots" through the use of secondary sources (media accounts, right-wing literature, and research monographs) and primary sources (face-to-face interviews, telephone interviews, and mailed questionnaires). Like Smith, Aho found that the hedgehogs are "exceptional only in their ordinariness" (p. 67). The most violent among them are average white men who have been "Boys' State representatives, high school yearbook editors . . . rock 'n' roll musicians . . . one-time teen athletes, a champion amateur golfer, and a high school teacher with a masters degree in counseling" (p. 66). Aho examined the profiles of each Order member and discovered nothing in their backgrounds to predict a shift from libertarianism to radical politics later in the life course. He describes these terrorists as "likable" and "good workers" who were "very polite" as young men. In a particularly telling description of one Order member, Aho interviewed the man's mother, who said, "He was a good little boy, except for his politics" (p. 66).

Aho (1990) also found a strong reliance on *The Turner Diaries* as a blueprint for terrorism among the Identity adherents. He traced numerous parallels between the book and the activities of actual groups operating in the Northwest, including the use of code names, the creation of "hit lists," the assassination of unreliable Identity devotees, and the initiation of members through ritual oath taking.

Further glimpses into the social processes that shape the dynamics of right-wing radicalism and the individual transforma-

tion from libertarianism to terrorism are splendidly detailed in
James William Gibson's *Warrior Dreams: Violence and Manhood in
Post-Vietnam America* (1994). Through his ethnographic study of
paint ball games and gun shows sanctioned by the National Rifle
Association (NRA), Gibson provides rare insights into the pathology
of modern American masculinity. He traces the rise of the Order and
the CSA to a "cult of the warrior," which emerged in response to
America's defeat in Vietnam, the emergence in 1978 of *Soldier of
Fortune* magazine, and the feminist movement. With this *zeitgeist* as
a backdrop, Gibson wrote:

> It is hardly surprising, then, that American men—lacking con-
> fidence in the government and the economy, troubled by the
> changing relations between sexes, uncertain of their identity or
> their future—began to *dream*, to fantasize about the powers and
> features of another kind of man who could retake and reorder the
> world. And the hero of all these dreams was the paramilitary
> warrior. (p. 11)

Like Smith and Aho, Gibson (1994) argues that the Christian
Identity movement "provided the most comprehensive mythology
for the far-right . . . in the 1980s." But he takes us a step closer to
understanding the epistemic setting of terrorism by distinguishing
religion from fantasy:

> [It was] *The Turner Diaries* that offered a second, more succinct
> formulation of how warriors could achieve a sacred order. . . . [I]t
> became an incredibly influential book—and for very particular
> reasons. Whereas Christian Identity basically told a story about
> the fall of the white man . . . [*The Diaries*] is built on the premise
> of a white government looking back on its successful rise to
> power. (p. 220)

Historians will eventually wrestle with two competing theories
on the Oklahoma City bombing. The first will probably become the
lesser-known of the two explanations. This theory will hold that
McVeigh blew up the Oklahoma City federal building on April 19,
1995, because on that day former CSA member Richard Wayne
Snell—an Identity adherent—was executed in the Cummins Unit of
the Arkansas State Prison on the standing executive order of former
Arkansas Governor Bill Clinton—who, as everyone knows, was
currently the titular head of the federal government. Hence, a con-

spiracy was behind the bombing. Its roots extended deep into the Ozark Mountains and the CSA and its criminal conspirator, the Order. The Oklahoma City bombing, then, was a conspiratorial retaliation waged by the far Right against Bill Clinton for the Snell execution. This theory is worth pondering. Snell was executed on the evening of April 19, 1995. His last words were directed at the sitting governor of Arkansas, Jim Guy Tucker: "Governor Tucker," Snell said before his execution, "look over your shoulder. Justice is coming." Earlier that day, at precisely 9:02 a.m., the fertilizer bomb had gone off beneath the day care center of the Murrah building (Hamm, 1997).

The second theory will hold that McVeigh bombed the Murrah building in retaliation for the government's actions at the Branch Davidian compound near Waco on April 19, 1993. As McVeigh saw it, FBI agents had killed some 80 men, women, and children at Mount Carmel. The prosecution will show that McVeigh made a "pilgrimage" to Mount Carmel and came away with a deep-seated hatred for the federal government. He had also learned, through newsletters and the like, that April 19, 1992, was the date that Bureau of Alcohol, Tobacco and Firearms (ATF) agents made their initial attempt to serve a search warrant on Randy Weaver (another Christian Identity adherent) at his mountain cabin near Ruby Ridge, Idaho. Later, Weaver's wife and 14-year-old son were killed by federal sharpshooters. Hence, McVeigh's bombing of the Murrah building was meant to redeem the sins of Waco and Ruby Ridge.

Both theories have an academic grounding in Michael Barkun's *Religion and the Racist Right: The Origins of the Christian Identity Movement* (1994b). Barkun identifies three key beliefs of Christian Identity. First, Identity believes that white "Aryans" are descendants of the biblical tribes of ancient Israel and thus are on earth to do God's work. Second, Identity holds that Jews are not only historically unconnected to the Israelites but also are the very children of the Devil, the biological offspring of a sexual encounter between Satan and Eve in the Garden of Eden. Third, Identity believes the world is on the verge of the final, apocalyptic struggle between good and evil, a struggle that demands Aryans do battle against the worldwide Jewish conspiracy. "By any criteria," Barkun writes, "these are beliefs that place Identity at the farthest margins of American religion, but they also suggest its potential political volatility" (p. ix).

Because numerous factors are likely to affect beliefs in the perceived victimization by the Jewish conspiracy, however, Identity adherents will almost certainly vary in the extent to which they embrace the goals of Identity and, therefore, in their extent of involvement in political violence. Barkun makes a monumental contribution to the terrorism literature by identifying this variation. He notes,

> The Order eventually grew to almost forty members, although some individuals had relatively tenuous connections. In time, tensions arose between committed Identity believers and others in the organization. . . . Although the Order never split, it did divide into Identity and non-Identity wings. (p. 231)

According to Barkun (1994), the Identity wing of the Order was responsible for its string of armored truck robberies, assassinations, and bombings. Also within this wing *The Turner Diaries* had its greatest effect (p. 229). Finally, Barkun speculates on the potential for Identity violence through an examination of the incidents at Waco and Ruby Ridge. "The Waco and Weaver episodes," he writes, "suggest that the potential for violence in Christian Identity depends upon both the beliefs and strategies adopted by Identity groups and the responses made by local and national authorities" (p. 242). The last sentence of his analysis could well have foretold the Oklahoma City bombing: "Therefore, the potential for Identity-related violence in the future depends as much upon the responses made by law-enforcement agencies as it does upon change internal to the movement" (p. 242).

## The Neo-Nazi Connection

Along with *The Turner Diaries* and Christian Identity, Smith, Aho, Gibson, and Barkun also acknowledge the existence of a neo-Nazi motif as a driving force behind the rise of U.S. right-wing terrorism during the 1980s. This is important for the current discussion because, as recent events indicate, a transatlantic conspiracy of neo-Nazi sympathizers may have been connected to the Oklahoma City bombing. This connection can be traced to Elohim City, a German neo-Nazi who lived there, and a telephone call made to the German by McVeigh two weeks before the bombing (Annin & Morganthau, 1996).

My own work in this area (Hamm, 1993, 1994b, 1995) is consistent with studies conducted by Canadian and European criminologists who have found that a critical factor in the development first of discontent and then of political violence among neo-Nazi youth is *information* transmitted via international travel, cyberculture, and the import of hard-to-find racist books, journals, films, and most important, music (Aronowitz, 1994b; Back, Keith, & Solomos, 1995; Baron, 1989; Fangen, 1995; Jensen, 1993; Lööw, 1993). My studies are based primarily on structured interviews with 36 Skinhead gang leaders conducted in the United States between 1989 and 1992. These Skinheads were predominantly young white males from working-class backgrounds who reported no early childhood trauma nor any abuse by their parents. The majority of them were either enrolled in high school, were high school graduates now working blue-collar jobs, or were attending a university.

These youths overwhelmingly embraced a neo-Nazi ideology that was, in order of statistical importance, antiblack, antigay, and anti-Semitic. (Many of them were tattooed with the swastika, the Iron Cross, or the mark of the Waffen SS.) They came to their extreme beliefs through exposure to (a) underground "zines" produced and distributed by adult neo-Nazis associated with the White Aryan Resistance (WAR) of Southern California, a likely recipient of the Order's largesse after its 1984 armored truck robberies; (b) religious material produced and disseminated by adults associated with the Christian Identity movement and the racist Church of the Creator; and (c) white power heavy metal music produced and distributed by neo-Nazi sympathizers in England, France, the Netherlands, and Germany.

The average Skinhead in the study had been involved in roughly five self-reported assaults against antiracist Skinheads, black males, gays, or Jewish institutions during the previous two years. At the time of these assaults, most of the Skinheads were intoxicated on beer and armed with clubs, knives, steel-toed military boots, brass knuckles, or loaded firearms. All the assaults were group projects. Accordingly, I concluded, "Instead of viewing the Skinheads as a street gang, we must define them for what they truly are. Because of their overt racist political violence, and links to a homologous international subculture of neo-Nazism, the Skinheads constitute what can best be described as a *terrorist youth subculture*" (Hamm, 1993, p. 65).

The white power music scene not only provides us with a way of understanding the transatlantic nature of neo-Nazism but also provides researchers with a mechanism for entering this modern terrorist youth subculture and monitoring its growth. Nowhere has this mechanism been more fully explored than in the work of Swedish criminologist Helene Lööw of Stockholm University (1993, 1995a, 1995b). Lööw has interviewed dozens of players in white power bands across Europe, Canada, and (over the Internet) the United States.

> The modern racist propagandist is not, like in the 1930's, a party strategist or skilled speaker, but a combination of rock star, speaker and street fighter . . . [who] walks stiffly back and forth over the stage. He is the high priest of the ritual, the leader that controls the public in the very same way the national socialist speaker of the 1930's did. (Lööw, 1995b, p. 28)

Through this rich ethnography, Lööw documents the spread of neo-Nazism throughout North America, Britain, France, Sweden, the Netherlands, and Germany. She describes, for example, how WAR and the Church of the Creator were imported to Sweden—via the white power music scene—where activists created zines dedicated to increasing violence against foreigners and homosexuals. Yet Lööw warns that it

> is wrong to describe the underground world of "White Power" as an exclusive youth culture, even if most of the "members" are young. There exists no age barriers—everyone who believes in the concept of racism and who is accepted by the network is considered a "brother or sister"—despite their age, sex, social position, or education. (1995b, p. 17)

Hence, not only does Lööw explain the transatlantic nature of neo-Nazism, but she also unpacks its transgenerational appeal. For instance, Smith (1994) documents the fact that Frank Silva, 39, is now serving a 40-year federal prison sentence for his activities in connection with the Order. Lööw shows how Silva has become a celebrity among European Skinheads through his various penitentiary interviews. At another point in her research, Lööw attended the annual "Hitler Fest" in Stockholm and explained how both musicians and their audience have been inspired by Hitler, WAR, and the poetry of former Order member David Lane, 58, currently serving a 190-year federal sentence (Smith, 1994). Lööw also shows how the symbols and regalia of German national socialism have been combined with those of the American Ku Klux Klan and the South African Aryan Brotherhood to produce a hybrid of neo-Nazi banners and uniforms for modern European youths. Finally, and perhaps most illustrative of the transatlantic and transgenerational nature of neo-Nazism, Lööw traces the events that led to the creation of the "Day of the Martyrs"—December 8. Next to April 20 (Hitler's birthday), this is the most important day in the mythology of European neo-Nazism: On December 8, 1984, Order leader Robert J. Mathews was killed by FBI agents in a shootout on Whidbey Island, Washington (Aho, 1990).

The production and distribution of mail-order neo-Nazism has increased dramatically in the 1990s. In fact, it is estimated that the international marketing of Nazi memorabilia, racist and anti-Semitic literature, and Nazi T-shirts, stickers, banners, videos, uniforms, posters, jewelry, and white power heavy metal music has become a $100 million-a-year commercial enterprise (Hamm, 1994d; Jensen, 1993). A large portion of this material originates in the United States and is distributed by such groups as WAR, Resistance Records of Milwaukee, and the National Socialist German Workers' Party/Exile & Edification Organization (NSDAP/AO) of Lincoln, Nebraska (Hamm, 1993; Kaplan, 1995; Schmidt, 1993).

This enterprise is no doubt a result of the proliferation of new information technologies created by computers. With it has come the transatlantic penetration of neo-Nazism into modern societies of the digital age. Les Back et al. (1995), of the University of London, have convincingly demonstrated how it is even possible for nationalistic movements of markedly different persuasions to establish common networks within the Internet and cyberculture. They show, for instance, how the Aryan Crusader's Library—an on-line virtual networking resource run by a neo-Nazi Skinhead at the University of Texas—includes a category entitled "The African Quarter," which is produced by the Nation of Islam. Back and his associates argue, "The establishment of these strange acquaintances in cyberspace point to where opposing, and sometimes deeply antagonistic racial and nationalistic ideologies, can associate around common terms of reference . . . particularly around shared anti-Semitism" (p. 9). Therefore, it is possible "for staunchly nationalistic sensibilities to be maintained while fascist culture is globalized" (p. 9).

Moreover, the British sociologists show how a variety of computer networks are being used by neo-Nazi groups to develop and sustain an international system of communication to inform activists of events as diverse as the planning of a memorial march for Rudolf Hess in Berlin and the recording of names of antiracist activists, hostile judges, and journalists in such places as Billings, Montana, and Birmingham, Alabama. In Sweden alone are more than 20 active neo-Nazi computer bulletin boards with international linkages. Back et al. (1995) conclude by reminding Americans of something they already know too well: Many of these international bulletin boards post detailed instructions for making powerful fertilizer bombs like the one used in Oklahoma City (for a concise discussion of these postings, see Stern, 1996).

A review of neo-Nazism in the 1990s would not be complete without a discussion of Germany. Since 1991, racist Skinheads and other right-wing extremists—often trained in explosives and hand-to-hand combat—have grievously injured more than 20,000 foreigners, asylum seekers, Jews, leftists, punks, anarchists, and people with handicaps (Aronowitz, 1994a; Hamm, 1994a; Willems, 1995). German sociologists, however, have been less interested in the cultural antecedents of these crimes (the free flow of information within and across national borders) than in generational factors. Moreover, right-wing extremists are viewed as part of a "new" Germany that has been transformed by the demise of communism and the revival of national and regional identities. Their violence, then, is explained in terms of a peculiar behavioral characteristic of the "children of the wall" or the "children of industrialization."

According to the German sociology community, these youths become headline news as a result of their protests against established institutions, the generation gap, the plundering of natural resources (especially in the former East), the colonization of their immediate social environment by Third World immigrants, and increased competition between these immigrants and host-country youths over low-wage jobs. All of this has been exacerbated by Germany's recent financial recession, massive spending commitments made to bring the former East infrastructure up to Western standards, and rising unemployment (Lauk, 1994). Thus, the young extremists have been found to have poor school records, poor job skills, and a host of personal problems (Heitmeyer, 1993; Kühnel, 1995a; Willems, 1995).

German scholars have therefore constructed classic structural models of social movements explicating the conditions necessary for the emergence of right-wing terror. I focus here on but one of them: Wolfgang Kühnel's (1995b) model of violent and xenophobic networks. At the macrostructural level, Kühnel argues that social, ethnic, and regional differences generate tensions that allow for the emergence of Skinhead and fascist subcultures prone to terroristic violence. These subcultures spread throughout the polity as a result of collective perceptions of the tensions between the right-wing subcultures and the general population. They are then stabilized through structures of opportunity in the ever-changing world of politics and the media.

At the mesostructural level, conflicts between different actors (e.g., between youths and immigrants) simultaneously create conditions ripe for the emergence of terroristic subcultures, which are then spread via scandal created in the public sphere. Various political strategies are then employed by activists to stabilize the emerging social movement.

Political and economic processes leading to perceived deprivation provide the conditions necessary for the emergence of terroristic subcultures at the microstructural level. They are spread by in-group/out-group dynamics and stabilized by activist networks that mobilize resources for the movement's cause.

Finally, at the individual level, all the above-mentioned conditions coalesce to create people with a tendency toward aggressive problem solving. Their aggression is spread through society by modeling (what U.S. sociologists call *social learning*), the pronounced need for stimulation, and status ascription. Last, the stabilization of the movement is achieved through a closing of the mind, by tuning out ideas and ideologies from the rest of the world.

## Disengagement: The Memoirs

I end this chapter on a positive note. If the final stage in the construction of a terrorist subculture is a closing of the mind, then an intriguing question follows: Is it possible for the human mind to be reopened by tuning in ideas and ideologies from the rest of the world? On the basis of the emergent genre of literature that we might describe as the "stomp and tell" memoir, the answer appears to be affirmative. But it also appears to be a hard road back from what Barkun calls the "farthest margins" of political consciousness. The stomp-and-tell memoir teaches that the road to terrorism begins with an extended period of political indoctrination, proceeds to terroristic violence against social out-groups, and climaxes with the achievement of group status ascription. The road back is less exciting. It begins with a moment of awakening to one's own terroristic behavior, proceeds to a crisis in status ascription leading to immediate disengagement, and then comes a downward spiral of guilt, bottoming-out at profound self-loathing. And then, finally, comes a prolonged period of personal rehabilitation. This pattern is richly detailed in two recent stomp-and-tells that may soon find themselves at the top of every terrorism researchers reading list (see also Ezekiel, 1995; Prichard & Starr, 1994; Regan, 1993).

The first is David Greason's *I Was a Teenage Fascist* (1994). Greason's indoctrination in neo-Nazism led to his proclivity for random violence against Asians on the streets of Sydney, Australia, and catapulted him into a leading role in the British National Front and then to a leading role in the notoriously racist and violent National Action (NA) of Australia. (His story was used as a basis for the critically acclaimed movie *Romper Stomper*.) But at the peak of his popularity, things began to unravel for Greason because of internal conflict with an NA rival, named Jim, over leadership of the group. Recalling this conflict, Greason writes:

> [H]is name was in virtually every issue of the *National Socialist Bulletin* and *Stormtrooper*. He'd even had a write-up by a French anti-fascist writer. . . . He'd worked through the politics, but the guilt stuck to him like shit to a blanket. . . . Then everything happened very quickly . . . we quarreled continuously. . . . Everyone knew how much I hated Jim. . . . I couldn't see why I should have to do any of Jim's bidding, but in the interests of party unity, I agreed to withdraw. (pp. 224-225, 289-290)

During the next month, Greason also became wracked with guilt over the sorry story of my unedifying exit. I was so pissed off with Jim, really pissed off. But then it struck me. It was like two people fighting over a bag of shit. One says, Let go, and the other says, I will if you will, so they both let go, but one runs off with the bag. And you're standing there, thinking, You cheat, and then you realize that he's just run off with a bag of shit. (p. 294)

Years later, after an extended period of depression and rehabilitation through antiracist activity, Greason reflected on his experiences. Please indulge me the opportunity to quote him in full:

[F]ascist politics is not just about alienation and belonging. It's also about politics. I don't think I could have edged out of the far-fight had I not read Ted Murphy's dissection of National Alliance's policies in *Rabelais*. Just as my realization that our grand theories of the world didn't work came from reading and talking and reading again. . . .

Yet the decider doesn't necessarily come by having your beliefs challenged point by point. I don't think you drop intolerant politics because you've realized that *The Protocols of the Learned Elders of Zion* is fraudulent or that Hans Eysenck's theories on race are Eurocentric. You can't simply figure your way out of a life. It really falls apart when you're willing to give people the benefit of the doubt. It comes when you're sitting in a cab with some Vietnamese taxi driver and you're remembering those lines you've always trotted out when you're in an argument—Look, all people prefer their own, and it's nothing to do with hatred, but everything to do with what people have in common except this time you're thinking, on a one-to-one basis, here, now, in this RSL cab, could I have more in common with this Vietnamese driver than I have with a National Action member who keeps guns under his bed? We are what we talk ourselves into. (pp. 298-299)

### Führer-Ex

Few places on this planet are farther apart than Sydney, Australia, and Berlin, Germany. Yet Greason's trials are almost replicated step-by-step in Ingo Hasselbach's celebrated autobiography *Führer-Ex: Memoirs of a Former Neo-Nazi* (Hasselbach & Reiss, 1996). *Führer-Ex* is one of those rare books that illuminates things about the world we would rather not know but can't avoid because the story has such a riveting fascination.

Although Greason is careful not to say too much about his random attacks against Asians, Hasselbach's memoir simply teems with violence. *Führer-Ex* is nearly 400 pages long, and two thirds of it is dedicated to stories of indiscriminate street violence, bar fights, firebombings, and Hasselbach's incarceration in East German prisons, where he befriended several key members of Hitler's Waffen SS who were doing life sentences. On his release from prison in late 1988 (a year before the collapse of communism and the fall of the Berlin Wall), Hasselbach returned to his home in East Berlin and established what was not only East Germany's most formidable neo-Nazi organization but also what may well have been the strongest and most violent fascist presence of the post-Hitler era.

At the peak of his popularity, Hasselbach was the leader, or Führer, of some 4,000 Skinheads and other neo-Nazis who had taken over four adjoining houses in the center of East Berlin. They called themselves the Komerads, although their name mattered little. Hasselbach and his followers simply took squatters' rights over this inner-city property and cordoned it off with steel fencing and razor wire. Living inside the bunker were some 400 neo-Nazis. Like a pack of wild dogs, they made nightly sojourns to the East Berlin streets, where they brutally beat hundreds of foreigners, asylum seekers, punks, and anarchists. Their weapon of choice, however, was the Molotov cocktail. Their sport (for a classic discussion of crime-as-sport, see Sykes, 1978) was to see how many cars they could bomb on a given night.

Hasselbach spares us nothing. He tells us about his life growing up under communism, and his dramatic transformation from a peace-loving hippie to an angry punk to a full-blown neo-Nazi Skinhead. He tells us how he became a pain in the ass for the Stasi and ended up in prison, where he received his political indoctrination at the hands of Hitler's former henchmen.

Then Hasselbach tells us about the inner workings of his neo-Nazi cell. One Skinhead whom Hasselbach met in prison has more than 200 swastika tattoos festooning his body. He joins together with another dozen youths to show a continual stream of old movies about the Third Reich inside the bunker where hundreds of young East Berliners gather nightly to celebrate the glories of their grandfathers, many of whom served in the SS. Another group of Skinheads takes off for Bosnia, where they become self-styled mercenaries and take part in the killing and mass rapes. Even an indigenous folk idiom emerges. Hasselbach explains how the Komerads abandoned "white power rock" in favor of a softer, more plaintive acoustic-guitar-driven genre of folk songs celebrating the modern Nazi experience. One Skinhead becomes so obsessed with all of this that he dresses in a full Nazi battle uniform—complete with a sawed-off pump-action shotgun and hand grenades—and visits the battlegrounds of World War II. There he finds what he thinks is the skeleton of a Waffen SS officer. Overcome by emotion, he picks up the bones, cradles them in his arms, and takes them home to bed.

Hasselbach left the neo-Nazi movement in January 1993. I will explain why in a moment. He sat down to write *Führer-Ex* soon after. He did so, in his words,

> to fight the neo-Nazis and to fight the Cause. And the first step in fighting them was to tell the story of what made me one of them, of how I pulled others in, and of how a sewer of Third Reich wastewater flows beneath the clean streets of modern Germany. I've climbed out of that sewer, and I will now tell you what's down there. (1996, p. xii)

Hasselbach came to the United States on April 17, 1995. He did so because his mother's apartment had just been bombed and he was dodging repeated attempts on his life by the Komerads. In exile, Hasselbach took up residence at a New York City hotel. Using a laptop computer, he began to put the finishing touches on his manuscript. Two days later, the fertilizer bomb went off in Oklahoma City. This caused Hasselbach to consider his memoir in a wider context. In the Introduction, he writes:

> I don't know if whoever blew up the Alfred P. Murrah Federal Building in Oklahoma City read the army manual we worked from. If they didn't, I'm sure we had some other reading material in common. The right-wing extremist movement is a loose network of people with a great deal of hatred and potential for violence, and all over the world they are constantly exchanging information. . . . Virtually all of our propaganda and training manuals came from the right-wing extremist groups in Nebraska and California. Such materials are legal to print in the United States under the First Amendment. In Germany, they are not,

under the Constitution passed after the defeat of the Third Reich. (pp. viii-ix)

Hasselbach's awakening came on November 23, 1992. At about 1:00 a.m., two Skinheads threw Molotov cocktails into the home of a 51-year-old Turkish woman named Bahide Arslan in Mölln, one of western Germany's most prosperous cities located near Hamburg. In the ensuing fire, Arslan was burned to death as she lay atop her grandson. Another child, Arslan's granddaughter, Yelitz Arslan, 10, also burned to death in the blaze, along with her cousin, 14-year-old Ayse Tuknaz. Six other family members were hospitalized for severe burns and smoke inhalation (Hamm, 1994a). Hasselbach (1996) remembers:

> I woke up the next morning to the news on my clock radio; three people had been burned alive in a neo-Nazi attack in the town of Mölln in northern Germany. . . . Oddly enough, considering the thousands of attacks that had occurred in the last couple of years, this was the first with fatalities. . . .
> I felt a certain boundary had been overstepped. . . . I told my Komerads point-blank that this was a sad and awful event and we must at least re-think our methods if they were to lead to this. (pp. 322-333)

But like Greason, no one else sided with Hasselbach, and he became an outcast. His nemesis was a violent young Skinhead—a "brutal idiot" named Oliver:

> It was a humbling experience trying to get even one person to side with me, the so-called Führer, in this crowd. They all preferred the view of young Oliver, and some people threw back into my face my own words from previous meetings, when I had said the foreigners were simply a vehicle for politics.
> It was true. I'd thought like that not too long ago. But something had permanently snapped inside of me, and I couldn't think that way anymore. I couldn't think of these Turks just as foreigners. They were also people—dead people with families. (p. 324)

This conflict led to Hasselbach's disengagement from neo-Nazi violence and eventually to his rehabilitation, which reached exquisite clarity in that New York City hotel room shortly after the Oklahoma

City bombing. But before that, Hasselbach underwent a deep depression. After the Mölln bombing, he took to roaming the streets of East Berlin alone, adrift and depressed. Like Greason, he began to think a lot about human excrement.

> As I walked around, I thought about how I'd so badly screwed everything up. I had done only shit—and not merely worthless shit, as so many do. Evil shit. Shit that was getting women burned alive in their homes. Shit I couldn't even begin to explain now. . . . I went back and sat alone in the living room. . . . I started to think of hanging myself that night. I looked around for places to do it. (p. 330)

On the very day that I conclude this review, the newspapers are reporting the suicides of three British neo-Nazis in Arizona and California. Several things spared Hasselbach that fate. In his words, the "first step" he took was to reexamine everything he had ever read about the Holocaust. This was an important step because, as Alexis Aronowitz (1994b) has so courageously pointed out, East German high school students of the communist era were largely deprived of educational material on the Holocaust. Hence, they had to find such information on their own. This led some East German youths, like Hasselbach and his Komerads, to consider as viable the theories expounded by such virulently racist and anti-Semitic American groups as WAR and NSDAP/AO.

This period of reeducation was followed by a purging ceremony in which Hasselbach gathered together his mountain of neo-Nazi propaganda and burned it. Then he arranged for a television interview, in which Hasselbach condemned the movement and its ideology, ending his appearance by burning a picture of Hitler and declaring that he was stepping down as the so-called "Führer of the East."

Hasselbach (1996) then became a wanted man by the Komerads; he was especially fearful of "the cold-blooded nineteen-year-old Oliver" (p. 344). Posters bearing his picture and the words "Ingo Hasselbach—State Spy" soon appeared on every East Berlin street corner. He went into exile in Paris, became surrounded by people of every race and color, and began to feel "as though a heavy weight had fallen from me" (p. 340). Then Karin came into his life. They soon became lovers. Through her, he got to know a life beyond neo-Nazism. He soon met all sorts of people—in the theater, in the arts community, people who'd never been near a street fight. She made up an odd pet name for him—Führer-Ex.

But that wasn't the only personal experience that saved Hasselbach from the hangman's noose. If messages of hatred and intolerance can find receptive audiences around the world, then so can messages of fraternity and peace. This one blew straight off the corner of Haight-Ashbury circa the late 1960s. If he was depressed, Hasselbach said, he kept listening to Neil Young. He has every album Young ever made.

## Conclusions, Trends, and New Directions

In her 1994 keynote address before the American Society of Criminology, U.S. Attorney General Janet Reno (1995) challenged social scientists to find new ways to disseminate their research as widely and as quickly as possible. "Current information is critically important," she said. "Find out what we can do about violence, try to develop a clearinghouse where we can get information out across the country as soon as it's happening" (p. 8).

The collection and dissemination of research on U.S. terrorism could certainly benefit from such a clearinghouse. It appears that university libraries are not up to the task of identifying and cataloging the massive body of academic literature on the subject. In this chapter, for example, I have cited 47 sources on domestic terrorism and hate crime that became available to social scientists between 1986 and 1996. Yet only six of them (13%) are cataloged in the university databases. Missing are such important works as Barkun's *Religion and the Racist Right*, Aho's *The Politics of Righteousness*, Gibson's *Warrior Dreams*, and Hasselbach's *Führer-Ex*.

The work of Jeffrey Kaplan provides a model case study of this problem. In 1995, Kaplan published an ambitious 51-page article in *Terrorism and Political Violence* called "Right-Wing Violence in North America." Kaplan meticulously worked through everything published on the Order, CSA, and transatlantic neo-Nazism. He provides original interviews with neo-Nazi Skinheads, an Identity preacher who once ministered to the Order, and offers no fewer than 15 pages of detailed footnotes on right-wing violence in North

America since 1986. Yet if you go to your university library and punch-up "domestic terrorism" on the computer, Kaplan's fascinating study will not be listed.

This report carries a second implication for social science. Just as Attorney General Reno laments the fact that research is often published "three years too late" (1995, p. 6), so, too, does the responsibility befall the U.S. Department of Justice of providing comprehensive and timely statistics on domestic terrorism to advance social scientific knowledge. In all likelihood, the official FBI report on the Oklahoma City bombing will not appear in university libraries until 1998, and then it will most likely offer limited empirical and substantive information about that terrible event.

And what of the future? What shape and form will U.S. terrorism have taken by the time that report is released? Predicting future trends is always risky, but if anyone has a crystal ball, perhaps it is those social scientists who have made a career of studying U.S. terrorism. I have asked a dozen of the nation's leading terrorism researchers for their ideas on the future and conclude by summarizing them.

First, to a person, each researcher sees the continued potential for antigovernment violence. Some see the Federal Bureau of Prisons as especially vulnerable to this threat. In recent years, federal prosecutors have exercised extraterritorial jurisdiction to put some high-profile international terrorists behind bars in U.S. penitentiaries. The European experience with terrorism shows that terrorist groups often make demands involving the release of terrorists held in prison. As more and more international terrorists are incarcerated in federal facilities, the potential for international terrorism against federal prisons and federal courts may increase.

Nearly every researcher also sees the continuation of U.S. right-wing antigovernment violence directed against judges and other local law enforcement officials. Some see the virtually unregulated availability of military-style firearms as a long-standing part of this problem. Others see the U.S. military as a potential breeding ground for extremists of the future. And still others see the unregulated use of cyberculture—with its plethora of postings on bomb making—as an utterly intractable part of the problem.

But the overarching theme of these predictions was that right-wing U.S. terrorism would only increase as we approach the millennium. The new millennium is extremely important to Christian

Patriots because, as Barkun (1994b) reminds us, "Identity believes the world is on the verge of the final, apocalyptic struggle between good and evil, a struggle which demands that Aryans do battle against the Jewish conspiracy" (p. ix).

I agree with all of these predictions on right-wing U.S. terrorism, but I offer one addition to the mix. More than anything else, the Oklahoma City bombing of April 19, 1995, has taught us that American terrorists are events oriented. Therefore, special days in the mythology of terrorist subcultures should not be ignored by agents of the federal government who are responsible for the security of prisons, post offices, military bases, courts, and federal buildings. Certainly, April 19 is an especially foreboding day. In the future, the next day—April 20, Adolf Hitler's birthday—may also become important. But if we have learned anything about the transatlantic and transgenerational appeal of neo-Nazism, it is that the future high holy day will be December 8. The Day of the Martyrs.

# 5

# The Patriot Movement
## *Past, Present, and Future*

### BRIAN LEVIN

America's Patriot antigovernment movement, barely noticed before
the bombing of a federal building in Oklahoma City, represents the
greatest threat of domestic terrorism to the United States at the end
of the 20th century. Assessing the threat from this movement, however, is in many ways an easier task than describing exactly what it
is. The Patriot antigovernment movement represents a newly formed
broad coalition of previously autonomous and loosely related social
and political ideologies. Its component ideologies represent a wide
spectrum internally regarding goals, methods, and leadership. The
ideological range is expansive: including wholly nonviolent fundamentalists and libertarians on the more moderate end of the scale,
and a small but influential number of white supremacists and Constitutionalists[1] on the other end, who believe that America exists for
white Christians only.[2] Methods, too, can range quite dramatically
from mainstream legal challenges, lobbying, and rambling political

diatribes all the way to fraud, intimidation, and terrorism. In this chapter, I analyze the terrorist threat of the Patriot antigovernment movement by examining both the historical factors that have led to its creation and its current characteristics.

Modern Patriot extremism fits neatly into established terrorist typology. Patriot offenders fall into at least one of these three main types of terrorists:

1. Ideologically Motivated

   *Beliefs*
   - Theological
   - Political
   - Hybrid

   *Citizenship*
   - Domestic
   - Foreign

2. Psychologically Dangerous

   *Sociopath*
   - Desires sense of power, knowledgeable about consequences

   *Mentally unstable*
   - Irrational or delusional

3. Self-Serving or Revengeful

   *Benefit*
   - Offender gains financial, reputational, or other enhancement

   *Revenge*
   - Offender settles an actual or perceived grievance against an individual or institution

Although the Patriot movement is a recent phenomenon, its component parts are hardly new. Paramilitarism, fundamentalism, tax protestation, anti-Semitism, white supremacy, nullification initiatives, gun rights, cults, libertarianism, conspiracy theories, and isolationism are recurrent political and social forces that have affected American history. It is not the component ideological parts of this movement that are new, but rather their relationship to one another. An understanding of how and why this relationship was forged is essential to analyzing not only the threat of the Patriot movement but also its evolution.

## Historical Roots of Resistance to Federal Authority

The extent of federal authority during the early history of the United States has been the subject of both political debate and factional violence. The formation of the nation itself and ratification of the Constitution involved a careful yet somewhat imperfect balancing of state and federal power. In fact, the Constitution's Bill of Rights, when first enacted in 1791, restricted only the hands of the federal government and not the states from interfering with various enumerated rights. This situation leads many commentators to observe that the goals behind the Bill of Rights were as much to restrict federal authority as they were to protect the exercise of fundamental rights because individual states still had significant latitude to interfere with civil liberties.

### Early Rebellion

This country's long history of renegade antigovernment paramilitary organizations extends back to the postrevolutionary period. In 1786, the first major challenge to federal authority occurred when dispossessed and disenfranchised poor Massachusetts farmers launched Shay's Rebellion against Commonwealth Courts and a federal military arsenal. The factional violence fueled support at the Constitutional Convention for a strong centralized federal government proficient at preventing such insurrections.

In 1794, another group of armed farmers launched the Whiskey Rebellion in protest over a new 30% tax on whiskey, a popular commodity. These militant rural Pennsylvania farmers threatened federal tax collectors, U.S. marshals, and those farmers in compliance with the new tax. After Pennsylvania, Governor Thomas Mifflin refused to end the intimidation of federal agents and citizens in the Commonwealth, President Washington and Treasury Secretary

Alexander Hamilton convinced the governors of adjacent states to call out 15,000 militia troops, and the rebellion promptly ended without further violence ("Whiskey Rebels," 1975, p. 1232).

### Nullification Politics and Klan Extremism

The Nullification Doctrine, a political concept that dates back to 1798, is embraced in altered form by modern-day Patriots. The doctrine incorrectly contends that states can void repugnant federal laws within their jurisdiction. Today's Patriots and Constitutionalists believe this "right" of nullification extends beyond the states to individual "sovereign" citizens as well. For instance, Michigan militia leader Norman Olson (1997) contends, "No man-made law can abolish the citizen militia since such a law would be in fact an unlawful act designed to dissolve the power vested in the people" (p. 13).

In 1798, Virginia's Thomas Jefferson and Kentucky's James Madison introduced the Nullification Doctrine to America by drafting state resolutions designed to void the sweeping Alien and Sedition Acts, which punished not only antigovernment plots but also defamatory criticism and dissent against government officials. The unconstitutional Alien and Sedition Acts were, in large part, repealed two years later when a Jeffersonian political victory threw the Federalists out of office. Nullification would continue to be an influential political doctrine in 19th-century America, peaking, but not ending, with the Civil War ("Nullification Doctrine," 1975, p. 813).

After the Civil War, antigovernment backlash in the South against the Union victory and Reconstruction federal civil rights laws ranged from the political to the terroristic. The Ku Klux Klan (KKK), the nation's largest and most enduring terrorist group, founded in Pulaski, Tennessee, in 1866, waged a violent campaign against newly freed black slaves who exercised their rights and the whites who supported Reconstruction (Chalmers, 1981).

A companion political and legislative backlash against federal authority also took place during the post-Civil War years. State Jim Crow Laws and Black Codes perpetuated the oppression and segregation of blacks, and the Posse Comitatus Act generally restricted the use of military troops from enforcing federal authority against civilians, as had been the case during Reconstruction. Federal courts also became ensnared in the political backlash against federalism by abandoning interpretations of federal laws that would limit the power of individual states and protect minorities ("Jim Crow Laws," 1975, p. 579; Levitas, 1996).

Although many political leaders were distrustful of the reach of federal power, they were also fearful of violence perpetrated by organized armed extremists. Legislation in the later half of the 19th century was enacted to address the threat posed by renegade private armies and terrorist groups. In 1886, the U.S. Supreme Court upheld the right of the states to ban unauthorized paramilitary training and military organizing (*Presser v. Illinois*, 1886).

Today, more than 100 years later, in addition to a federal ban on paramilitary training, 41 states have laws banning private armies or paramilitary training (see Figure 5.1; Civil Disobedience Act, 1968; Halpern & Levin, 1996, pp. 133-134). Outrage over Klan atrocities led to the passage of the Federal KKK Acts, laws that are still used today to punish violent deprivations of civil rights. The Klan's influence ensnared the whole South, and its membership soared to over 500,000 before it was "officially" disbanded in 1869 by its founder, a former Confederate general, Nathan Bedford Forrest (Chambers, 1981).

The Klan's second incarnation came in 1915. A Georgia preacher named William Simmons broadened the scope of Klan bigotry to include Catholics, Jews, and new immigrants, in addition to African Americans. He also sculpted Klan ideology to embrace Christian fundamentalism and fanatical patriotism—trends present today in the ideological framework of the Patriot movement. A new technological medium, the motion picture, broadcast a glorified and heroic Klan image to the nation in the then-popular D. W. Griffith film *Birth of a Nation*. By the mid-1920s, the Klan had 4.5 million members throughout the East, with a disproportionate representation in Indiana. Lynchings committed or inspired by the Klan were a common terror tool in the South. Thousands of mostly black Americans were murdered by Klansmen or their sympathizers over the span of several decades. Before being co-opted by racists, lynching had previously emerged as a punishment of choice by frontier vigilantes from the revolutionary era into the late 1800s (Bullard, 1991, pp. 14-18; "Ku Klux Klan," 1975, p. 618; "Lynching," 1975, pp. 668-669; Ridgeway, 1995, p. 52).

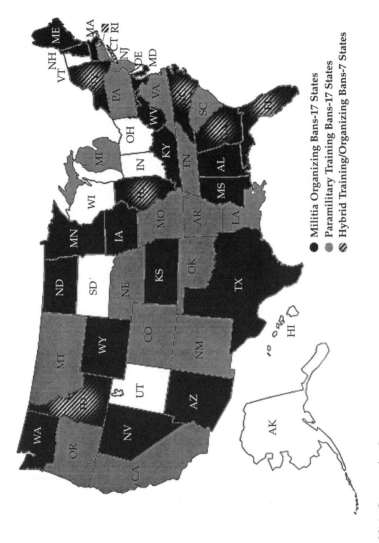

**Figure 5.1.** Militia Statutes by State

● Militia Organizing Bans-17 States
● Paramilitary Training Bans-17 States
▨ Hybrid Training/Organizing Bans-7 States

By 1925, internal quarrels, corruption, and highly publicized sex scandals led to a steep decline in Klan influence and membership until a revival during the civil rights era (Bullard, 1991, pp. 14-18; "Ku Klux Klan," 1975, p. 619). Although the Klan today, with only 5,000 members nationally, is a mere shadow of its former self, Klan methods and ideology have played a key role in the evolution of antigovernment politics and paramilitary extremism.

### The Silver Shirts

Another influential extremist organization that aided in the development of armed antigovernment paramilitarism in the United States was the fascist Silver Shirts of the 1930s. The Silver Shirts were the American analogue to Hitler's Brown Shirts, and their proclaimed goal was to further the "work of Christ militant in the open." Many key paramilitary and white supremacist leaders of the post-World War II era were members or associates of the Silver Shirts. These same leaders would later play a crucial role in fomenting conspiracy theories and bigotry as a mainstay of far Right paramilitary extremism for decades to come. The Silver Shirts were led by William Pelley, a conspiracist, Hitler fanatic, and virulent anti-Semite who had accused Herbert Hoover of being a puppet of international Jewish bankers who had crafted the Great Depression. The Silver Shirts peaked in the mid-1930s with about 15,000 members, but the advent of World War II and several high-profile espionage convictions resulted in the organization's dissolution (Ridgeway, 1995, pp. 62-64).

Although the Silver Shirts' existence was short-lived, the group's influence on right-wing American paramilitary extremism extends to the present day. Henry Beach, who decades later founded the racist antitax Posse Comitatus movement, was a Silver Shirt. Another prominent Silver Shirt racist, Gerald K. Smith, is considered a patriarch to succeeding generations of right-wing racist extremists. A Christian minister turned anti-Semitic populist, Smith was a close advisor to another controversial populist, Louisiana Senator Huey Long, whose rising political career abruptly ended in assassination in 1935. Smith, like Pelley, railed against the threat of an international Jewish conspiracy for most of his life. Anti-Semitic scapegoating was a popular tool for many extreme right-wing demagogues who sought to exploit fear of jazz era decadence, the Depression, communism, capitalism, immigration, the perceived decline of morality, and international conflict. The most prominent mainstream purveyors of anti-Semitic conspiracies in the 1920s and 1930s were popular radio personality Father Charles Coughlin and industrialist Henry Ford, who published and disseminated anti-Semitic tirades in his newspaper, *Dearborn Independent,* and in the republished *The Protocols of the Elders of Zion* (Ridgeway, 1995, pp. 55-62, 66). Although thoroughly discredited as a fraud, the *Protocols* are still circulated today within the Patriot movement as a genuine secret document outlining a Jewish conspiracy to control the world.

### The Racist Religion of Christian Identity

An associate of Smith, Wesley Swift is a religious patriarch to many modern-day militias and white supremacists. After World War II, Swift served as an ordained minister in an evolving new and virulent racist religious movement called the Church of Jesus Christ Christian, or Christian Identity. One Swift follower and Identity adherent was Silver Shirt alumnus Richard Butler, now the aging patriarch of Aryan Nations, one of America's most influential neo-Nazi hate groups. William Potter Gale was another follower of Swift and his bigoted Identity theology (Ridgeway, 1995, p. 33). Gale, who died in 1988, founded the violent anti-Communist California Rangers militia in the 1960s and was a chief architect of the modern Posse Comitatus movement—the forerunner of today's antigovernment Freemen and Common Law Court movements. In 1987, Gale was convicted for his part in a plan to assassinate a federal judge and Nevada IRS officials.

Identity's racism and anti-Semitism are eerily reminiscent of the mainstream bigotry present in many Christian denominations of years past. The wellspring of this bigotry, however, is much newer and far more peculiar. Christian Identity is the progeny of British Israelism, a 19th-century belief that contends white Christians are the real Israelites. Under Identity theology, Jews are the spawn of Satan and people of color are subhuman "mud people," the product of a faulty first creation. American Identity liturgy preaches that America is a divinely bestowed white Christian homeland to be won in an apocalyptic battle against the Jewish-dominated U.S. government, race traitors, and minorities. Today, Identity adherents and other white supremacists refer to the U.S. government as the Zionist Occupational Government (ZOG). After the great millennial end battle, believers contend, the second coming of Christ will take place.

In many ways, Swift's racist Christian Identity theology mimics mainstream ultra-conservative fundamentalist Christian religions. Identity theology is intensely scriptural and distrustful of many of the values accepted in the more progressive mainstream society.

The cloak of traditional fundamentalism made Christian Identity an easy theology for conservative Christian racists to embrace. With varying degrees of speed and intensity, mainstream conservative American religions, by the end of the 20th century, had rejected their previous positions of silence or support regarding racial supremacy. Civil rights era violence and the eloquence of Dr. Martin Luther King Jr. and his progeny steered mainstream Christianity into a role that increasingly valued tolerance and equality. The Christian denominations of yesteryear that justified both slavery and segregation no longer existed for the modern racist fundamentalist, making Identity a natural theological refuge.

Identity's fundamentalist traditions, decentralized structure, survivalist tendencies, and virulent distrust of the government enable the sect to recruit some ultra-conservative disenfranchised whites into its web of racial hatred and anti-Semitism. Identity not only provides a structured theological framework for virulent hatred and scapegoating against selected enemies but also a biblical justification of violence against these enemies.

### The Posse Comitatus Movement

In addition to Identity, another building block of the modern Patriot tradition is the Posse Comitatus movement. *Posse comitatus* is Latin for "power of the county," and the tradition dates back to medieval England, where the local sheriff enlisted residents to enforce laws against criminals and critics of the crown (Levitas, 1996). In the United States, posses were sometimes called on by law enforcement to apprehend criminals on the Western frontier. The modern

Posse Comitatus was formed by ex-Silver Shirt Henry Beach in Portland, Oregon, in 1969 (Ridgeway, 1995, p. 129). Just as Christian Identity established a biblical religious structure for the amorphous antigovernment and bigoted beliefs of "sovereign white Christians," the Posse Comitatus did the same in the legal and political arena. In much the same fashion that Identity interprets the Bible, the Posse movement embraces simple, contorted, fundamentalist beliefs about the Constitution. It rejects the notion of America's monetary system, the income tax, the judicial system, the federal reserve, civil rights for minorities, most post-Civil War constitutional amendments, as well as state and federal authority over residents. The Posse Comitatus movement refers to whites as independent "sovereign citizens" who need not comply with most modern legislation, particularly taxes (Ridgeway, 1995, pp. 129-138).

During the 1970s and 1980s, Posse Comitatus membership extended throughout the nation, with a concentration in the West, Plains states, south-central United States, and Wisconsin. Like their Patriot progeny of the 1990s, the Posse issued threatening edicts against government officials, disseminated counterfeit checks and cash, stockpiled weapons, conducted paramilitary training, murdered law enforcement officers, and established their own "sovereign" courts and communities. In 1975, Posse extremists even formed a conspiracy to assassinate Vice President Nelson Rockefeller (Ridgeway, 1995, p. 133). Posse membership benefited from mainstream conservatism, antitax sentiment, racial polarization, distrust of government, aggressive marketing techniques, the farm crisis, and strategic alliances with parallel racist movements.

The folk hero and martyr of the Posse Comitatus movement is Gordon Kahl, a grandfatherly-looking North Dakotan and World War II veteran. In 1983, the 63-year-old Kahl killed two U.S. marshals and injured three others when they tried to arrest him for violating his probation on a previous tax evasion conviction. Several months later, Kahl himself was killed in a pitched firefight with lawmen in rural Arkansas that also left a local sheriff dead (Corcoran, 1990).

One Freemen-style autonomous "sovereign" community, Tigerton Dells, Wisconsin, flourished briefly before being broken up by authorities in the mid-1980s. Tigerton Dells was presided over by Identity minister James Wickstrom, a convicted felon and former associate of William Potter Gale, who now operates the influential American Patriot Fax Network.

## The Modern Ku Klux Klan

During the late 1970s and the 1980s, the Klan relied on two distinct strategies to promote its cause. Both strategies have since emerged in the modern Patriot movement. One strategy, that of mainstreaming racism, was pioneered by David Duke. Duke left the Klan and started his own group, the National Association for the Advancement of White People (NAAWP). Duke's strategy was to mainstream and subtly disguise his bigotry by exploiting racial divisions less directly than the more confrontational KKK style. He wore suits and submerged his racial views into mainstream political discussions of affirmative action, crime, drugs, federal authority, welfare, gay rights, and education. Duke was elected to the Louisiana House of Representatives and was narrowly defeated in bids for governor and the U.S. Senate in the late 1980s. In 1988 and 1992, Duke unsuccessfully ran for president on the Populist Party ticket (Schwartz, 1996, pp. 36-38). Bo Gritz, a Green Beret Vietnam War veteran and popular Patriot-style survivalist, was briefly the Populist Party's vice presidential nominee. In 1992, Gritz advocated the establishment of armed civilian militias during his own Populist Party presidential candidacy (Stern, 1996, p. 36).

Although Duke's political performance was often disquieting, it never resulted in his ascension to any high political office. Nevertheless, Duke's influence and knowledge of U.S. politics are evidenced by the increasing prevalence of the race baiting present in other, more successful mainstream political initiatives such as President Bush's Willie Horton ads, the racially polarizing reelection practices of North Carolina's Senator Jesse Helms, and the success of anti-immigrant and anti-affirmative action referendums in California. Like Duke, today's Patriot movement also has a less shrill, nonviolent political side that seeks to elect officials and influence legislation by exploiting general discontent.

The other Klan strategy was more violent and extreme. The Klan could no longer count on the mainstream membership and political support that sustained it in the South during the turbulent civil rights era. During the 1980s, many Klan factions adopted not only a disturbing new violent and militaristic style but also an increasing solidarity with other hatemongers they previously distrusted, notably neo-Nazis. During the 1980s in North Carolina and Texas, Klan paramilitary units terrorized minorities with impunity until federal courts enjoined them. In the late 1970s and the 1980s, Klan members and their associates committed numerous murders, bombings, and other violent attacks on minorities, eerily reminiscent of the Klan's previous waves of terror. Although the Klan's violent shift and militaristic style increased membership off its early 1970s lows to about 11,000 in 1981, there was an unintended consequence (Klanwatch, 1990, p. 47): Prominent watchdog groups like Klan-watch, the Anti-Defamation League (ADL), the American Jewish Committee (AJC), and the Center for Democratic Renewal engaged in a variety of successful strategies against the Klan and other or-ganized hate groups that included monitoring, grassroots activism, legislative initiatives, and civil lawsuits. The Klan and other hate groups suffered a series of crushing legal blows for their connections to acts of hate violence in cases litigated by the Justice Department's Civil Rights Division and the Southern Poverty Law Center (SPLC). These losses resulted in the imprisonment of many racist leaders and the crippling of several prominent violent hate groups, including Alabama's United Klans of America, California's White Aryan Resis-tance, the Invisible Knights of the KKK, the Church of the Creator, the Arizona Patriots, and Arkansas' Covenant, Sword, and Arm of the Lord (CSA) militia.

One of the most influential Klan leaders of the 1980s was Louis Beam, a Vietnam War veteran and former Grand Dragon in David Duke's Texas Knights of the KKK, who pioneered the concept of Klan militia with the formation of the Texas Emergency Reserve (TER). In the early 1980s, the TER terrorized refugee Vietnamese fishermen in Galveston Bay until a federal court enjoined its activities as a result of a lawsuit brought by the SPLC (*Vietnamese Fishermen's Association v. Knights of the Ku Klux Klan*, 1982). A subsequent lawsuit against Steven Miller's Confederate Knights of the KKK enjoined paramilitary activities and the intimidation of black citizens in North Carolina (*Person v. Miller*, 1988).

### Aryan Militancy

In 1981, Beam joined ex-Silver Shirt Richard Butler's Aryan Nations, an influential neo-Nazi Identity group based in Hayden Lake, Idaho. Beam was and continues to be a trendsetter in the antigovernment hate movement. He pioneered many methods used by the Patriot movement today: modern paramilitary organizing, extremist computer networks, closer ties between Klan members and Nazis, and the strategy of an antigovernment guerrilla insurgency against public officials and minorities.

An Aryan Nations offshoot group, the Order, launched just the kind of insurgency envisioned by Louis Beam. In 1983 and 1984, the group committed murders, numerous armed robberies netting over $4 million, and other felonies as part of its plot to assassinate civic leaders and to foment an antigovernment race war. Most of the stolen money has never been recovered and is believed to have been distributed to a variety of prominent hate groups. In 1984, The Order founder Robert Jay Mathews stated, "A secret war has been developing for the last year between the regime in Washington and an ever growing number of white people who are determined to regain what our forefathers . . . died for" (Bullard, 1989, p. 15). Later that year, Mathews was killed in a fire following a ferocious gun battle with FBI agents in Whidbey Island, Washington. The remaining members were convicted on federal charges and are still considered "prisoners of war" by the extremist Right (Bullard, 1989, p. 16).

The Order's name and methods were based on a popular 1978 racist novel *The Turner Diaries*, authored under the pseudonym Andrew Macdonald by another influential neo-Nazi, William Pierce. Pierce, a former college physics professor, presides over the West Virginia-based National Alliance, a neo-Nazi group that actively advocates militia organizing by white supremacists (*False Patriots*, 1996, p. 37; Macdonald, 1978).

*The Turner Diaries* is influential to the ideology of the antigovernment hate movement. Like Posse Comitatus and Christian Identity, the novel galvanizes bigotry and antigovernment sentiment into a simple, cohesive, and accessible message. Moreover, its glorification of violent guerrilla attacks by small, committed bands of racist warriors is considered not only inspirational but also instructional within the world of far Right extremists.

*The Turner Diaries* racist folklore of random acts of violence directed against one's enemies had a profound effect on unaffiliated hatemongers such as racist Skinheads, who also embrace the book. Although the vast majority of hate crimes are not committed by hard-core hatemongers, a disproportionate number of bias-motivated homicides are committed by Skinheads. By the late 1980s and early 1990s, neo-Nazi Skinheads were the most common identifiable cause of bias-related homicides in the United States (e.g., see SPLC, 1994, pp. 17-18; 1995a, pp. 14-15; 1996, p. 7). According to an ADL (1993) study, Skinheads committed dozens of bias homicides over a period of several years.

By the end of the 1980s, the world of organized hate and right-wing extremism was down, but not quite out. Although these groups had committed more violent acts of domestic terrorism than any other ideological category of terrorists during the 1980s, they were also the focus of a relentless string of prosecutions and civil suits. One of the few notable prosecutorial losses came in 1988 when Louis Beam, Richard Butler, and almost a dozen others were acquitted on sedition and other charges by a federal jury in Fort Smith, Arkansas. The indictment alleged a plot to "overthrow, put down and destroy by force the government of the United States and work for a new Aryan Nation" through the bombing of federal buildings and sabotage of infrastructure targets (Dees, 1996, pp. 41, 43-44).

In a post-acquittal interview, Klan defendant Robert Miles summed up the state of right-wing extremism this way: "Who knows? What movement? What's left of it?"; meanwhile, Beam proclaimed himself a "Seditionist" ready to continue his fight against the government "till we get our country back" (Dees, 1996, p. 44).

## The Genesis of the Patriot Movement

By the early 1990s, far right-wing extremism was at a crossroads. Previously popular centralized group structures made extremist organizations susceptible not only to infiltration by authorities but also to civil and criminal liability for the conduct of their associates. A traditional mainstay enemy, international Jewish-inspired communism became an anachronism with the recent downfall of the Soviet Union. In addition, displays of overt bigotry limited the racist far Right's ability to recruit from a broad pool of potential members.

Social surveys indicated broad discontent and insecurity among the general public concerning economic shifts, taxes, crime, and a bloated and inequitable federal bureaucracy (Levin, 1993). Furthermore, Americans no longer trusted or felt connected to the institutions on which they relied in the past to provide them with common goals and an identity. According to annual opinion polls, from 1974 to 1994 the percentage of Americans expressing a great deal of confidence·in various institutions declined drastically. For example, those reporting a great deal of confidence in the White House dropped from 28% to 18%; in the U.S. Supreme Court, from 40% to 31%; and in Congress, from 18% to 8%. Similar declines in confidence were evidenced in organized religion, the press, corporations, universities, and traditional medicine. In addition, 83% of Americans thought government regulations manifested a threat to their rights and freedoms (U.S. Department of Justice, 1995, pp. 144-145). Still, the extreme Right lacked the ability to form a cohesive coalition among themselves. Right-wing extremists also lacked the ability to exploit the growing fear and frustration manifested in the politics of white, mainstream Americans.

That all changed in 1992 when violent rioting in Los Angeles and disturbances in other major U.S. cities left 60 dead and more than $1 billion in property damage. Television broadcasts of racial assaults and lootings, coupled with an anemic police and national guard response, were just the kinds of images needed to unify the extreme Right. Militia advocate Larry Pratt stated that the Los Angeles riots were a "great lesson in self-defense" that illustrated the "importance of having an armed militia to organize quickly and effectively to defend people in their homes and in their stores and their livelihoods" (Dees, 1996, p. 54). And the impression that the government allowed violent disorder to reign against innocent, unarmed, white citizens was hardly limited to extremists; it struck a chord with mainstream whites as well. In the 30 days following the acquittal of the police officers charged in the Rodney King beating, the rate of interracial hate crimes of all sorts soared throughout the United States (Levin, 1993).

### Tragedy at Ruby Ridge

Another violent tragedy later that same year made the government appear to many not just as an impotent bystander but as a violent aggressor against its own citizens. Christian Identity adherent and self-proclaimed white separatist Randy Weaver was wanted on charges of selling two sawed-off shotguns to a federal informant. Weaver and his wife, Vicki, had moved to a wood cabin on an isolated hill in Ruby Ridge, Idaho, to raise their family under fundamentalist Identity-style principles and to isolate themselves from the rest of society. A plywood sign with red letters at the entrance to Weaver's property proclaimed, "Every Knee Shall Bow to the Yashua Messiah" (Walter, 1995, p. 5).

On August 21, 1992, a deadly gun battle broke out between Weaver, his teenage son Samuel, family friend Kevin Harris, and U.S. marshals surveilling his remote property. By day's end, Samuel Weaver and William Degan, a decorated U.S. marshal, lay dead, along with the Weaver family dog, Striker. Kevin Harris was severely wounded. Before the siege ended on August 31, 1992, Weaver's wife, Vicki, was mistakenly shot and killed, as she cradled her infant, by an FBI sharpshooter who had reportedly relied on an improper change to the bureau's "deadly force" guidelines (Walter, 1995, pp. 201-209, 242-243).

Weaver, represented by famed Wyoming defense attorney Gerry Spence, was eventually acquitted on all charges except his original failure to appear in court. In 1995, the Weaver family settled a lawsuit with the government for more than $3 million. As a result of the incident, Congress held extensive hearings, and several FBI officials, including FBI Deputy Director Larry Potts, were relieved of their duties (SPLC, 1995c, p. 15). One veteran agent faces criminal charges for destroying evidence in the matter after the fact (Associated Press, 1996; "Guilty Plea," 1996).

The tragedy at Ruby Ridge not only made the soft-spoken Weaver a folk hero but almost immediately galvanized previously semiautonomous far Right ideological movements under one umbrella coalition. Patriot zealot Chris Temple, referring to the Weaver tragedy, stated, "All of us in our groups . . . could not have done in the next 20 years, what the federal government did for our cause in 11 days at Naples, Idaho" (Dees, 1996, p. 31).

### Estes Park, Colorado: The Patriot Movement Is Born

In October 1992, Identity Pastor Pete Peters convened an invitation-only gathering of 160 "Christian men" at a lodge in Estes Park, Colorado, to forge a new coalition of antigovernment Patriots.

The gathering was dominated by racist Identity leaders, including Richard Butler, Louis Beam, and Chris Temple. Peters began the conference by invoking the Weaver tragedy in a lengthy address on the evils of government. Butler did a Hitler salute on stage while proclaiming to be a "100% bigot." In a long, rambling diatribe, Beam urged cooperation while he railed against the violent federal government: "When they come for you, the federals will not ask if you are a constitutionalist, a Baptist, Church of Christ, Identity Covenant believer, Klansman, Nazi, homeschooler, Freeman, New Testament believer, [or] fundamentalist. . . . Those who wear badges, black boots, and carry automatic weapons and kick in doors already know all they need to know about you. You are enemies of the state" (Dees, 1996, p. 51).

In 1992, Beam also published a detailed *Turner Diaries*-style plan for a guerrilla insurgency against the government in his journal *The Seditionist*. The strategy called *leaderless resistance* advocates the development of small, autonomous, guerrilla cells to target government officials, minorities, and infrastructure sites for violent strikes. Beam explained, "Since the entire purpose of Leaderless Resistance is to defeat state tyranny . . . all members of phantom cells or individuals will tend to react to objective events in the same way through usual tactics of resistance" (Beam, 1992, p. 5).

The meeting included Klan members, neo-Nazis, Posse Comitatus associates, and other overtly racist ideologues. Also present were a smattering of non-Identity attendees without any apparent racist agendas, including antiabortion activists, home school supporters, and extreme gun rights advocates. One non-Identity attendee, Larry Pratt, head of the Washington, D.C.-based Gun Owners of America, railed against the Fourteenth Amendment and advocated the establishment of armed civilian militias, in part, by invoking the imagery of the Los Angeles riots. The Fourteenth Amendment, enacted in 1868, guarantees equal protection and citizenship rights regardless of race. The amendment is frequently attacked by both antigovernment racists and extreme gun rights advocates (SPLC, 1995b, pp. 4-5). Pratt, who subsequently spoke at similar gatherings, later served as a national cochair on the presidential campaign of Pat Buchanan in 1996.

The 1990s Patriot militia movement was born at the Estes Park gathering. In addition, an important coalition was formed between

Identity and other racist extremists on the one hand and nonracist, ultraconservative, and fundamentalist activists on the other. All were bound together by visceral antipathy toward the federal government.

Two other critical incidents further solidified the Patriot antigovernment movement's broad coalition. The first was the fiery end to the 51-day Branch Davidian siege at Waco, Texas, which resulted in the deaths of 78 people on April 19, 1993. Waco soon became a Patriot rallying cry. The second event was the passage of the Brady Bill by Congress in November 1993. The legislation established a waiting period for the purchase of guns and banned certain types of assault weapons. Many saw the legislation as a tyrannical attempt to first disarm and then enslave American citizens. To Patriot adherents, Ruby Ridge, Waco, and the Brady Bill represented a sweeping premeditated assault on the survival of arms-bearing citizens by a tyrannical government.

By 1993, the fledgling antigovernment Patriot movement was spreading its hateful conspiratorial messages throughout the United States through pamphlets, radio shows, videos, weapons expos, conferences, newsletters, meetings, and fax networks. The emerging umbrella Patriot ideology appealed to individuals representing a wide range of preexisting subcultures and personalities, including survivalists, libertarians, ultrafundamentalists, millennialists, white supremacists, gun rights advocates, agrarians, and cynics.

In October 1993, two Patriot leaders, Lynda Lyon and George Sibley, were arrested for the murder of Opelika, Alabama, police sergeant Roger Motley after a high-speed chase and a standoff. Motley was shot to death by Lyon while taking Sibley into custody for failing to obey his commands after a minor disturbance in a shopping center parking lot. Motley was the first police fatality at the hands of a 1990s Patriot extremist (SPLC, 1993, p. 1). By year's end, Klanwatch noted another disturbing trend: 35 white supremacists were arrested in 13 states on weapons and explosives charges (SPLC, 1994, pp. 1-3).

During 1994, militia organizing and paramilitary training quickly spread throughout the United States (see Figure 5.2). The Militia of Montana (MOM) was formed in February by John Trochmann, his brother David, and nephew Randy Trochmann. MOM soon became one of the nation's two most influential militias through a combination of good timing and clever marketing.

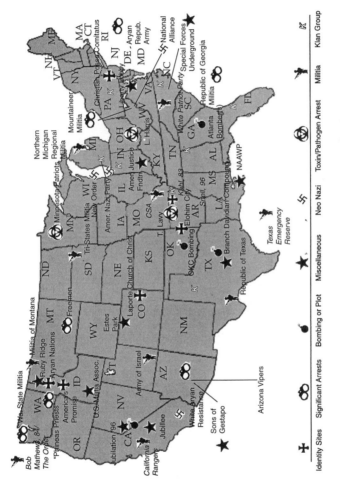

**Figure 5.2. Important Patriot Sites and Organizations**

SOURCES: Klanwatch, the Anti-Defamation League, the American Jewish Committee, and the Stockton College Center on Hate and Extremism.

NOTE: Italicized groups are listed for historical purposes.

John Trochmann previously led United Citizens for Justice, a Weaver support group, with Louis Beam and Chris Temple, a former campaigner in Bo Gritz's political forays and a writer for the racist Patriot publication *The Jubilee* (Dees, 1996, p. 45; Stern, 1996, p. 36). Trochmann had been a featured speaker at Richard Butler's 1990 Aryan World Congress and at Pete Peters's 1992 Estes Park Conference (Dees, 1996, p. 50; *False Patriots*, 1996, p. 56).

John Trochmann traveled throughout rural Montana, speaking to hundreds at a time about perceived conspiracies and the need for the establishment of unauthorized militias and secret paramilitary cells. Soon MOM was selling paramilitary training manuals, the newsletter *Taking Aim,* videos, and militia startup kits to thousands of customers throughout the United States via mail order out of Trochmann's Noxon, Montana, garage (*False Patriots*, 1996, p. 56).

In April, Norman Olson and Ray Southwell formed the Northern Michigan Regional Militia, which reportedly grew to at least 6,000 members—the largest of any in the United States (Stern, 1996, pp. 96-98). Convicted Oklahoma City federal building bomber Timothy McVeigh even attended a meeting of the Michigan Militia (Dees, 1996, p. 161). After the Oklahoma City bombing, Olson and Southwell abruptly left their posts in the Michigan militia after they circulated a press release blaming the Japanese government for the explosion (Dees, 1996, p. 232).

During 1994, disturbing examples of antigovernment violence and intimidation also began to concern authorities and monitoring groups. Freemen in Montana commandeered courthouses, tax protesters beat and stabbed a California county clerk, an Identity zealot critically wounded a Missouri state trooper in an assassination attempt, militia associates in Michigan armed with sophisticated weapons and reconnaissance equipment surveilled police in Michigan, and federal authorities in Virginia broke up a militia that allegedly had plans for sabotage (*Anti-Government Terrorism*, 1995; *False Patriots*, 1996, pp. 31-33). The media in 1994, however, tended to concentrate instead either on the quirky ideology of many militia members or on their rural paramilitary training sessions.

By the end of the year, Patriot violence, organizing, and the emergence of white supremacist leaders within the movement caused alarm among watchdog groups and various government officials. Analysts were concerned about an apparent upsurge in membership, an escalation in the level of violent rhetoric in Patriot literature and at gatherings, disturbing instances of violence and intimidation, and the jockeying of white supremacists for leadership roles in the movement. In October 1994, the SPLC sent a package to U.S. Attorney General Janet Reno, describing the increasing level of militia activity and its connection to white supremacy as "a recipe for disaster." That same month, the ADL (1994) also issued a comprehensive report entitled *Armed and Dangerous* detailing militia activity in more than a dozen states.

On April 10, 1995, the AJC's Ken Stern issued a report whose cover letter warned of the danger of militia violence to federal targets on April 19 because of the date's symbolic significance to Patriot followers (Stern, 1996, p. 13). MOM's March 1995 *Taking Aim* newsletter revolved almost entirely around the importance of April 19 to the Patriot movement (Dees, 1996, pp. 132-133).

## Microcosm of the Movement: Timothy McVeigh

At 9:02 a.m. on April 19, 1995, a massive explosion collapsed the entire front portion of Oklahoma City's Alfred P. Murrah Federal Building, killing 168 people—the single worst act of domestic terrorism in U.S. history. Less than an hour and a half later, the alleged bomber, Timothy McVeigh, would be in custody in Perry, Oklahoma, just south of the Kansas border. McVeigh was pulled over by a trooper for driving without a license tag and was arrested for carrying a concealed handgun (Marks, 1995, p. 128).[3]

According to the AJC's Ken Stern (1996), McVeigh, who was later convicted of the bombing, "was the essence of what Louis Beam meant by the 'Leaderless Resistance'. . . movement and [what] its literature was designed to produce" (p. 187). The 26-year-old Army veteran left the service after a failed attempt to join the Special Forces following a stint in Desert Storm. McVeigh's nomadic and undistinguished post-Army existence looks like a microcosm of the extreme Patriot movement itself. He frequented Patriot expos, made an emotional Waco pilgrimage, collected antigovernment literature, wore fatigues, refused automobile registration, conducted paramilitary training, built and detonated bombs with codefendant Terry Nichols, and hawked *The Turner Diaries* at gun shows. The antigovernment *The Turner Diaries* might well have been the inspiration for the Oklahoma City bombing. On pages 39 to 40, Pierce describes in explicit detail the aftermath of an early morning ammonium nitrate and fuel oil (ANFO) truck bomb attack on the FBI's Washington headquarters:

> The scene in the courtyard was one of utter devastation. The Pennsylvania Avenue wing of the building, as we could then see, had collapsed, partly into the courtyard in the center of the building and partly into Pennsylvania Avenue. A huge, gaping hole yawned in the courtyard pavement just beyond the rubble of collapsed masonry, and it was from this hole that most of the column of black smoke was ascending. (Macdonald, 1978, pp. 39-40)

In the days before the Oklahoma City bombing, McVeigh placed several telephone calls to Pierce's National Alliance message center (Hamm, 1997, p. 198). He also placed calls to Elohim City, an armed Christian Identity compound in eastern Oklahoma led by Reverend Robert Millar (Dees, 1996, p. 136). Unconfirmed reports alleged that McVeigh visited Elohim City five times prior to the date of the bombing (Stern, 1997, p. 9). During the evening of April 19, 1995, Millar follower and convicted double murderer and racist Richard Wayne Snell was executed in Arkansas. In November 1983, Snell and CSA leader James Ellison plotted to use a van to blow up the Alfred P. Murrah Federal Building (Hamm, 1997, p. 5). Militias made Snell's execution a cause célèbre. The March 1995 issue of *Taking Aim* described Snell's case as a "Patriot to be executed by the Beast" (Dees, 1996, p. 133).

Snell's last words were a cryptic Identity warning: "Governor Tucker, look over your shoulder. Justice is on the way. . . . Hail [God's] Victory. I am at peace" (SPLC, 1995b, p. 3). A newspaper article reported that a state prison official alleges that Snell repeatedly stated, "There was going to be a bomb, there was going to a [sic] explosion" on the day his death sentence was to be carried out (Stern, 1997, p. 9). After retrieving Snell's body from Arkansas, Millar brought it to Elohim City, where he laid it in an open casket for 3 days. Millar left the casket open in the mistaken belief that Snell was possibly a resurrected savior who would lead Identity followers in their end battle against the government (SPLC, 1995b, p. 3).

Media reports citing U.S. Department of Justice sources allege a connection between McVeigh and several white supremacist bank robbery defendants who had visited Elohim City (Boettcher, 1997). One inhabitant of Elohim City at the time of McVeigh's calls was Michael Brescia. Brescia and others who were present at Elohim City at the time of the bombing faced federal charges for a string of Midwestern bank robberies perpetrated by a group known as the Aryan Republican Army (ARA). Brescia's Elohim City roommate at the time was an ultra-right-wing German citizen, Andreas Strassmeir. Strassmeir was alleged to have met McVeigh at a gun show. An Oklahoma City bombing victim has even named Strassmeir and Brescia as defendants in a wrongful death civil suit over the death of two children in the federal building bombing. Neither man has been criminally charged in connection with the bombing (Stern, 1997, pp. 9-10). Millar denies speaking to McVeigh, and the relationship between McVeigh, Elohim City, and Snell's execution remains a mystery (SPLC, 1995b, p. 3).

The bombing of the Murrah building was the most horrific example of an emerging pattern of Patriot-inspired violence during 1995. Other bombings or bomb plots against courthouses, government offices, and the offices of civil rights groups also took place throughout the year. Shootings and armed confrontations between police and Patriot extremists also occurred with regularity (*False Patriots*, 1996, pp. 31-33). A coalition of Patriot groups met in Gregory, South Dakota, over the summer and declared war on the federal government (SPLC, 1995c, p. 2). Other groups stockpiled illegal weapons, engaged in coordinated surveillance of "enemies," or planned attacks with mass toxins and pathogens (Dees, 1996, pp. 201-202; *False Patriots*, 1996, pp. 31-33). On October 9, 1995, Amtrak's Sunset Limited passenger train was derailed by saboteurs near Hyder, Arizona, leaving 1 dead and 83 injured (*False Patriots*, 1996, p. 22). The perpetrators left behind a copy of *An Indictment of the ATF and FBI* (1997), protesting law enforcement abuses at Waco and Ruby Ridge.

A similar pattern of threats and violence continued in 1996. The most noteworthy Patriot incidents included the 81-day Freemen standoff in Brussett, Montana; the arrests of militia members in Arizona, West Virginia, and Washington on conspiracy, explosives, and weapons charges; the arrest of Identity followers for bombings and bank robbery in Washington; the arrest of several white supremacists for a string of Midwestern bank robberies (Slobodzian, 1997, pp. A1, A10); the nationwide distribution of an antigovernment attack plan by militias during the Freemen standoff; and various acts of intimidation by renegade common law courts. These courts are illegitimate "tribunals" convened by sovereign citizens who issue edicts, judgments, penalties, and threats against transgressors— usually government officials or creditors—under a hodgepodge of faulty legal and historical theories (Hanson, 1996). In 1996, Klan-watch counted 112 common law courts conducting operations in 34 states (C. Valient, personal communication, March 22, 1997). The practice of using false legal or financial instruments as a tool of intimidation is now called "paper terrorism." Federal investigators also examined a possible link between three jailed Christian Identity "Phineas Priest" bomb suspects and the July 1996 Centennial Olympic Park bombing (Morlin & Walter, 1997, p. 1).

Patriot extremism continued to make headlines in 1997. In Atlanta, journalists received letters claiming responsibility for bombings outside a Sandy Springs, Georgia, abortion clinic in January and an explosion in February at an Atlanta nightclub catering primarily to gays and lesbians (Harrison, 1997, pp. A1, A10). The letters, signed "Army of God," were replete with antigovernment references and terminology popular with the Patriot movement. An underground guerrilla training manual entitled *Army of God Manual* (1997) has been widely circulated within the extreme fringe of the antiabortion movement for several years. The 1997 Atlanta bombings involved tandem dynamite-based devices, with the more powerful bomb programmed to detonate last. Presumably, the second, more powerful blast was intended to harm responding law enforcement officers.

The FBI is also seeking two Washington state men on 16 charges in connection with a February 15 shootout with Ohio police following a traffic stop. The men, brothers Chevie O'Brien Kehoe and Cheyne C. Kehoe, are Patriot adherents. Chevie Kehoe is also being sought on federal firearms charges and is wanted for questioning in connection with the June 1996 murder of an Arkansas gun dealer, his wife, and 8-year-old daughter (Associated Press, 1997a).

Influential Christian Identity minister Mark Thomas pled guilty in federal district court in Philadelphia in February for his role in a string of Midwestern bank robberies committed by the ARA. The plea agreement mandates Thomas's cooperation with federal investigations into the activities of other right-wing extremists (Slobod-zian & Fazlollah, 1997, pp. A1, A10). The 47-year-old Macungie, Pennsylvania, resident was described by the ADL as someone who "has emerged both as one of the most significant links between the 'Christian Identity' and neo-Nazi skinhead movements, and one of the leading hate groups in the American Northeast" (ADL, 1997a, pp. 150-152). Thomas, formerly the head of the Pennsylvania Ku Klux Klan, was head of the Commonwealth's Aryan Nations chapter at the time of his arrest.

In Wise County, Texas, in April, four extremists were arrested by federal authorities for plotting to commit an armed robbery, blow up natural gas storage tanks as a diversion, and kill responding police officers. The suspects are alleged to be Ku Klux Klan members (Parks, 1997, p. 24A).

In May, seven members of another Texas antigovernment group faced a variety of state and federal criminal charges. Members of the Republic of Texas face numerous charges following a kidnap-ping, a 6-day standoff, and a plot to distribute $1.8 billion in fraudulent financial instruments. Another Republic of Texas mem-ber was killed by Texas police after he fled the group's Fort Davis "embassy" following the April standoff (Slover, 1997, p. 1A).

Republic of Texas members contend that the state's annexation by the federal government in 1845, rendering Texas an independent republic, is invalid. One faction of the group was led by "ambas-sador" Richard McLaren, who waged a "paper war" against Texas businesspeople and government officials from his ramshackle Fort Davis compound. McLaren's compound was the scene of the tense 6-day standoff.

In April, three Colorado militia members were arrested by federal authorities after a raid on the home of the group's ringleader uncovered six fully automatic AK47s, land mines, and other ex-plosive devices. The head of the cell, Ronald Cole, a Branch Davidian sympathizer, had previously gone to the federal courthouse in Den-ver to protest the Timothy McVeigh trail (Chronis & Pankratz, 1997, p. A1).

In northern California, at least six antigovernment sym-pathizers were arrested on explosives charges after the home of a Yuba City Freemen sympathizer was accidentally damaged when stored explosives detonated in April (Wallace, 1997, p. A18).

In May, Los Angeles authorities arrested five alleged militia men who were accused of "planning domestic terrorism" throughout southern California. Scores of firearms and grenade launchers, thousands of rounds of ammunition, and military equipment were confiscated (Associated Press, 1997b).

## Criminal Patterns of Patriot Activity

My preliminary analysis of almost 60 Patriot-related criminal incidents reported in the press or obtained by monitoring organizations from January 1994 to December 1996 revealed the following patterns (shown in Figure 5.3):

22%   Explosive-Related Incidents (Theft, possession, manufacture, or detonation, sometimes accompanied by plan for use in specified or unspecified future attacks)

15%   Threats (Generally against government officials)

12%   Failure to Comply With Regulations (Environmental, tax, or other regulations)

10%   Weapons Offenses (Possession of banned or altered weapons or illegal paramilitary training)

10%   Larceny/Fraud (Theft, embezzlement, counterfeiting, securities fraud)

9%   Premeditated Assaults/Confrontations (Violence generally directed against law enforcement or government officials)

5%   Armed Robberies (Includes banks and journalists)

5%   Violent Spontaneous Confrontations (Generally traffic stops or suspect's appearance at official proceeding)

5%   Standoffs (Barricade-type events involving law enforcement)

5%   Toxins/Pathogens

2%   Infrastructure Attacks[4]

Recent acts of Patriot violence revealed two general types of trends. The first trend is one toward well-orchestrated acts of "high intensity" violence by small bands of assailants. These high-intensity events include single mass catastrophic events, such as the Oklahoma City bombing; planned, coordinated, serial events, such as a

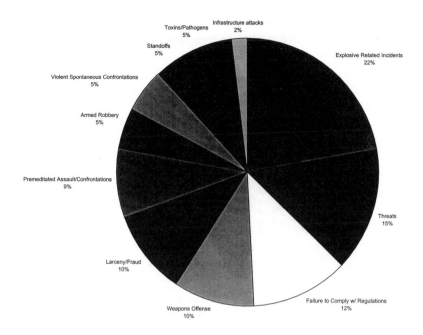

**Figure 5.3.** Patriot-Related Crimes from January 1994 to December 1996

coordinated set of "Order style" armed robberies or smaller connected bombings; and armed "Waco style" standoffs involving fortified compounds or residences.

Moderate-intensity events, the second trend, will be far more prevalent than high-intensity ones. Moderate-intensity events may be violent, but the risk of mass fatalities is less severe because the crimes often (a) are not as well planned, (b) involve a lone assailant or a single event, (c) involve less powerful weapons, (d) are directed against property, or (e) are only in the planning stage. Moderate-intensity events include confrontational traffic stops, police intervention in domestic matters, computer hacking, and noninjurious destruction of infrastructure targets such as power, transportation, and communication systems or unoccupied structures.

Several other disturbing trends have also emerged. Group structure increasingly revolves around small, secretive, "leaderless resistance"-type associations. Small cells are less likely to be infiltrated or discovered by law enforcement. The smaller number of members also reduces the risk posed by unsupervised individuals whose mistakes can result in detection, prosecution, or civil lawsuits. Furthermore, technology, information, and dangerous weapons and material are more affordable and accessible today than ever before, enabling even a few committed individuals to commit acts of mass terrorism while still maintaining a low profile. Patriot extremists are increasingly keeping low profiles. Several recent violent incidents have involved either previously unknown extremists or an absence of claims of responsibility.

Expertise regarding tactics can be obtained anonymously through the Internet and other sources without the necessity of enlisting an "outsider" for assistance. The Internet also allows Patriot ideologues to spread hatred and strategies to a broad range of would-be guerrillas without the direct relationship necessary to make them legally responsible for the terrorism they may inspire. The Internet also allows the transfer of encrypted information in a manner that is more secure than standard telephone or mail communications. Computers and the Internet also present an opportunity for increasingly sophisticated Patriot extremists to hack, infiltrate, and disrupt government and commercial computer networks.

Reflecting an overall societal trend, guns and explosives remain the most popular weapons. Although these traditional weapons are still the most common tools for Patriot extremists, a few Patriots have recently been apprehended with mass toxins and pathogens. Unfortunately, deadly substances like ricin and anthrax are inexpensive and easily obtained or synthesized—thus guaranteeing their future use. Popular Patriot Internet sites, books, and videos outline in explicit detail instructions for the manufacture and dissemination of not only explosives but also mass poisons and pathogens. A few recent Patriot crimes have involved suspects armed with ricin and bubonic plague. A small amount of ricin, a hard-to-detect ultratoxic plant protein, can annihilate the population of a medium-sized U.S. city. The presence of many well-fortified Patriot and Identity compounds like Millar's Elohim City make future additional standoffs with law enforcement a virtual certainty. The Ruby Ridge, Waco, Freemen, and Republic of Texas sieges illustrate the difficulties presented to authorities by small, well-fortified compounds. Residents of Patriot compounds are often isolated, committed ideologues who are well trained and well armed. Some are conditioned to respond violently to law enforcement or subscribe to apocryphal paranoid prophecies.

An evolving standoff strategy is emerging on the part of authorities. These new law enforcement tactics include (a) the off-site arrest of ringleaders, (b) the isolation and containment of other dangerous members, (c) the use of trusted intermediaries in negotiations, (d) the controlled escalation of events related to timing and access to resources by fugitives, and (e) the negotiated release of innocent third parties.

## Patriot Ideology

Although Patriots agree that the government should be distrusted, the level of antipathy and rationales for it vary significantly. There is general agreement in the movement that government authority has been used corruptly and expanded in a manner that threatens the exercise of perceived fundamental rights. During recent senate hearings, John Trochmann protested, "The High Office of the Presidency has been turned into a position of dictatorial oppression" (*Appearance Before the Senate*, 1995). The more extreme segments of the movement further contend that many government functions are not only disagreeable or poor policy but also are part of a coordinated international conspiracy to strip citizens of their arms and liberties before enslaving them. The Patriot journal *The Spotlight* rhetorically inquired: "Is America on the brink of occupation by military troops under United Nations control?" (*False Patriots*, 1996, p. 10). Extreme Patriot ideology contends that whites are sovereign citizens whose rights are delineated, not by the government, but rather by a cobbled assortment of historical writings whose meaning is often subject to their fanciful interpretation. These sources include the Bible, English common law, the Magna Carta, the Declaration of Independence, the Articles of Confederation, and selected misinterpreted sections of the Constitution. Patriots, for instance, dismiss constitutional provisions that they disagree with, like the Fourteenth Amendment. They derisively refer to minorities as illegitimate "Fourteenth Amendment" citizens whose status was improperly conferred by an illegal exercise of federal authority. They also maintain that all federal laws enacted after 1933 are void because President Roosevelt altered the nation's legal system to one operating under maritime law.

A misinterpretation of the Second Amendment's "right to bear arms" clause is also central to Patriot and militia claims of government abuse of fundamental rights. Patriots mistakenly claim that the Second Amendment provides a fundamental right to individual gun ownership and militia organizing. According to Patriots, the Second Amendment extends to private citizens a right to armed rebellion against tyrannical governments. Although this dangerous interpretation, called the "insurrectionist theory of the Second Amendment," has been rejected by every federal court decision and by most credible legal scholars, it is still actively promoted by both Patriots and the National Rifle Association (NRA). "*[T]he Second Amendment is not the source of the right to form militia nor to keep and bear arms.. . .* In fact, the right to form militias and to keep and bear arms existed from antiquity" (Olson, 1997, p. 11). Nevertheless, for more than a century, every federal court decision on the subject has consistently upheld governmental regulations on private gun ownership, approved of bans on private militia activity, or ruled that the Second Amendment only allows states to maintain a regulated national guard.

Extremist Patriots also contend that a so-called New World Order exists to impose a one-world government on all nations, including the United States. President George Bush's 1991 description of post-Soviet Bloc international alliances during the Gulf War has been given a twisted new meaning. According to Patriot conspiracists, the United Nations, the Olympics, the Council on Foreign Relations, the General Agreement on Tariffs and Trade (GATT), the North American Free Trade Agreement (NAFTA), and the Trilateral Commission are all players in a secret international conspiracy to enslave American citizens. Similarly, "Wise Use" Patriots argue that environmental and zoning regulations represent a coordinated effort to deny sovereign citizens their "God given" land rights.

Patriots not only misinterpret laws, they contort other facts as well. Popular Patriot conspiracy theories include government plots to establish concentration camps in the Midwest, to secretly inject microchips into people along with vaccinations, to amass Hong Kong police in Mexico in preparation for an offensive strike against U.S. citizens, to control the weather, and to spy on people by using black helicopters.

## Patriots and Politics

Like earlier extremist movements, the Patriot movement received an infusion of support from the mainstream conservative political back-lash of the early 1990s. This widespread support was short-lived, however. The acceptance of Patriot politics by the mainstream populace was limited to a small but somewhat elastic population of politically frustrated conservatives, reformists, survivalists, and libertarians. Acceptance of shrill calls for "revolution" by politicians and commentators has since been replaced by a general preference for moderation. By 1996, the angry white male who saw the government as the enemy was eclipsed in political influence by the so-called soccer mom who had a more moderate and collaborative view of government. This political moderation is linked to a variety of factors:

> The lack of unifying and charismatic mainstream conservative political leaders
>
> The perception that mainstream conservatism was leaning toward the extreme and was too combative
>
> A good economy
>
> Diffusion of right-wing frustration by the success of several high profile, conservative, social and political reform initiatives

Many successful conservative reforms were, in fact, given attention by the "system," thus obviating the necessity for an alternative, and sometimes violent, political paradigm. Examples include welfare reform, anti-immigrant initiatives, anti-affirmative action laws, antigay marriage legislation, tax and budget reform, a relaxation of concealed sidearm possession by many jurisdictions, tax and budget initiatives, in-depth legislative hearings on Waco and Ruby Ridge, and the lack of another nationally notable violent confrontation involving federal law enforcement.

Politicians popular with the Patriot movement had a difficult time during the 1996 elections. Texas Republican Steve Stockman, a vocal militia advocate, narrowly lost his congressional seat in Texas; conservative Republican gun rights advocate Helen Chenoweth barely held on to her congressional seat in Idaho; and Colorado Patriot leader Charles Duke barely registered with Colorado voters in his bid for U.S. Senate.

The mainstream electorate in 1996 did not invigorate or connect with antigovernment politics as it had done in 1994. Still, by the end of the decade, it was clear that millions of Americans were either lost to the traditional two-party system or had given up voting altogether. Anything from a Waco-like trigger incident to a horrendous government scandal to an economic downturn could turn many of these aloof and drifting citizens into future Patriot supporters.

Last, Patriot politics are often local—both geographically and ideologically. Even if ultraconservatives had done well in the mainstream, their acceptance by the movement would be extremely limited. Because this movement is a decentralized one run by sovereign independent citizens, leaders are often distrusted as enemies or dismissed as ineffectual by the movement's more hardcore elements. Although it is unlikely that any future leader will exert direct control over this amorphous movement as a whole, an eloquent charismatic figure could increase membership and indirectly (and legally) inspire adherents to undertake additional violent acts. The political glue that holds the disparate parts of the Patriot movement together is a fickle one whose bonds strengthen or weaken as a result of a complex interplay of social, political, and economic factors. For the foreseeable future, the Patriot movement will be made up of a more or less permanent core of aloof citizens. Their politics range from libertarianists to mainstream single-issue advocates to fundamentalists on one end, to a few violent Christian Identity-related factions including Freemen, common law court supporters, militiamen, and other so-called sovereigns. All components of the Patriot movement will undoubtedly receive sustenance from a continuing array of real and perceived government scandals and abuses. The terrorist threat primarily rests in the decentralized violent core of Identity-related zealots and other committed fringe extremists who informally share information and methods but who act in small groups—secretly, autonomously, and violently.

## The Growing Danger
## of Identity Influences

The emergence of a small, violence-prone Identity segment of the movement eclipsed the moderate, libertarian, and survivalist components, causing discernible fissures. The difficulty for analysts was assessing those members of the nonviolent camp who had actually adopted a peaceful stance, as opposed to those whose stated motives were disingenuous.

Christian Identity and white supremacy will continue to play a disproportionately dangerous and important role in the Patriot movement. In March 1997, Klanwatch reported that 101 of 858 Patriot organizations had "ties to racist groups or leaders, or expressed racist anti-Semitic belief" (C. Valient, personal communication, March 22, 1997). Racist-type Patriot groups were monitored in 32 states. Of the more than 380 militias monitored, dozens were confirmed by Klanwatch to have racist ties. The group also monitored major Identity congregations in at least 20 states, in addition to several well-armed Identity compounds. Many prominent Identity leaders and white supremacists, such as the Aryan Nations' Richard Butler and Louis Beam and the National Alliance's William Pierce, are actively exploiting militias as a vehicle for recruitment. Furthermore, public and private intelligence analysts contend that many more prominent Patriot leaders are not public about their white supremacist beliefs or associations.

Identity influence is a particularly dangerous component of the Patriot movement. Identity injects a violent and well-entrenched millinealistic urgency into the movement. Many Identity followers believe the year 2000 will be the time of an apocalyptic end-battle against the evil Zionist occupational federal government. The violence of political terrorism is sometimes checked by the hierarchy of a dominant authoritative organization, the achievement of a particular specific objective or benefit, or the desire to achieve political or social acceptance of their cause. The primary goal of Identity ideology of destroying modern American society through guerrilla warfare and replacing it with a divinely ordained whites-only homeland does not leave much room for the less violent alternatives that are present in other nontheological terrorist movements.

And although their numbers are minuscule, possibly less than a 1,000, a small subset of Identity followers are dangerous zealots committed to using "biblically" justified violence to achieve their goals.

## Conclusion

Patriot terrorism is influenced by several important factors. These include the literature and rhetoric of the Patriot subculture, Identity theology, technology, the availability of the tools of violence, the terrorist acts of their cohorts, offensive acts committed by their perceived enemies, and fears over the coming millennium. The Patriot movement suffered a temporary membership setback after the Oklahoma City bombing, with less extreme members abandoning the movement in disgust. Since then, though, a remaining core of committed followers have remained with the movement, although they are maintaining a lower profile. By mid-1997, Klanwatch reported a 6% increase in the number of Patriot groups over the previous year (Southern Poverty Law Center, personal communication, March 5, 1997). The ADL found a decline in the number of states with militia activity but reported a significant increase in militia-related crime and common law court intimidation (ADL, 1997b).

One thing is sure: Violence by a fringe group of Patriot extremists will continue. Many of these acts will be committed by small, autonomous, leaderless resistance cells or lone offenders. Still, antigovernment extremists are tied together through informal means as diverse as the Internet, Patriot publications, and expos and paramilitary trainings. Although most cases will involve the traditional mainstays of guns and bombs, a smaller number will involve an evolving array of dangerous mass weapons that are increasingly accessible and glorified in Patriot literature. Most violence will continue to be directed against government targets, although an increasing number of attacks will likely involve infrastructure targets and other entities lambasted in Patriot literature. Although some attacks will be claimed, many attacks will not involve claims of responsibility with the perpetrators, instead invoking a strategy called "propaganda of the deed," wherein the target itself indicates the motive. These targets include media outlets, financial institutions, abortion clinics, international gay establishments, and civil rights groups, all of which are culled from an expanding list of perceived enemies.

## Notes

1. Constitutionalists are also known as Freemen and Christian Patriots.

2. Individuals or groups referenced in this chapter adhere to a broad range of constitutionally protected beliefs. The inclusion of a particular individual or group in this chapter does not mean or imply that they engage in, encourage, or promote illegal activity.

3. Another U.S. Army veteran, Terry Nichols, was charged in connection with the Oklahoma City bombing. Like all criminal defendants, he is presumed innocent until a trier of fact concludes that the evidence presented establishes guilt beyond a reasonable doubt.

4. This 2% figure refers to one incident of sabotage to a railroad. Another incident directed against infrastructure targets was classified under the heading "Explosive-related incidents."

# Two Decades of Terror
## Characteristics, Trends, and Prospects for the Future of American Terrorism

BRENT L. SMITH
KELLY R. DAMPHOUSSE

Although much has been written about international terrorists, our understanding and concern regarding domestic terrorist groups has been limited. Before 1995, the news media and related publications generally surmised that the threat of major terrorist activity in America was confined to international terrorist organizations. Americans had grown accustomed to reading about international terrorists and

AUTHORS' NOTE: The authors thank the FBI's Terrorist Research and Analytical Center, the Administrative Office of the U.S. Courts, and the U.S. Sentencing Commission for assistance in data collection. We also thank the State University of New York Press for permission to reprint tables from Brent L. Smith's *Terrorism in America: Pipe Bombs and Pipe Dreams* (1994).

feared, to a certain degree, an increased risk of terrorist attacks by foreigners on U.S. soil. Evidence of this new threat seemed clear when the World Trade Center (WTC) was bombed in 1993. The bombing of the Alfred P. Murrah Federal Building in Oklahoma City in 1995 and the 1996 bombing at the Atlanta Olympics forced Americans to reexamine the social causes of violent political extremism within our own borders. Not since the 1960s, when violent leftist extremism threatened social stability in the United States, have Americans focused their attention so keenly on the groups and individuals who seek radical change to U.S. society.

Seemingly unnoticed, however, this variety of homegrown terrorist organizations had been emerging since the late 1970s. Although the spectacular antiwar, civil rights, and student movements of the 1960s and 1970s had dissipated, the 1980s saw the rise of some of the most spectacular and dangerous groups in U.S. history. How to study this phenomenon has been an ongoing problem among students of terrorism. Empirical efforts to study terrorism have, in many ways, created more conceptual problems than they have solved. Each published work seems to compound the vagueness of the concept, rather than provide conceptual clarity to the subject (Wardlaw, 1989). Scholars have defined, refined, and redefined terrorism to accommodate personal preferences regarding what should or should not be labeled "terroristic." Unfortunately, these variations in definitions of terrorism have given legitimacy to the aphorism "One man's terrorist is another man's freedom fighter." Because the Federal Bureau of Investigation (FBI) has jurisdiction over all "officially designated acts" of terrorism, this study uses the FBI's definition of terrorism: "the unlawful use of force or violence to intimidate or coerce a government, the civilian populace, or any segment thereof, in furtherance of political or social goals" (FBI, 1991b, p. 25). Although acceptance of the FBI's definition of terrorism is somewhat restrictive, its use provides insight into the polity's efforts to investigate, prosecute, and sanction those persons or groups it has deemed to be violent threats to political stability.

An examination of domestic terrorism since 1980 challenged many of our assumptions. We learned, for example, that terrorism was not the exclusive tool of violent leftists. As a result, we were forced to reevaluate our previous notions regarding the motivations of terrorists. We also learned about the impact of prosecution strategies on domestic terrorism. This chapter reviews changes in the patterns, characteristics, and tactics of U.S. terrorists and federal investigative and prosecutorial strategies and takes a prospective look into the near future of terrorism in the United States. To do this, we use a unique data set derived from the court records of federally indicted domestic terrorists to describe the groups that commit terrorist acts, as well as draw conclusions about the success or failure of prosecutorial strategies in combating terrorism.

## Methods

Terrorists are tried and convicted of a variety of criminal offenses.[1] Consequently, it is difficult to distinguish between traditional offenders and terrorists by using usual governmental data sources. Since the early 1980s, however, the FBI's Terrorist Research and Analytical Center has published an annual report that specifies which crimes have been investigated under the FBI's Counterterrorism Program. In 1989, the FBI released to the senior author of this chapter the names of persons indicted as a result of these investigations for the period 1982 to 1988. The original list was supplemented with those indicted in 1989 by using the FBI's annual report (FBI, 1990). The U.S. Department of Justice matched the final list of 213 names with federal court docket numbers assigned throughout the United States and Puerto Rico. These people, representing 21 terrorist organizations, had been indicted for more than 1,300 federal law violations. A check of persons and incidents mentioned in the FBI's annual reports for the same period indicated that 288 persons were officially investigated for "terrorism/terrorism-related" activities. Overall, our original sample included 71% of known, officially labeled, federally indicted terrorists during that period.[2] Table 6.1 provides a summary of the number and group affiliations of persons in that sample. Demographic and sentencing data were obtained from applicable federal district courts and supplemented by data from the Administrative Office of U.S. Courts. Of the 213 terrorists in the sample, 129 had been convicted in federal courts at the time of data collection. The data set includes information on almost all the indicted right-wing terrorists, as well as the majority of the most infamous left-wing group members in the 1970s and 1980s. These data were supplemented with data on U.S. terrorists during the 1990s.

All the terrorists in our sample were investigated and prosecuted as part of the FBI's Counterterrorism Program. The single distinguishing feature of this group is that they threatened the use of violence "for the purpose of furthering political or social goals" (Office of the Attorney General, 1983, p. 13). The attorney general's guidelines are explicit in requiring the establishment of political motivation before a terrorism investigation can be initiated. Although individual-level data are not available to confirm the political motives of the defendants, the federal government clearly labeled the defendants as having such motives on the basis of group affiliation and other criteria prescribed by the guidelines.

## Patterns and Trends

In the 1980s, the FBI designated 219 crimes as official acts of terrorism.[3] The number of terrorist acts in the United States increased steadily during the early part of the decade, from 29 in 1980 to 51 in 1982. This increase was largely the result of international terrorism and the acts of Puerto Rican terrorists. As a result of this increasing terrorism, the FBI escalated its Counterterrorism Program and relaxed the Levi Guidelines (a fairly restrictive set of rules that limited the extent to which the FBI could be involved in internal security investigations) in early 1983. Although it is difficult to prove empirically the deterrent effect of this "tightening of the system," it is clear that the level of terrorism dropped significantly for the rest of the decade. By 1985, only seven acts of terrorism were reported. Although a brief flourish of terrorist activity occurred in 1986 (when some organizations were able to regroup and recover after the early success of the FBI), by 1987, federal indictments had begun to take their effect on the organizations; and by 1989, only four officially designated acts of terrorism were recorded by the FBI.

The 1980s reflects four distinct patterns of American terrorism and counterterrorism. First, the decade began with all-time high levels of domestic terrorism. Second, this period was followed by

**TABLE 6.1**   Sample Characteristics of Persons and Groups Indicted for
Terrorism/Terrorist-Related Activities: 1980-1989

| Name Of Group | Number of Persons Indicted | Total Number of Indictees[a] |
|---|---|---|
| **Domestic Terrorism** | | |
| *Right-Wing* | | |
| 1   Aryan Nations | 3 | 3 |
| 2   Arizona Patriots | 10 | 10 |
| 3   Covenant, Sword, and Arm of the Lord | 17 | 22 |
| 4   Ku Klux Klan | 1 | 1 |
| 5   The Order | 28 | 48 |
| 6   The Order II | 5 | 5 |
| 7   Sheriff's Posse Comitatus | 4 | 5 |
| 8   White Patriot Party | 7 | 9 |
| *Left-Wing* | | |
| 9   El Rukns | 7 | 7 |
| 10   Macheteros | 19 | 20 |
| 11   Armed Forces of National Liberation (FALN) | 5 | 5 |
| 12   May 19th Communist Organization | 7 | 11 |
| 13   United Freedom Front | 8 | 9 |
| 14   New African Freedom Front | 9 | 9 |
| 15   Provisional Party of Communists | 1 | 1 |
| *Single Issue* | | |
| 16   Evan Mecham Eco-Terrorist International Conspiracy (EMETIC) | 5 | 5 |
| Subtotal | 136 | 170 |
| **International Terrorism** | | |
| 1   Japanese Red Army | 1 | 1 |
| 2   Provisional Irish Republican Army | 16 | 21 |
| 3   Omega 7 | 4 | 7 |
| 4   Libyans | 7 | 7 |
| 5   Palestinian/Syrian | 4 | 4 |
| Subtotal | 32 | 40 |
| Grand Total | 168 | 210 |

SOURCE: Reprinted from *Terrorism in America: Pipe Bombs and Pipe Dreams* by Brent L. Smith, by permission of the State University of New York Press © 1994.
NOTE: a. *Indictees* refers to the total number of individuals indicted. In 42 cases, the same persons were named in more than one indictment. Consequently, the number of indictees may exceed the number of persons for each group. The three indictees for whom group information was not known were excluded from these analyses.

intense efforts on the part of federal law enforcement agencies to address this growing problem. Third, following the early success of federal law enforcement, some terrorist groups were able to reorganize and rebound from the devastating series of arrests that occurred in Phase 2. This revitalization was relatively short-lived. Fourth, the decade closed with the ominous arrival of the environmental terrorists.

Since 1990, a variety of groups—left-wing and right-wing, single issue, and international—have been investigated and the focus of recent indictments. Table 6.2 provides a summary of these groups. Three trends emerged in the 1990s. First, the noticeable decline in Puerto Rican terrorism since the 1993 plebiscite in which Puerto Ricans voted to maintain their commonwealth status was a blow to the independence movement. Second, Puerto Rican terrorism, which in number of acts committed dominated U.S. terrorism statistics during the late 1970s and 1980s, has been relegated to second place as right-wing terrorism surged in the 1990s. Third, changes in federal law and prosecutorial strategies, which previously sought the expulsion of suspected international terrorists but which now seeks to extradite and imprison international terrorists in federal prisons, has increased the frequency with which the United States is targeted by international groups.

## Typologies of Terrorist Groups

Most empirical work describing what we know about terrorist groups has been based on examinations of international terrorists (e.g., Clutterbuck, 1980; Russell & Miller, 1977). These studies have told us that terrorists are young (18-35 years of age), male, middle to upper class, and well educated (Rubenstein, 1987). Because relatively few terrorist acts take place in the United States, it has been assumed that extremists in the United States are closely related in ideology to their European counterparts—political leftists with anarchist overtones (Wilkinson, 1987). This view of the American terrorist is evident in the news media and in academe. Our investigation, however, suggests that domestic terrorism since 1980 has not been overwhelmingly leftist. Over half (103) of the 170 terrorists in our study were associated with right-wing groups frequently referred to as being a part of the Christian Identity movement.[4] The remainder of those

**TABLE 6.2**    Terrorist and Violent Antigovernment Groups Active in the
United States Since 1990

| Left Wing (Domestic) | Right Wing (Domestic) |
|---|---|
| Pedro Campos Revolutionary Group (PACRF) Popular Liberation Army Boricua Revolutionary Front | Up the IRS (90, 91) American Front Skinheads McVeigh et al. "Sons of Gestapo" Viper Militia |
| Single Issue/ Environmental/Other | International |
| Earth Night Action Group Yahweh (Black Hebrew Israelites) Animal Liberation Front | Provisional IRA Sikhs (unnamed group) Mujahideen-e Khalq Organization (MEK or MKO) (Iranian; anti-Khomeini) Abdel-Rahman group Anti-Serbian group (unnamed group) Abu Nidal Organization (ANO) |

SOURCE: Data compiled from annual reports of the FBI's Terrorist Research and Analytical Center, Federal District Courts, and Federal Archives.

indicted in our study were left-wing (62) and environmental or single-issue (5) terrorists. During the same period, 40 people were indicted by the FBI for international terrorism.

Although Peter Fleming, Michael Stohl, and Alex Schmid (1988) have identified more than 50 typologies categorizing the varieties of terrorists, most fall short of the requirements of mutual exclusiveness, validity and reliability, and functional utility. Our study focuses on "domestic" terrorists, and we divide them into three categories: (a) right-wing, (b) left-wing, and (c) single-issue terrorists. Because our sample has relatively few single-issue terrorists, we focus on the first two categories.

Right-wing groups have been described as having "a belief in the intrinsic superiority of their own race or nation group and the need to make their own race or national group supreme over other groups . . . and a belief in the necessity and desirability of war as a means of realizing national or racial destiny" (Wilkinson as cited by

Fleming et al., 1988, p. 177). Left-wing terrorists, in contrast, have been characterized by egalitarianism (to an extreme), hatred of capitalism and racism, and opposition to militarism. Except for single-issue terrorists (e.g., animal rights activists), indicted U.S. terrorists fall easily into one of these two categories. Right-wing groups are characterized by their link to the Christian Identity movement and have included the Aryan Nations; the Arizona Patriots; the Covenant, Sword, and Arm of the Lord (CSA); and various factions of the Ku Klux Klan (KKK). Placing the remaining groups into the leftist category is more problematic. The El Rukns (a Chicago street gang) appears to have little in common with Puerto Rican freedom fighters like the Armed Forces of National Liberation (or FALN, after its Spanish name) and the Macheteros (Machete Wielders). These remaining groups, in contrast, bear a striking resemblance on at least five fronts: (a) their ideology and beliefs, (b) their views on economics and the distribution of wealth, (c) their bases of operation, (d) their tactical approach, and (e) the targets they select. In fact, in these five characteristics we are also able to distinguish right-wing from left-wing terrorists. These distinctions are summarized in Table 6.3 and discussed below.

### Left-Wing Versus Right-Wing Worldviews

Left-wing terrorists in the United States have tended to adopt a political focus, whereas right-wing terrorists appear to be driven by religious beliefs. The Christian Identity movement provides the ideological link for most violent rightist groups. The movement is based on the belief that Aryans (instead of Jews) are God's chosen people. It is anti-Semitic, antiblack, and argues that America is the "promised land." Right-wing religious terrorists advocate the use of terrorism as a prelude to Armageddon (the war that will establish the kingdom of Christ) (Hoffman, 1988). In contrast, left-wing extremists have traditionally been sympathetic with Marxism and, as a result, view religion as the "opiate of the masses." For Karl Marx, religion served only to maintain the false consciousness that allowed capitalism (and all its travails) to continue. Capitalism, for Marx, is destroyed through worker revolution, resulting in a classless society (Marx & Engels, 1970). Although left-wing terrorists differ in many

**TABLE 6.3**   Characteristics of Left-Wing and Right-Wing Terrorist
             Groups in the United States

| | Type of Group | |
|---|---|---|
| *Characteristic* | *Left-Wing* | *Right-Wing* |
| Ideology | Political focus; primarily Marxism | Religious focus; ties to Christian Identity movement |
| Economic Views | Procommunist/socialist; belief in Marxist maxim "receive according to one's need" | Strongly anticommunist; belief in Protestant work ethic, distributive justice |
| Base of Operations | Urban areas | Rural areas |
| Tactical Approach | Cellular structure; use of safe houses | National networking; camps and compounds |
| Targets | For funding: prefer armored truck robbery | For funding: prefer armored truck robbery |
| | Terrorist (symbolic) targets: seats of capitalism or govern-ment buildings | Terrorist (symbolic) targets: federal law enforcement agencies or opposing racial or religious groups |

SOURCE: Reprinted from *Terrorism in America: Pipe Bombs and Pipe Dreams* by Brent L. Smith, by permission of the State University of New York Press. Copyright 1994.

respects, they share a common disdain for capitalism. This com-monality has resulted in leftist groups seeking funding from similar sources.[5] Ironically, Marx envisioned revolution by the masses, not by terrorism, a point well established by Marx's expulsion of Michael Bakunin from the International Workingmen's Association in 1872 because of Bakunin's advocacy of the use of terrorist tactics. Failing to awaken the proletariat through nonviolence, however, leftist groups have resorted to terrorism, even inflicting pain and suffering on members of the working class.

Right-wing extremists believe that people should be rewarded on the basis of the value of their labor. According to this philosophy, humans are motivated by rewards and punishments and possess an innate desire for distributive justice (see Homans, 1974). Added to the rudiments of the Christian Identity movement, right-wing groups hold a strong belief in the Protestant ethic (Weber, 1976). This belief results in little sympathy for the economically disadvantaged. The logical conclusion of this thought process is opposition to affirmative action, welfare, and other programs that exclude nonminorities. This is tied closely to strong antitax beliefs and a desire to maintain control over public funds at the local level. Left-wing extremists, in contrast, hold to the Marxist doctrine "from each according to his abilities, to each according to his need" (Marx, 1956, p. 258). Because capitalist societies unleash and encourage a manipulative greed in humans, left-wing terrorists in the United States typically aspire to create a new social system bereft of the greed they see as characterizing modern America. Thus, groups such as the FALN, the Macheteros, and the New African Freedom Fighters (NAFF) all vehemently opposed the presumed exploitation of blacks, Hispanics, and the working class (e.g., Fernandez, 1987). They also perceived affirmative action plans as inadequate, resulting in a perpetuation of the corrupt status quo. Such programs were deemed to be efforts to pacify the masses and to debilitate the formation of the collective consciousness.

### Operational and Tactical Differences

Right-wing and left-wing terrorists in the United States also differ in their bases of operation. Left-wing extremists (e.g., FALN, Macheteros, May 19th Communist Organization [M19CO], El Rukns) were active in New York, Chicago, Hartford, New Jersey, and Washington. In essence, they located their activity in large urban areas. In contrast, right-wing extremists (e.g., Aryan Nations, The Order, CSA) were based in rural areas of Montana, Idaho, Arkansas, and Arizona (among other locations). One explanation for this tendency for left-wing groups to focus their efforts in the city whereas right-wing groups tend to work in rural areas may be a consequence of social structural forces. Many members of left-wing groups are African Americans, Hispanics, and Puerto Ricans, who live, for the most part, in urban areas. Another, more complex reason has to do with the ideological and tactical differences between the two groups. Whereas right-wing terrorists have been active only in the last few decades, left-wing extremists have been active since the 1960s. The failure of the rural campaign of Che Guevara in Bolivia in 1967 chilled the enthusiasm of leftists for terrorism in rural settings. Instead, the attention of left-wing terrorists has been turned toward the city because (a) it offers opportunity to directly strike the heart of capitalism and (b) it offers anonymity to the terrorists (Marighella, 1971).

Right-wing terrorists, having never been exposed to the late 1960s writings of the leftist theoreticians, have failed to learn the lessons widely publicized in leftist publications following Guevara's failure in Bolivia. The isolation of contemporary right-wing extremist groups in rural settings allowed them to be rather easily identified, resulting in many arrests and prosecutions in the 1980s. Although apparently fatal, the choice of these rural settings was not accidental. On the basis of their beliefs associated with the Christian Identity movement, right-wing extremists viewed the survival camps as a necessary preparation for Armageddon required by God of His followers. At the same time, movement from the city represented flight from the inner-city pollutants of minorities, tolerance for homosexuality, and a liberal press. These new rural communities (some of them reaching a population of more than 100 people) housed entire families and often had a church as the center of social life.

The paradox of domestic terrorist groups is that although they want to create public support for some specific goal, the work they do (terrorism) requires that they maintain a clandestine existence (Laqueur, 1977). They face the dilemma of requiring broad public exposure while, at the same time, remaining secretive. To facilitate this dilemma, leftist groups have adopted the use of cellular structure encouraged by South American revolutionaries Abraham Guillen (1973) and Carlos Marighella (1971). Right-wing extremists, however, have not had the same level of contact with the leftists of the 1960s and have had to struggle with the paradox of publicity and secrecy on their own. Christian Identity extremists chose to build popular support by creating "survivalist" camps. Unfortunately for the terrorists, the established "fixed fronts" were easy targets for governmental responses (Laqueur, 1977, p. 184). At the same time, right-wing groups tended to link their organizations nationally instead of developing independent, autonomous cells. The result of these two organizational tactics was that, by 1987, many major leaders of right-wing terrorist groups across the country had been arrested and indicted as a result of federal terrorism investigations.

By the early 1990s, right-wing extremists began moving to a cellular model as well, a strategy most frequently described as "leaderless resistance."

Most violent extremist groups select targets for two purposes. First, they seek targets that will provide funding for future group operations. Marighella (1971) referred to this as "the appropriation of government resources." Although some groups (e.g., the El Rukns) have tried to obtain funding from external sources (e.g., Libya), most have had to rely on robbery to fund the revolution. Thus, most domestic terrorists have had to stoop to "common" criminality to support their causes. These acts have included some of the largest armored truck robberies in U.S. history. This is one of the few similarities between the two polar types of terrorists.

Second, right-wing and left-wing terrorists differ substantially regarding the selection of *politically motivated* targets. Both groups seek targets that, on their destruction, will result in the furtherance of the political or social causes they represent. For the extremist, the act of terrorism is largely a staged media event and is highly symbolic. Thus, the type of target selected by terrorists depends on their ideological bent. Right-wing groups, for example, have often spoken of striking out against the "Zionist Occupational Government" (ZOG). Until the Oklahoma City bombing in 1995, however, their efforts had been confined primarily to attacks against Jewish persons and property or against groups who appear supportive of "immoral" activities (e.g., adult theaters, homosexual rights organizations).

Left-wing extremists have been much more politically oriented in their target selection. Rather than focus on churches and synagogues, leftist terrorists have tended to focus on (a) representatives of government (e.g., courthouses, employees, military recruiting centers) and (b) large corporations (e.g., banks, oil companies). Ominously, the efforts of the right-wing extremists appear to have turned their attention to a broader spectrum of targets as threats have been received about the possible poisoning of large urban areas such as Washington, D.C. ("Group Weighed Cyanide Assault," 1988) and the indiscriminate bombing of federal facilities or public places as exemplified by the Oklahoma City bombing and, quite probably, the bombing at the Olympic Games in Atlanta in 1996.

In summary, left-wing and right-wing terrorists can be categorized along five dimensions. Right-wing terrorists tend (a) to

be associated with the Christian Identity movement, (b) to be opposed to federal government programs and taxation, (c) to be located
and active in rural parts of the country, (d) to be more nationally
organized, and (e) to focus their "political" attacks on Jews, minorities, liberal organizations, and more recently, federal agencies that
exemplify their ideological and religious beliefs (e.g., the FBI, BATF,
IRS, EEOC). Left-wing terrorists, in contrast, tend (a) to follow, at
least loosely, a Marxist doctrine, (b) to be anticapitalist, (c) to be
located and active in urban areas, (d) to be organized cellularly, and
(e) to focus their "political" acts on corporations or businesses affiliated with the defense industry. Further examination of our data
also reveals that previous demographic descriptions of international
terrorists may be only partially applicable to generalizations about
U.S. terrorists.

### Demographics

As noted previously, our descriptions of terrorist group members stem largely from examinations of international terrorists (e.g.,
Russell & Miller, 1977). Although these descriptions closely resemble
violent, left-wing extremists in the United States, right-wing extremists differ substantially. This is an important failure because, as
we have already shown, the majority of domestic terrorists indicted
in the United States since 1980 were members of *right-wing* organizations. For example, the average age at indictment for the terrorists in
our sample was 35 (see Table 6.4), considerably older than the estimate of 20 to 23 years of age provided by previous research (National Governors Association, 1978; Russell & Miller, 1977). Although a few crimes committed by those indicted occurred years
earlier, the majority took place within the year prior to the indictment. A conservative estimate, then, places the average age of
domestic terrorists at 30 to 33 years of age. Part of this discrepancy
may be that prior studies included all of the groups' members in their
calculations. It may be that older, more experienced members of an
organization are more likely to commit acts of terrorism. Another
explanation may be that previous studies focused on left-wing
groups. Many leftist terrorists who were arrested in the 1980s had
been active for more than a decade. Our data support this notion. The

average age of the right-wing terrorists was 39 years. More than one third were over the age of 40. In contrast, less than 20% of left-wing terrorists were 40 years of age or older.

Although terrorism remains a predominately male phenomenon, the proportion of females involved in extremist violence is far greater than for "traditional" crime (see Table 6.4). Although females in America make up only about 8% of arrests for serious offenses (FBI, 1990) and only 5% of prison inmates, 15% of people indicted for domestic terrorism were females. There is a sharp division in the two groups regarding female involvement. About 27% of indicted left-wing terrorists were females, whereas only 7% of indicted right-wing terrorists were females. In most cases, the women were married to actively violent right-wing extremists.

Over 70% of left-wing terrorists were members of minority groups (mostly black or Hispanic). In contrast, only about 3% of right-wing terrorists claimed to be minorities (see Table 6.4). Similarly, descriptions by government agencies and other reports regarding the educational attainments of international leftist terrorists are fairly accurate reflections of violent, American, left-wing extremists. They are generally well educated, with over half having graduated from college. Only 12% of right-wing terrorists, however, held college degrees, whereas one third had not graduated from high school. This differing level of education for the two groups is highly related to their occupational differences. Violent leftists were more likely to have members who were physicians, attorneys, teachers, and even government workers. By contrast, terrorists associated with the Christian Identity movement were more likely to have members with minimal job skills. Interestingly, both leftists and rightists found U.S. prisons to be fertile grounds for recruitment.

## Prosecution

Few crimes evoke greater fear of instability in Western democracies than terrorism (Wolfgang, Figlio, Tracy, & Singer, 1985). Despite this concern and the salience of the topic for criminological theory, few studies have examined in detail governmental responses to terrorism. Conflict theorists, such as Austin Turk (1982), suggest that

**TABLE 6.4**   Demographic Characteristics of Left-Wing and Right-Wing
Terrorist Groups in the United States

| Demographic Characteristic | Type of Group[a] | |
|---|---|---|
| | Left-Wing | Right-Wing |
| Age | Average age at indictment: 35—18% over age of 40 | Average age at indictment: 39—36% over age of 40 |
| Sex | 73% Male | 93% Male |
| | 27% Female | 7% Female |
| Race | 29% White | 97% White |
| | 71% Minority | 3% American Indian |
| Education | 54% college degrees | 12% College degrees |
| | 12% GED equivalent or less | 33% GED equivalent or less |
| Occupation | Mixed, but many professional workers: physicians, attorneys, teachers, social workers, etc. | Mixed, but a large number of unemployed or impoverished self-employed workers |
| Place of Residence | Urban | Rural |

SOURCE: Reprinted from *Terrorism in America: Pipe Bombs and Pipe Dreams* by Brent L. Smith, by permission of the State University of New York Press © 1994.
NOTE: [a]Left-wing domestic terrorists included members from the following groups: El Rukns, Macheteros, FALN, May 19th Communist Organization, United Freedom Front, New African Freedom Front, and the Provisional Party of Communists. Right-wing domestic terrorists included members of the Aryan Nations; Arizona Patriots; Covenant, Sword, and Arm of the Lord; Ku Klux Klan; the Order; the Order II; Sheriff's Posse Comitatus; and the White Patriot Party.

public perceptions regarding the egregiousness of the offense and support for governmental intervention determine selection of one of the two basic strategies used to prosecute terrorists (Smith, 1994). The first involves explicitly politicizing the crime by charging the defendant with offenses like seditious conspiracy, treason, or some "terrorism specific" statute. This approach was used rarely during the 1980s.

The second strategy involves prosecuting terrorists as conventional offenders. Recent analyses of the prosecution of U.S. terrorists during the 1980s confirm that, with the exception of the very infrequent use of "treason, sedition, and subversive activities" (USC Title 18, § 2384), federal investigators and prosecutors chose to pursue prosecution of terrorists as "conventional" criminals (Office of the Attorney General, 1983; Poveda, 1990). The tendency to avoid the creation of political crimes such as terrorism may be because of the inability to create practical, working definitions of such offenses that succeed in meeting constitutional criteria (Fleming et al., 1988; Smith, 1985; Wardlaw, 1989). Previous research indicates that efforts to create specific political offenses like terrorism have been doomed because motive was a salient, defining characteristic of the crime (Smith, 1988).

Another reason explicitly politicizing the crime or using terrorism-specific statutes have not been used extensively is that they are extremely difficult to prosecute successfully. Table 6.5 shows the outcomes of the 10 most frequently used federal statutes during the 1980s for the prosecution of persons indicted under FBI terrorism investigations. Explicitly politicized charges (treason, sedition, and subversive activities) were seldom used, and for good reason: They had the highest acquittal rates of the statutes used to prosecute terrorists. These charges prominently appeared in three major trials against terrorists in the 1980s and early 1990s: (a) the 1989 trial of United Freedom Front (UFF) members; (b) the 1988 trial of extreme right-wing group members in Fort Smith, Arkansas; and (c) the 1990 trial of May 19th Communist Organization members in Washington, D.C. Each of these trials had similar outcomes: The Fort Smith trial resulted in acquittal for all the defendants. The trial against UFF members in Massachusetts resulted in acquittal on the major counts, and the judge declared a mistrial on the remaining verdicts. In Washington, although one defendant was convicted and sentenced to 20 years, charges against the other defendants were dropped after the judge ruled that the indictment was repetitious of charges for which they had been convicted previously (Smith, 1994).

Recent events, however, may signal a change in the traditional federal prosecutorial approach to dealing with terrorists. The first event was the creation of "hate crime" legislation that specifically includes motive of the perpetrator as an element of proof. This legislation is indicative of a trend to allow motive to play an increasingly important role in the creation of federal legislation. The second event has been the expansion of federal "terrorism-specific" statutes. The indictment of the alleged perpetrators of the April 19, 1995, bombing of the federal building in Oklahoma City represents the first use of these statutes (e.g., see USC Title 18, § 2332). The third event was the successful prosecution of the WTC bombers in October 1995. Their conviction marked the first successful usage of federal "seditious

**TABLE 6.5**   Outcomes of the 10 Most Frequently Used Federal Statutes for Terrorism/Terrorism-Related Activities: 1980-1989

| USC Chapter | OUTCOME[a] | | | | |
|---|---|---|---|---|---|
| | Trial Conviction | Guilty Plea | Dismissed Because of Plea[b] | Acquittal or Mistrial | Total |
| Racketeering | 147 | 2 | 78 | 100 | 327 |
| | 45.0% | 0.6% | 23.9% | 30.6% | |
| Machine guns, etc. | 86. | 9 | 95 | 21 | 211 |
| | 40.8% | 4.3% | 45.0% | 10.0% | |
| Conspiracy | 32 | 42 | 12 | 26 | 112 |
| | 28.6% | 37.5% | 10.7% | 23.2% | |
| Racketeer Influenced Corrupt Organizations (RICO) Act | 22 25.9% | 20 23.5% | 23 27.1% | 20 23.5% | 85 |
| Firearms | 22 | 0 | 17 | 35 | 74 |
| | 29.7% | 0.0% | 23.0% | 47.3% | |
| Explosive Materials | 14 | 5 | 27 | 22 | 68 |
| | 20.6% | 7.4% | 39.7% | 32.4% | |
| Stolen Property | 13 | 0 | 12 | 13 | 38 |
| | 34.2% | 0.0% | 31.6% | 34.2% | |
| Robbery or Burglary | 4 | 1 | 3 | 4 | 12 |
| | 33.3% | 8.3% | 25.0% | 33.3% | |
| Emergency Economic Powers | 0 0.0% | 1 4.8% | 20 95.2% | 0 0.0% | 21 |
| Mail Fraud | 2 | 0 | 11 | 7 | 20 |
| | 10.0% | 0.0% | 55.0% | 35.0% | |
| Treason, Sedition, Subversive Activities | 4 18.2% | 2 9.1% | 0 0.0% | 16 72.7% | 22 |
| TOTAL | 346 | 82 | 298 | 264 | 990 |
| | 34.9% | 8.3% | 30.1% | 26.7% | |

SOURCE: Reprinted from *Terrorism in America: Pipe Bombs and Pipe Dreams* by Brent L. Smith, by permission of the State University of New York Press © 1994.
NOTES: a. Excludes cases pending and cases for which outcome is unknown. Of 1,363 counts in the sample, case results were available for 1,117 counts. The remaining 127 count results for other federal statutes are not presented here
b. Dismissed because of plea on this or other counts.

conspiracy" statutes against terrorists in a decade. These signs all suggest that, for at least one type of political offender—terrorists— political motive may be an important determinant in prosecution (Smith, 1994) and sentencing (Smith & Orvis, 1994). Smith (1994), for example, previously noted that terrorists are less likely than nonter- rorists to receive probation and that they receive longer sentences, on average, than nonterrorists for conviction of identical federal crimes.

Explanations for why this strategy is used differ greatly. *Conflict theory,* for example, suggests that this strategy is used by the polity to hide the intent to harshly punish politically motivated offenders when public sentiment would not justify such a reaction. Conse- quently, the polity takes advantage of the relaxed rules of due process at the sentencing stage to sanction terrorists more harshly than similarly situated nonpolitical offenders. In contrast, *consensus theory* asserts that to achieve the moral will of the people, an ex- pedient approach to restore stability is to convict as quickly as possible to get the offender off the streets and then, at sentencing, to address the real extent to which the public desires harsher punish- ment. This approach serves two functions for the government. First, it increases the probability of successful prosecution (Smith & Orvis, 1994); second, it removes offenders who are "dangerous or threaten- ing to society" (Tittle, 1994, p. 24).

The decision by the Department of Justice to focus its efforts on the prosecution of terrorist groups, rather than of individual acts of terror, significantly affected prosecutorial strategies. Efforts were concentrated on breaking up the organizational structure and leader- ship of the terrorist group. Consequently, *among terrorists,* an individual's role in the organization (leader or follower) was the most significant factor associated with sentence length. As a result, the actual perpetrators of some terrorist incidents in the United States received minimal sanctioning in exchange for testimony regarding group leaders. With terrorists striking more indiscriminately and with greater loss of life (the WTC bombing and the Oklahoma City bombing), whether such a prosecutorial approach can be maintained in the face of mounting public pressure to maximize the punishment of the *actual perpetrator(s)* is yet to be determined. Changes in prosecutorial strategies may significantly affect the high conviction rates currently enjoyed by federal prosecutors.

Despite the introduction of new sentencing guidelines, the sentencing phase in judicial proceedings clearly continues to allow for more discretion than during trial. The absence of a jury, a reduction in the standard of proof from "beyond a reasonable doubt" to the standard used in civil suits of "preponderance of the evidence," and the allowance of "uncharged and unconvicted conduct" as evidence all provide for upward departures in the sentencing of terrorists. Introduction of the new federal sentencing guidelines did little to alter these procedures. Although the guidelines created a new formula for sentence computation that restricted the range of sentences, the use of "uncharged and unconvicted conduct" can still be raised at sentencing. The standard of proof continues to be the lesser "preponderance of the evidence," and sentencing remains under the authority of the judge, rather than a jury of one's peers. Consequently, federal courts have allowed upward adjustments under the guidelines for a variety of behaviors relevant to terrorism: cases in which the defendant made threats against the president of the United States; took hostages; was an organizer, leader, or supervisor in criminal activities involving five or more persons; and, most important, where reliable information indicates that the criminal history category does not adequately reflect the seriousness of the defendant's past criminal conduct or the likelihood that the defendant will commit future crimes (U.S. Sentencing Commission, 1991). Although the defendants' behavior in these cases might warrant more severe sanctioning, further analysis of the relationship between political motivation and punishment severity is necessary to determine whether criminality, rather than political belief, is the primary determinant of sentence length (for a more detailed discussion of these issues, see Smith & Damphousse, 1996).

## Prospects for the Future

The nature of domestic terrorism in the United States during the past two decades has revealed itself to be a game of cat-and-mouse between terrorist groups and those trying to prosecute them. The interactions between these two opposing forces have led to a series of interesting trends. First, in the immediate post-Watergate era, the

FBI operated under the "Levi Guidelines," a fairly restrictive set of rules that limited the extent to which the agency could be involved in internal security investigations (Poveda, 1990). During this period, domestic terrorists, particularly leftist groups such as the UFF and the M19CO, successfully avoided capture and prosecution through a strategy that involved a cellular structure and very limited recruiting efforts.

With congressional pressure mounting, William French Smith revised the guidelines in 1983, allowing the FBI greater flexibility and raising the priority of terrorism investigations. The results were dramatic. Leftover violent leftists from the 1970s were arrested in large numbers from 1984 to 1987. Because of their cellular structure and clandestine strategy, attrition from arrests took its toll, minimal recruitment provided no replacements, and leftist terrorism declined dramatically after 1985.

The arrests and subsequent convictions in the 1980s of members of the most prominent left-wing groups from the 1960s and 1970s apparently signaled the end of that generation of violent leftists in the United States. Similarly, results of the plebiscite in Puerto Rico in 1993 revealed little support for the independence movement and momentarily has curtailed activities of the Puerto Rican terrorist groups. Although the ideology of leftist groups like the Weather Underground, the Black Liberation Army (BLA), the UFF, and the M19CO may re-emerge in later groups, the intergenerational ties that link many extreme leftist terrorist groups were broken during the 1980s. The radical leftist literature that arose following Che Guevara's failure in Bolivia signaled a shift in leftist tactics from a rural revolutionary model to one advocating urban terrorism through a cellular organization. If similar groups do appear again in the late 1990s, the lessons learned by the leftists of the 1960s may have to be relearned by subsequent generations of left-wing terrorists.

Likewise, the "war in '84" by the extreme Right resulted in arrests in 1985 as the FBI and federal attorneys successfully investigated and prosecuted scores of right-wing group members from the Order, the Sheriff's Posse Comitatus, the CSA, the Aryan Nations, and the White Patriot Party (WPP) (Smith, 1994; Smith & Morgan, 1994). The 1988 trial of extreme right-wing groups' leaders was a turning point for the extreme Right. Despite their acquittal, the leaders of the extreme Right recognized that efforts to nationally network organizations could lead to wholesale civil litigation and criminal indictments. Although continuing efforts to recruit heavily from two extremist segments of the population (militia organizations opposed to gun control legislation and the Skinhead movement [Smith, 1995]), the extreme Right spent the early 1990s devising a strategy known as "leaderless resistance" (J. Roy, personal communication, April 20, 1995), an approach reminiscent of the extreme Left's cellular model of urban terrorism. How the application of this model will affect the prosecution of right-wing terrorists in the late 1990s is yet to be seen.

Since adoption of U.S. Attorney General William French Smith's guidelines for terrorism investigations in 1983, the federal government has made two additional alterations worthy of note. The first involved passage of the Extra-territorial Jurisdiction Act, later amended, which expanded the FBI's authority and jurisdiction to include acts of terrorism committed against U.S. citizens outside the usual jurisdictional boundaries of the United States. The capture and subsequent imprisonment of Fawaz Younis in 1989 for his involvement in a Beirut airport airline hijacking marked the first usage of the statute. By the mid-1990s, a contingent of international terrorists were incarcerated in U.S. prisons. Although such a policy may send a clear deterrent signal, it will also increase targeting of Americans, coupled with demands for the release of terrorists held in U.S. prisons, a dilemma European countries have faced for years.

Second, recent federal legislation has focused on the creation of terrorism-specific statutes (e.g., see USC Title 18, § 2332). Although this legislation avoids the creation of a specific crime called "terrorism" by focusing on the target selection of the perpetrator rather than on his or her motive, these statutes clearly move in the direction of "explicitly politicizing" such offenses. This approach marks a significant departure from the 1980s, when terrorists were overwhelmingly prosecuted for "traditional" or "conventional" crimes. Whether this approach, with its more severe penalties and intended deterrent effect, will outweigh the potential costs of politicizing terrorists' behaviors and setting them apart from common criminality remains to be seen.

In conclusion, the greatest immediate threat from terrorist groups in the United States will probably come from violent fringes of the extreme Right. For these persons, the threshold over which the violent extremist steps is strewn with religious symbolism. All right-wing groups that turned to terrorism during the past two decades had developed some relationship with Christian Identity theology. Although most Christian denominations teach that the second coming of Christ will be preceded by "great tribulation," most also teach that believers will either be protected from these adversities or "raptured" prior to Christ's return. Christian Identity theology suggests neither; adherents are urged to prepare for mortal combat to deal with the coming Armageddon, the great battle wherein Christ will vanquish his enemies and establish his reign on earth. For many Christians, the end of the millennium is highly significant. It is a commonly held belief among many denominations that the year 2000 (or thereabouts) represents the end of six 1,000-year periods. Believing that the beginning of the next millennium is fulfillment of the statement that "on the seventh day, God rested," the return of Christ is seen as imminent. Fear of the coming tribulation is being used by Christian Identity militants as a rationale to attract recruits. The movement can be expected to continue to increase in size as fear of this possibility expands. Among the general Christian community, fear of a one-world government, a single universal currency, a cashless society, and the increasingly sophisticated technological ability of government to monitor the religious activities of citizens add fuel to fears regarding "the great tribulation." Some of these people will be drawn into the Christian Identity movement.

Although we cannot dismiss the threat of leftist violence, the threat of right-wing, antifederal violence is the greatest threat for several reasons. First is the aforementioned religious significance of a new millennium. Second, unlike the violent extremists of the Left in the 1970s and 1980s who decided to go underground, the violent extremists of the Right are busy perfecting strategies to maintain an aboveground presence for recruiting purposes while developing an underground cellular network. For the Left in the 1970s and 1980s, the choice was exclusive: Either stay aboveground and continue to recruit but limit terrorist activities, or go underground and turn to terrorism. The Christian Identity movement is attempting to maintain both an aboveground presence through its religious outlets while others in the movement go underground. We have yet to see whether the so-called leaderless resistance approach will minimize civil and criminal liability for spokespersons of the violent fringes of the Christian Identity movement.

Usually, *symbolic catalysts* propel extremist groups to violence for short periods of time. Sometimes, single precipitating events push extremists over the edge and serve as the impetus for violent extremism. The next few years will be critical for federal efforts to minimize antigovernment violence on the right. One reduction strategy is to explore alternative intervention methods that minimize the potential creation of these symbolic catalysts.

## Notes

1. Although Chapter 113B of the *Federal Criminal Code and Rules* is entitled "Terrorism," it has been used sparingly and does not include motive as an essential element, focusing instead on target selection (*Federal Rules,* 1995, p. 763).

2. The sample includes persons affiliated with the following groups: Aryan Nations; Arizona Patriots; Covenant, Sword, and Arm of the Lord; Ku Klux Klan; the Order; the Order II; Sheriff's Posse Comitatus; White Patriot Party; El Rukns; Macheteros; Armed Forces of National Liberation; May 19 Communist Organization; United Freedom Front; New African Freedom Front; Provisional Party of Communists; Jewish Defense League; Earth First; Japanese Red Army; Libyans; Omega 7; Palestinian/Syrians; Provisional Irish Republican Army; and three persons of groups unknown.

3. The data described here were derived from information provided in the annual reports of the FBI's Terrorist Research and Analytical Center.

4. Actually, not all right-wing groups identified themselves with this philosophy, whereas many who *did* advocate these religious beliefs did *not* resort to violence to achieve their goals.

5. Moammar Gadhafi was simultaneously providing support for groups and individuals as diverse as the El Rukns, Vernon Belcourt, and Kwame Ture (Stokely Carmichael).

# PART 3

# FIGHTING TERRORISM

In one way or another, all the chapters in Part 3 deal with fighting terrorism. The first offering, Chapter 7, "Prosecuting Domestic Terrorists: Some Recommendations," by Tomas C. Mijares and Wayman C. Mullins, calls for the cooperation of all levels of government in combating terrorism. According to Mijares and Mullins, cooperation removes the need to pass new laws to punish terrorists; it allows the implementation of already existing criminal statutes, such as the Racketeer Influenced and Corrupt Organizations (RICO) Act, to attack terrorists and prosecute them. They also encourage private citizens to bring civil actions against extremists and terrorists. Mijares and Mullins's recommendations are simple, straightforward, and capable of yielding fruit.

Chapter 8, "An International Legislative Approach to 21st-Century Terrorism," is what Douglas A. Kash recommends. According to Kash, the newfound call to religious fanaticism that reverberates throughout the impoverished societies of the world necessitates a multinational approach to fighting terrorism. The first, albeit most important, step in the cooperative direction is to agree on a legal definition of terrorism. Only then, Kash believes, will the United States and its allies begin to counter 21st-century terrorism.

Part 3 concludes with a discussion of various sensory-enhancing technologies and their use in terrorist situations. In Chapter 9, "Domestic Law Enforcement's Use of Sensory-Enhancing Technology in Terrorist Situations," David B. Perkins and Tomas C. Mijares provide the reader with the latest on ambient light magnification, audio amplification, infrared lighting, and radar. They also explore the constitutional questions these surveillance technologies raise.

# 7

# Prosecuting Domestic Terrorists
## *Some Recommendations*

### TOMAS C. MIJARES
### WAYMAN C. MULLINS

On August 21, 1992, federal agents were conducting surveillance on white separatist Randall C. Weaver, who was wanted for failing to appear in court on a weapons charge. When U.S. Marshal William Degan left his position of cover to repair a malfunctioning surveillance camera, he encountered Weaver's son, Sammy, who had been alerted to the marshal's presence by the family dog, Striker. A shootout ensued, leaving both Degan and Weaver's 14-year-old son dead. After a 12-day standoff, during which Weaver's spouse, Vicki, was killed, Weaver surrendered. Weaver was later acquitted of all charges except for his failure to appear in court. On August 15, 1995, without admitting guilt, the federal government agreed to pay the Weaver family $3.1 million to settle lawsuits stemming from the deaths of Vicki and Sammy Weaver.

This tragedy that was Ruby Ridge is just one of several major government efforts against extremists that turned into a public relations nightmare while gaining sympathy and support for the targeted groups. At other times, the monetary cost of the operation was so high that it affected the decision-making process. U.S. Attorney General Janet Reno admitted after the siege at the Branch Davidian compound near Waco, Texas, that a major factor in her deciding whether to mount the assault was the expense of maintaining a strike force at the scene.

Should these costly operations be continued, considering the risks involved? With this in mind, we examine the efficacy of law enforcement efforts directed toward extremist individuals and groups. Then we make some recommendations about managing and prosecuting the extremist Right.

## Two Important Cases

### Robert Jay Mathews

On December 7, 1984, FBI agents cordoned off the area around three safe houses on Whidbey Island, a small, relatively inaccessible island in Puget Sound, Washington. The bureau made arrests at two of the residences. In the last house remained a teenage boy and Robert Jay Mathews, leader of the Order, an underground terrorist group sworn to bring victory to the Aryan race by destroying the federal government and ridding the country of minorities and Jews. After allowing the boy to surrender to the authorities, Mathews opened fire. On December 8, 1984, Mathews died as a result of the firestorm created when the flares fired by federal agents ignited the ammunition stored in the house.

Mathews was rumored to have masterminded several armed robberies, including that of a Brinks armored truck near Ukiah, California, which netted the Order more than $3 million. Mathews also was suspected of the murder of an Order member who was believed to be an informant. Following Mathews's death, authorities found in Weaver's home and in his various hiding places detailed plans for the destruction of highways, power plants, telecommunication sites, and ships in Puget Sound.

Authorities hoped that Mathews's death would cripple the Order and severely curtail the activities of the Aryan Nations; neither occurred. Instead, Mathews earned the rank of martyr, and the Aryan Nations, a center for white supremacist organizing and Identity teaching where Mathews recruited his followers, became a magnet for the violent fringe of the extreme Right. The Order was reborn as the Bruder Schweigen Task Force II (or the Order II), with its members rededicating themselves to the overthrow of the federal government.

With renewed vigor, Richard Butler, founder of the Aryan Nations, began holding regularly scheduled meetings of the extreme Right at his compound in Hayden Lake, Idaho. At one of the first of these conclaves, Butler and other extremist leaders drew up the Nehemiah Township Charter, which was legally filed in Kootahana County, Idaho, as the U.S. Constitution. The charter was drafted, in large part, as a direct response to the death of Mathews at the hands of federal authorities.

### James Ellison

After Mathews died in 1984, several Order members joined up with the Covenant, Sword, and Arm of the Lord (CSA) at its compound in Marion County, Arkansas. By the spring of the following year, the links between the Order and CSA became apparent. As federal agents closed in on the compound, Order members David Tate and Frank Silva made their escape. By April 20, 1985, both were taken into custody for killing one Missouri state police officer and seriously wounding another after a routine traffic stop. Two days later, after a three-day standoff, CSA leader James Ellison and four Order members were arrested at the CSA compound by federal agents. Authorities found stockpiles of illegal weapons, land mines, and a rocket launcher. Members were charged with a variety of crimes, including firebombing a synagogue and attempting to blow up a natural gas line.

One year after his arrest and conviction, and in exchange for a reduction of his sentence, Ellison agreed to testify against others in the violent, extreme Right movement. In April 1987, 14 members of the extreme Right were charged with sedition: Louis R. Beam, Jr. (former Grand Dragon of the Knights of the KKK); Richard Butler (leader of the Aryan Nations); Joseph Richard Scutari (Aryan Nations and the Order); Bruce Carroll Pierce (Aryan Nations, the Order, and alleged triggerman in the murder of Denver radio commentator Alan Berg); David Eden Lane (Aryan Nations, the Order, and participant in the Berg murder); Robert E. Miles (leader of the Mountain Church of Jesus Christ the Savior); Ardie McBrearty (intelligence chief and legal advisor to the Order); Robert N. Smalley, Richard Wayne Snell, and Lambert Miller (CSA); William and Ivan Wade (CSA, Posse Comitatus, and KKK); Andrew Virgil Barnhill (the Order, CSA, and KKK); and David M. McGuire (Ellison's son-in-law).

In federal court in Fort Smith, Arkansas, Ellison told of a secret meeting at the 1983 Aryan Nations Congress in Hayden Lake during which he and other violent extremists planned for a race "war in '84." Despite Ellison's testimony, which satisfied his commitment to the government, the jury remained unconvinced. All 14 men were acquitted of all charges on April 7, 1988. Shortly thereafter, Ellison was released from prison, whereupon he resumed control of the CSA.

Why was there no conviction? Among the most plausible of many explanations was that the jury simply did not believe the men were guilty. Some jury members may even have thought it unfair to retry some of the defendants for crimes for which they were already serving time. Another explanation rests with the creditably of the testimony of those trying to reduce their own sentences. Whatever the reason, the Fort Smith verdict says that no matter how offensive someone's thoughts, they are still only thoughts. Or, in other words, "Extremism is not terrorism."

### Extremism Is Not Terrorism: The Legacy of Fort Smith

The Fort Smith decision affected law enforcement's efforts against the extreme Right. First, it severely hampered the government's proactive policy of arresting members of extremist groups that articulate unpopular, albeit violent, beliefs. Second, it served to further unify the leadership of the extreme Right into an even tighter cohesive unit. Unlike the fragmented left-wing groups of an earlier era, far Right extremist leaders have always cooperated with each other, with some individuals belonging to several groups simultaneously. Fort Smith made a bad situation even worse.

Today's extremist leaders actively sponsor paramilitary training centers and other activities as they prepare for Armageddon (e.g., see Coates, 1987; Dees, 1996; Stern, 1996).

## Some Recommendations

If law enforcement has been ineffective in its prosecution of domestic terrorist groups, what can be done to reverse the trend? First, an effort must be made to avoid elevating common criminals to an almost romantic status within the media and society as well. Members of extremist groups are often directly involved in a wide variety of criminal activities. In many cases, focusing on their racist rhetoric may actually help their recruitment efforts while hampering their prosecution by detracting from the criminality of their deeds.

Second, authorities should concentrate on using already existing laws to prosecute domestic terrorists for traditional criminal activities. In this way, the prosecution is handled by local officials who are versed in the intricacies of the local criminal codes. At the federal level, the Racketeer Influenced and Corrupt Organizations (RICO) statutes, used successfully against organized crime, can be employed to prosecute terrorists who are wont to commit a variety of offenses—such as counterfeiting and weapons smuggling—covered under the RICO statutes.

Third, private citizens should be encouraged to initiate civil action against domestic terrorists, just as Beulah Mae Donald did after her 16-year-old son, Michael, was abducted and killed in Mobile, Alabama, in 1981. After Michael's abductors, James (Tiger) Knowles and Henry Francis Hays, were convicted of murder and for violating Michael's civil rights, Mrs. Donald brought a civil suit against the Klan, arguing that it is liable for the actions of its members just as a corporation is for its employees. She won a $7 million judgment. In May 1987, the Klan turned over to Mrs. Donald its national headquarters building in Tuscaloosa that was later sold for about $50,000. Capturing the assets of extremist organizations may indeed prove beneficial in deterring and countering terrorism.

Finally, authorities from different legal jurisdictions must agree to work together against domestic terrorist activity. Although the subjects of the Branch Davidian incident may not qualify as terrorists, this disaster illustrates the need for interagency cooperation. Interviews of surrounding law enforcement and protective agencies indicate that earlier contacts with David Koresh yielded a wealth of information about the compound's infrastructure and, more important, the inhabitants' attitudes. Waco may have been avoided had this information been made available to the Bureau of Alcohol, Tobacco and Firearms (ATF).

# 8

# An International Legislative Approach to 21st-Century Terrorism

## Douglas A. Kash

[T]ransnational criminality has become one of the most pressing problems confronting contemporary society. . . . [V]iolence within nations and across national boundaries strains public institutions because of the social and political upheaval it causes, most brutally epitomized in terrorism. . . . [Terrorism] can no longer be tackled by Governments individually. Its political, economic, social, cultural and human costs can only be substantially reduced by nations acting in concert.

*(Perez de Cuellar, 1990, pp. 42-43)*

AUTHOR'S NOTE: Special thanks to Sharad Khandelwal, a 3rd-year law student at the University of Michigan Law School, for his critical research and analysis of international criminal law and policy.

163

The reality of present-day terrorism and the continuing threat it poses for the future must be confronted with a determined and unified effort by the world community. Yesterday's amateur extremists have matured into today's lethal terrorists. Significant advancements in counterterrorist approaches have been evenly matched by new terrorist techniques. The relative ease with which these terrorists can obtain weapons of mass destruction makes the situation even more troublesome. No one nation can address these issues alone.

A multinational approach is needed like the one articulated in the *Report of the Eighth U.N. Congress on the Prevention of Crime and the Treatment of Offenders* (1990). Specifically, the report calls for international cooperation in crime prevention and criminal justice for the 21st century. Without a multinational legislative effort, the report warns, geographic boundaries, which limit the effectiveness of national laws, actually protect terrorists who take advantage of gaps in legal procedure. For decades, however, the main impediment to developing laws to prevent and punish terrorists has been the failure of the international community to adopt a legal definition of terrorism.

## A Definitional Dilemma

No single inclusive definition of terrorism has been accepted by the United Nations or in any generally accepted multilateral treaty. A policy combating terrorism simply cannot be developed unless all participants agree on the meaning of what is being addressed. In fact, not until 1979 did the U.N. General Assembly adopt a resolution condemning terrorism per se and providing that "all acts of terrorism that endangered human lives or fundamental freedoms were unequivocally condemned" (International Convention Against the Taking of Hostages, 1979). By 1985, the U.N. made further progress by adopting a resolution entitled Criminal Acts of a Terrorist Character, which incorporated its 1979 declaration. This resolution "unequivocally condemned, *as criminal*, all acts, methods and practices of terrorism whenever and by whomever committed" (Criminal Acts of a Terrorist Character, 1985). Although these pronouncements address terrorism as a concept, the global acceptance of a definition

nevertheless remains elusive—thereby postponing its criminaliza-
tion on an international level. Illustrative of this dilemma is the
proclamation of the late Richard Baxter (1974), U.S. Judge to the
International Court of Justice: "[W]e have cause to regret that a legal
concept of terrorism was ever inflicted upon us. The term is im-
precise; it is ambiguous; and above all, it serves no operative legal
purpose" (p. 380).

Moreover, "[t]he problem with legal definitions of terrorism is
that they account for neither the social or political nature of terrorism." Violence comprises perplexing social factors that "range
beyond narrow legal limitations and foreign policy restrictions."
Because political violence ordinarily occurs during the struggle for
legitimacy, "someone or some group must have the *power* to label
opponents. Groups can be labeled as terrorists whenever their opponents have the authority to make the label stick. Thus, legal
definitions do not account for all of the problems associated with
terrorism" (White, 1991, p. 5).

In its essential elements, *terrorism* is politically motivated
violence perpetrated against noncombatant targets by subnational
groups or clandestine agents. With new forms of violence such as
"terrorism for profit" and "religiously motivated terrorism" chal-
lenging the motivational element of terrorists, and with "computer
generated terrorism" redirecting the targets of terrorists, the definition of terrorism as a matter of necessity must be amorphous. One
alternative is for the definition to focus on the *act*, and not on the
motivation inducing such an act.

Initially, all nations should enact domestic legislation to implement their obligations found in current international treaties in an
effort to establish some common ground. By creating a standard
definition of terrorism, countries would be able to draft and implement similar, if not identical, legislative initiatives to address terrorism. A common definition and unified strategy will combat terrorists more effectively than unilateral efforts or piecemeal regional
conventions. Although a common definition remains ethereal, the
past few years have witnessed a flurry of activity on the international
legislative front. Following the lead of the United States, the major
economic and political powers have undertaken measurable steps to
defeat terrorism by using new laws as their primary tool. Within the
last few years, leading nations from around the world have met in a

series of summits to consider the implementation of new legislative initiatives to address terrorism.

## Halifax Summit

In the first of several recent international summits addressing terrorism and other forms of international crime, the Political-8 (with the inclusion of Russia, the G-7 is now the P-8) met on June 17, 1995, in Halifax, Nova Scotia. Discussing the inclusion of Russia in the summit, Canadian Prime Minister Jean Chretien remarked that the active cooperation of Russia is essential on transborder issues because it is viewed as a major source of weapons-grade nuclear material found on the international black market (Williams, 1995). This invitation to Russia, therefore, was a welcome expansion of a developing international coalition to fight terrorism. Although each country had been a victim of terrorism, none were closer to the source of most modern terrorist activity than those of the Middle East, who were noticeably absent because they were not invited.

The absence of a broader coalition of nations, particularly Middle Eastern states such as Egypt and Jordan, meant that modern methods for fighting international terrorism could not be readily pursued. These methods and measures include ratifying existing international antiterrorist treaties; resolving the political turmoil underlying terrorism; cutting off certain nations' financial and logistical support of terrorism; and sharing intelligence resources at the source of the terrorist activity. Instead, the meeting produced the typical rebuke of terrorism in the form of a hollow proclamation that the new era of global cooperation will give the United Nations "new teeth" to combat terrorism. This promise was supplemented by an initially promising, yet eventually unfulfilled, suggestion of a March 1996 meeting in Moscow to discuss nuclear smuggling.

## International Crime Control Act of 1996

In a speech before the U.N. General Assembly on October 22, 1995, President Bill Clinton called for the preparation of legislation to address international crime. The result of this directive was the International Crime Control Act of 1996. The act, which is not yet codified, focuses on five crucial areas to improve the ability to prevent, investigate, and punish terrorists and other types of international criminals.

The first section authorizes the U.S. attorney general to deny entry into the United States to anyone trying to avoid prosecution in a foreign country and to send convicted foreigners back to their home countries. The attorney general also has discretion to extradite criminals to countries with which the United States does not have an extradition treaty. The second section targets terrorists' financial support networks by expanding the list of money laundering "predicate crimes" to include terrorism and public corruption against foreign governments. Criminal law will also be broadened to authorize the investigation and punishment of terrorists and other organized criminal groups that commit serious crimes against U.S. citizens. The third section deals with eliminating the statutes of limitation for all federal criminal offenses committed outside the United States. The fourth section addresses terrorists' methods for the transshipment of "precursor chemicals" used to manufacture narcotics and provides extraterritorial jurisdiction for financial crimes. The final section authorizes law enforcement authorities to train foreign law enforcement personnel and to more effectively share seized assets with foreign agencies.

Since Clinton's address, the U.N. Crime Commission passed a U.S.-cosponsored International Declaration on Crime and Public Security (IDCPS) (J. Dixon, personal communication, September 17, 1996). This declaration sought to promote bilateral, regional, multilateral, and global legislative cooperation regarding terrorism. All nations were encouraged to address terrorism and other transnational crimes by ensuring that law enforcement and other competent judicial authorities can cooperate effectively. Specifically, member states were ordered to take steps to implement the Declaration on Measures to Eliminate Terrorism (1995). The members agreed to develop and enforce domestic laws aimed at activities that undermine the legal foundations of civilized society. To promote the involvement of a greater segment of society in this effort, all agreed to strengthen their respective criminal justice, law enforcement, and victim assistance agencies. The IDCPS, adopted by the U.N. General

Assembly on December 12, 1996, further promotes the goals of regional anticrime and counterterrorist measures worldwide. Its enactment demonstrates a dedicated global effort in combating terrorism and signals a new commitment to its eradication.

## Ottawa Summit

Following the Halifax Summit, the P-8 met at a second antiterrorist summit in Ottawa, Canada, on December 12, 1995. The attendees eventually agreed that a more internationally comprehensive approach was needed when they "called on *all* nations to ratify the major international anti-terrorism agreements by 2000 . . . stop international trafficking of nuclear, biological, and chemical [NBC] weapons . . . [and] intensify international training efforts and information sharing by governments" (U.S. Department of State, 1996). All nations also agreed to convene a ministerial-level meeting of foreign and security ministers to address specific measures to deter, prevent, and investigate terrorist acts. Nevertheless, although the eight nations realized that a new approach was necessary, the enactment of that approach remained elusive. Although each country agreed, in principle, to the necessity for addressing terrorism, chronic disagreement as to the extent and nature of terrorism and how best to combat it continued to prevent the formation of a consensus opinion.

## Sharm el-Sheikh Summit

The March 13, 1996, summit at Sharm el-Sheikh, Egypt, signaled the emergence of a new approach to fighting terrorism by gathering the world's first counterterrorism summit including 30 world leaders. This summit's goal was to demonstrate an international commitment to isolate nations that support terrorism and to promise more financial support for the Palestinian Authority. The conference was convened after four separate suicide bombers in Israel killed 59 people and wounded dozens more. Realizing the futility of earlier counterterrorism pronouncements, leaders who previously had called for the destruction of Israel stood shoulder-to-shoulder with their former enemy to condemn terrorism. At this "Summit of the Peacemakers," Western heads of state mingled with Arab leaders to produce a diverse coalition of countries bringing to the table new ideas, perspectives, and most important, new power in attempting to enact the vague promises of previous meetings. Unfortunately, those earlier promises for a unified counterterrorism stand and peace in the Middle East have largely failed.

The conference was designed to address increasing cooperation between intelligence agencies of different governments (particularly those of the Middle East), the continuation of the peace process, and the ending of terrorism by cutting the flow of money from private Arab individuals to terrorist groups. One such benefactor is Osma Bin Laden, the heir to a wealthy Saudi family fortune, who finances terrorist groups throughout the Middle East. The U.S. State Department labeled Bin Laden a major sponsor of Islamic extremist activities throughout the world; he not only donates his own money but also solicits contributions from other wealthy religious businessmen and Islamic leaders (Gerth & Miller, 1996). Unfortunately, the only summit accomplishment was a series of counterterrorism "working groups" that convened two weeks later at the U.S. State Department.

Sharm el-Sheikh was criticized as a lost opportunity because specific agreements and treaties were not reached. Although the meeting did not deliver as advertised, its most important aspect was that new players were invited to a forum designed to help develop a successful antiterrorist strategy. Critically important was that, for the first time, fighting terrorism through the creation of a viable peace process, which delegitimates the use of violence for political ends, was seriously explored. The presence of the Arab nations also energized the traditional ways of fighting terrorism. For instance, U.S. efforts to isolate Iran and other terrorist-sponsoring nations will continue to be ineffective unless Iran's nearest neighbors actively comply. At Sharm el-Sheikh, the attending Arab nations sided with Israel in targeting Iran's main beneficiary, the Islamic Resistance Movement (Hamas). In fact, the only Middle Eastern countries not invited were Iran, Iraq, and Libya, each of which is an active supporter of international terrorism. Notwithstanding the limited achievements of the conference, the P-8 rallied their nations to three more summits to further discuss areas of concern and to identify specific counterterrorism measures.

## Lyon Ministerial

In June 1996, the P-8 met in Lyon, France, and adopted 40 recommendations prepared by their representatives in the Senior Experts Group to combat terrorism and related transnational crimes. The Lyon Summit organized these recommendations into four key areas. First, each government will share information regarding investigations, extraditions, and prosecutions of terrorists and other fugitives. In addition, governments will host exchanges of law enforcement and judicial personnel. Second, each country should develop money-laundering and asset forfeiture statutes to freeze or seize assets worldwide. Third, countries must share information and technology relating to secure borders, antiforgery equipment, and black markets that support terrorist activity. Fourth, all signatories are expected to develop countermeasures to terrorists' use of modern technology to wage warfare against civilian financial institutions and government databases.

## Paris Ministerial

As agreed to in Lyon, P-8 members met in Paris on July 30, 1996, to continue the international campaign to combat terrorism discussed at earlier ministerial meetings. British Foreign Minister Malcolm Rifkind declared that it is now necessary to toughen up the codes so that international terrorists have no place to hide (Seiff, 1996). To that end, the P-8 adopted measures nearly identical to those endorsed in Lyon. All eight representatives agreed to ensure the implementation of several legislative initiatives in their respective nations. The following is a summary of these measures:

1. *Securing the mass transportation infrastructure from terrorist attack.* Establish a system to track closely the manufacture, sale, transport, and resale of explosives. Introduce taggants into the manufacturing process of all materials used in explosives. All nations that manufacture automobiles were also encouraged to adopt a common standard for labeling vehicles and parts (which may later be crucial evidence in a postblast investigation). Additionally, it was agreed to urge the standardization of passenger

manifests to more quickly provide crucial information such as names, nationalities, destinations, and methods of payment.

2. *Declaring terrorist bombings an international crime and beginning the drafting of an international treaty that would require nations to prosecute or extradite all terrorists who bomb or otherwise threaten public safety.* This measure was recommended because, to date, no international convention addresses terrorist bombings except those on air and maritime transport.

3. *Criminalizing the possession of biological weapons to address the threat posed by individuals or terrorist groups.* The current biological weapons convention only prohibits abuse by nations, not by individuals or groups.

4. *Stopping terrorists from using computer encryption technology by developing uniform encryption technologies to penetrate terrorists' codes.* This measure will allow for legitimate government access to communication data to prevent or investigate acts of terrorism while simultaneously protecting the privacy of legitimate computer communications.

5. *Improving counterterrorist cooperation and coordination by expanding the training of all counterterrorist personnel to prepare for the most threatening forms of terrorism, including attacks via radioactive, chemical, biological, and toxic substances.*

6. *Deterring, prosecuting, and punishing terrorists by investigating the abuse of organizations, groups, or associations used by terrorists as a front for their own activities.* Nations were encouraged to adopt domestic legislation to ensure that acts of terrorism are considered serious criminal offenses and their perpetrators duly punished.

7. *Reexamining asylum, borders, and travel documents to tighten controls and the issuance of the necessary documents in order to hamper the movement of terrorists.*

8. *Expanding international treaties, agreements, and mutual legal assistance procedures to coordinate multinational investigations and to facilitate greater cooperation between law enforcement and judicial agencies worldwide.* This measure would also establish an international standard for heightened airport security measures.

9. *Adopting legislation to prevent the financing of terrorists by nations, private individuals, and organizations that claim to be charitable, social, or cultural.* Monitor cross-border monetary transactions and exchange information with foreign counterparts.

10. *Improving information exchange on terrorism through legitimate legal requests, particularly with accelerated methods of communication.* Such information includes activities and movements of suspected terrorists, travel documents, arms trafficking, and communication intercepts.

U.S. Attorney General Janet Reno proclaimed that the Paris agreements will strengthen the ability of the international community to deter terrorism before, and respond effectively after, it occurs (Nelson & Stout, 1996). Although these and other declarations are made for public consumption, the reality is that these measures are useless unless they are implemented by nations beyond the P-8, whose member nations already enjoy good working cooperation on these issues. These principles do not, however, identify those nations that willfully provide refuge to terrorists; this continues to be a leading factor in the perpetuation of terrorism.

The Europeans were reluctant to discuss U.S. proposals imposing international economic and political sanctions on countries sponsoring terrorism. Instead, they suggested that a policy of "constructive engagement" be used to promote change in certain countries. The closest the P-8 came to the U.S. proposal was to call on all states to prosecute terrorists and their supporters and to refrain from providing support to anyone involved in terrorist activity (Whitney, 1996).

## The Future of Terrorism Legislation

During the past two decades, many of the same concepts contained in the aforementioned proposals have surfaced before the international community. This time around, however, there is a newfound urgency, given the call to religious fanaticism that echoes throughout many of the world's impoverished societies. Compounding the problem is the fact that many of these religious zealots are freelancers who take it upon themselves to commit acts of terrorism in the name of the deity. Tracking them is difficult because they do not necessarily align themselves with any specific group. Those that do, join together in loose configurations, granting little to law enforcement authorities. Harvey Kushner (1994) warns that these terrorists will prove more deadly than past terrorists because it is "much harder to infiltrate groups [or individuals] that are not organized in any systematic way" (p. 43). In that case, many states will have to rethink their counterterrorist policies to guard against those that would welcome Armageddon. A future treaty will, it is hoped, address these and other issues by instituting a coordinated international legislative approach to 21st-century terrorism.

# 9

# Domestic Law Enforcement's Use of Sensory-Enhancing Technology in Terrorist Situations

DAVID B. PERKINS
TOMAS C. MIJARES

One of the most crucial needs in the response to a terrorist incident is the development of tools for gathering and analyzing information to be used in scenes involving hostile, armed, and barricaded subjects. In most situations, unaided human senses are insufficient to locate and identify the subject and to determine the extent to which any criminal activities are being perpetrated. The rescue of passengers and crew members during the 1976 Entebbe Airport hostage situation in Uganda; the 1977 raid by West Germany's GSG-9 (Grenzschutzgruppe Neun) at Mogadishu, Somalia; and the 1980 Iranian Embassy incident in London are noteworthy examples of how accurate information regarding the exact location, condition, and activities of terrorists and hostages was crucial to success. Although the rescue forces in each of these incidents possessed detailed information regarding area blueprints and the location of inanimate objects, rescue efforts were strengthened by a knowledge of the location of the terrorists and their victims.

The televised serving of a search warrant by the Bureau of Alcohol, Tobacco and Firearms (ATF) personnel at the Branch Davidian compound outside Waco, Texas, illustrates the need for all law enforcement responders to have information about the activities and locations of those being served. One of this chapter's authors was at the scene of a less well known, but more typically common, occurrence in domestic law enforcement: In 1988, officers from the Detroit Police Special Response Team attempted to arrest an armed, mentally disturbed subject who had barricaded himself in his second-story apartment after firing shots from a front window. Officers Frank Walls and Emery Esse, along with their immediate supervisor, Sergeant Ted Montgomery, had been advised that the subject would be to their immediate left as they made entry. This information had been developed from an analysis of the floor plan and a limited observation made by officers from an adjacent dwelling. Unknown to the officers, the subject used his cover to crawl to a position where he would be unseen by the entry team. After gaining entry, the officers approached the area where the subject was presumed to be. The subject had moved from this position, however, and was able to mortally wound Officer Walls with a single shot from a .35 rifle fired from the officers' right. Had the officers received updated information on the subject's location through technology capable of penetrating an opaque surface, a safer alternative tactic could have been developed.

By keeping their own activities from direct observation, terrorists and barricaded criminals can limit the tactical options of responding law enforcement personnel. Only with adaptations of various technologies can the human senses be improved enough to allow law enforcement responders to these situations to gather and analyze information, formulate a plan of action, and execute that plan while minimizing the risks to all concerned.

Thus, the purposes of this chapter are (a) to describe the utility and efficiency of current technologies, (b) to identify the legal and constitutional issues associated with the use of these technologies, and (c) to draw appropriate conclusions and recommendations for the continued development of these technologies.

# Operational Comparisons of Sensory-Enhancing Technology

Several technologies have been developed to enhance the normal human ability to receive input from the environment before processing the data into usable information. These technologies were originally developed for many different purposes but were later modified and applied to law enforcement and military needs. When used properly, these technologies can provide important information.

### Ambient Light Magnification

The most basic form of sensory enhancing technology is based on the refraction of visible light waves. Through a combination of convex optical lenses, the observer is able to view objects and persons safely and undetected. Even under conditions of darkness, police personnel have been able to employ technology that magnifies ambient starlight to produce a magnified usable view. Ambient light magnification technology requires an unobstructed line of sight to be effective, however.

Another type of light wave enhancement technology is much more intrusive. This technology involves the penetration of the walls of buildings to insert a plastic optical fiber. The tip of this fiber can be ground into a lens. The body of the fiber, which is approximately the diameter of a refill tube for a ballpoint pen, is used to transmit a signal from the lens to a video camera and a monitor from which the investigating officers can safely view the activities inside. This technology has been used several times by British forces in the investigation of terrorist activities of the Irish Republican Army (IRA).

### Audio Amplification

When sound is too faint to be heard at a particular location, various audio amplification devices have been used for assistance. These devices range from the very simple and inexpensive, such as a medical stethoscope, to the complex and costly, such as the parabolic microphone seen at televised professional football games to isolate the sounds of competition from those of the spectators. These reproduced conversations can be integrated with a voice stress analyzer, which measures variances in tone, pitch, and volume to determine the anxiety level of persons inside the targeted area.

### Infrared Light

Current technology allows the observation of activities through the detection of heat differential from a distance, followed by a computerized translation of input into infrared images that then become visible on a video telescreen (Laird, 1994). This technology allows the user to observe terrorist activity during the cover of darkness. As long as no surface masks the heat emitted from the persons under surveillance, this technology can be used to detect the location and activities of suspects, as well as the location, activities, and condition of any hostages.

In addition to its use in observing criminal activity, the ability of this technology to detect heat differentials through foliage allows infrared light to be used for rescue work and to identify the location of decomposing bodies covered by as much as a foot of soil. It can be used to detect the presence of humans who have been illegally crowded into freight cars during immigrant-smuggling activities. Most recently, the technology has been used to detect the "hot spots" in buildings and homes used for illegal drug processing (*United States v. Cusumano*, 1995; *United States v. Porco*, 1994).

### Radar

Radio Detecting And Ranging, better known as *radar*, was originally developed as an anticollision device using the constant speed of electromagnetic radiation. Objects illuminated with a beam of electromagnetic radiation generally reflect and scatter the beam in all directions, including back to the source of that beam. By using a device known as a *duplexer*, the radiation may be alternately transmitted and received at the same point. The radiation can pass through a variety of surfaces and can be adjusted to reflect from only specific types of surfaces. It can operate under varying atmospheric conditions and does not need light to be effective. Thus, radar is not a line-of-sight technology and can be used in many situations where the exact location of the target or human subject is not apparent. This technology has been modified by engineers from the Advanced Electronics and Technology Division of Hughes Missile Systems Company to detect human motion through nonferrous surfaces. According to Larry Frazier (1995), the signal processor restricts sensitivity to the normal range of motion that could be expected from human activity. And, according to Frazier (personal communication, May 8, 1996), this old technology found a new use when officers in Mesa, Arizona, used it to determine the exact location of a barricaded suspect.

## Legal Issues Associated with Sensory-Enhancement Technology

### Fourth Amendment Concerns

The new technology designed for surveillance purposes poses the ominous connection between technology and government intrusion. Many have offered extensive commentaries relative to the potential for both effective law enforcement and abuse of privacy rights inherent in the development of technology, and particularly in the context of the use of thermal surveillance in the war on drugs (e.g., see Moore, 1994; Suga, 1995; Wilson, 1995; Zabel, 1995). Lynn Pochurek (1994) suggests that the U.S. Supreme Court has carved out a "drug exception" to the warrant requirement of the Fourth Amendment that finds favor in this area of criminal investigation. As we explore later, certain parallels may exist between these drug interdiction efforts and future police efforts against terrorism.

Regardless of the nature of the surveillance devices discussed in the literature, the seminal case on privacy interests is *Katz v. United States* (1967). Pochurek (1994) states, "In *Katz* the Supreme Court handed down a decision that has become the modern touchstone of Fourth Amendment analysis [by] declaring that the Fourth Amendment protects people, not places" (p. 142). She further describes *Katz* as requiring the satisfaction of a twofold inquiry, which first asks the question whether an individual has displayed a subjective expectation of privacy, and second asks whether society recognizes this expectation to be reasonable. Michael Suga (1995) concurs that "if one of these [prerequisite] conditions is found to be absent, then there is no privacy interest that is protected by the Fourth Amendment" (p. 910). Lisa Hale (1995) has elaborated on these two broad tenets and has supplied insights into more specific principles for the application of thermal surveillance. She has identified these further principles as (a) the defining of protected areas by categories—that is, residences (where privacy expectations are highest), curtilage (areas in close proximity to the residence where privacy interests nonetheless remain strong), and open fields (where expectations of privacy are lacking); (b) the abandonment doctrine; and (c) the plain view doctrine.

Hale and Suga report a split in the lower federal and state court opinions. They seem to suggest emergence of a trend toward allowing the warrantless gathering of drug evidence by thermal surveillance. Collectively, these two authors note that courts have variously concluded that (a) a person has no reasonable expectation of privacy in "waste heat" escaping from a structure, even a home; (b) any expectation of privacy has been insufficiently displayed or abandoned through ineffective insulation efforts; (c) the monitoring of external heat is indeed akin to plain view surveillance; or (d) thermal surveillance is also similar to nonintrusive police canine sniffs (e.g., see *State v. Cramer*, 1992; *State v. McKee*, 1993; *United States v. Domitrovich*, 1994; *United States v. Penny-Feeny*, 1991; *United States v. Pinson*, 1994; *United States v. Porco*, 1994).

As Pochurek (1994) and Matthew Zabel (1995) also point out, some courts have declined to adopt such analogies and, therefore, have reached contrary results (see *State v. Young*, 1994; *United States v. Cusumano*, 1995; *United States v. Field*, 1994; *United States v. Ishmael*, 1994); and other courts have simply acknowledged the existence of the issue but avoided ruling on it, typically resorting to other grounds for their specific case holdings. Indeed, this apparent reluctance to meet the problem head-on was recently on display in the 10th Circuit through its *en banc* rehearing of a prior panel ruling in *United States v. Cusumano* (1996). The original three-judge panel, while ultimately upholding the defendants' convictions, nonetheless specifically denied the government its use of evidence gained through warrantless thermal surveillance of home marijuana cultivation, believing this tactic to be a violation of the Fourth Amendment.

The full court, emphasizing the need for judicial restraint on constitutional issues in the face of separate and sufficient independent sources of additional government evidence, later vacated that portion of the panel's ruling dealing with thermal surveillance, thereby effectively avoiding the issue.

Of those courts currently in favor of allowing the warrantless use of thermal surveillance, great stock is sometimes put in the notion that the devices do not send beams of light into the structure, nor do they penetrate its walls. Rather than physically probe the interior, these devices merely augment the user's own senses to natural phenomena outside the targeted structure. Because only heat escaping to the exterior wall surface is being monitored, these devices are said to be passive and incapable of detecting the sort of intimate human activity that unreasonably infringes on the privacy within. Zabel (1995) criticized this thinking extensively, stating that such distinctions as to the means of intrusion into privacy are irrelevant. Indeed, hypertechnical debate over "passive" versus "penetrative" methods would seem even less compelling in the long term when one recognizes the likelihood of improvements in thermal technology. This prospect, coupled with the use of equipment such as optical fiber lenses and improved radar devices, which do, in fact, penetrate, signals that the police will eventually be able to obtain almost limitless information from behind walls. The resultant impact on privacy becomes obvious as we stand on the brink of the 21st century.

### Terrorist Applications: Classic Cases

Although comparisons of drug interdiction activities with counterterrorist operations may be helpful, typically important fact differentials are present in these distinct arenas. For example, the case law is replete with instances in which courts have held that the only party who has standing to challenge governmental misconduct is the party whose individual constitutional rights have been intruded on (*United States v. Melucci*, 1989; *United States v. Pierce*, 1992; *United States v. Sanginette*, 1988). In *United States v. Karo* (1984), the Supreme Court stated, among other things, that valid Fourth Amendment challenges require that the complainant possess a justifiable interest in the privacy of the place intruded on. Usually, a terrorist scenario does not take place on the private property of the terrorist and is unlikely to present a situation in which the suspect will be found in a location where a justifiable interest in his or her personal privacy exists.

Because of the settings in which these contacts most often arise, the perpetrators are unlikely to display any subjective expectations of privacy. Indeed, as experience would seem to bear out, high notoriety and publicity may be their primary objectives. Nor would concocted assertions of privacy expectations under these circumstances likely be deemed reasonable by either society or the courts. The two precedent conditions of *Katz* for complaint about unreasonable search would be almost universally missing. Incidentally, it is likewise doubtful that any hostages will complain of rescue actions on a constitutional privacy basis. Indeed, a greater ultimate risk for the police relative to these victims may arise from the failure to employ available sensory-enhancing technology if harm to them is caused during rescue efforts. Such a failure may implicate a breach of duty theory toward the victims, with possible civil liability for the rescue forces, particularly for a counterterrorist tactical unit (Mijares & Perkins, 1995).

Finally, unlike the drug interdiction cases, the warrantless use of enhanced surveillance in classic terrorist situations is not being employed so much in aid of a search for evidence itself, but rather for responder, bystander, and victim safety. The whole field of "exigent circumstances" recognizes the balancing of individual freedoms and privacy interests against effective law enforcement and public safety. In *Karo*, the Supreme Court specifically noted that exigent circumstances may allow intrusions that would, under normal conditions, be deemed intolerable. This position is consistent with a significant body of precedent-setting cases handed down by both the high court and the lower courts when risk of armed violence is present in the facts (e.g., see *Arizona v. Hicks*, 1987; *Dorman v. United States*, 1970; *United States v. Shye*, 1974; *Warden v. Hayden*, 1967).

### Terrorist Applications: Nonclassic Cases

There are, of course, possible cases in which counterterrorist units may become engaged where the slight level of information available to them encourages the use of enhanced surveillance for more than the sake of safety. Consider a scenario wherein the police have been contacted by an unknown terrorist or informant and supplied with only limited details to suggest an impending violent act. During the course of follow-up investigation, enhanced sensory surveillance devices will assist the police investigative unit in at least two ways. First, the devices will certainly provide information to help safeguard both the responding police personnel and innocent bystanders in any subsequent arrest processes that occur. Second, in some situations, the information derived from these devices could further add to the totality of the circumstances corroborating the criminal activity itself (*Illinois v. Gates*, 1983). In this context, the use of such devices can be seen as closely analogous to use in the drug interdiction cases. The substantive purpose behind their deployment becomes, at least in part, a true search for evidence. And, in earlier stages of terrorist preparation, the surveillance might conceivably be made of locations, including a home, in which the would-be perpetrators have taken steps indicating subjective expectations of privacy and which expectations society is generally willing to recognize as being reasonable.

Even in these situations of preincident surveillance, law enforcement officials can at least argue that exigent circumstances and risks to societal security justify the means under an emergency doctrine approach. Edward Mascolo (1992) defined such a doctrine as one that allows officers to make warrantless entry of private premises for preservation of life, or general inquiry into unsolved crime, if there is substantial and imminent danger and no accompanying police intent to either arrest or search. He observes that the *doctrine of emergency* has not been defined in its overall concept and that courts usually engage in a case-by-case analysis. Protection of human life may become the crucial factor in the analysis, for life is deemed to take priority over the right of privacy.

Given the ever-increasing alarm of society over recurring incidents of both individual and mass violence, the courts may ultimately react to this priority in a manner similar to that of current drug interdiction cases by imposing something akin to a "terrorist exception" to the Fourth Amendment. In an environment such as this, law enforcement's use of advanced sensory-enhancing technology would seem likely to flourish.

## Conclusions and Recommendations

When used individually, sensory-enhancing technologies have not, to date, been completely accurate and reliable. Nor have they included the necessary redundancies to verify or expand on the information obtained. The current technology can only provide an approximation of the facts needed to make informed tactical decisions. Because the signals received by these technologies are usually converted into electronic impulses, eventually it may be possible to integrate these impulses into a virtual reality depiction of the situation. This development should provide accurate information for immediate and safer resolution of a terrorist incident with a barricaded suspect by providing an audio and visual record of the activities taking place within the perimeter occupied by the perpetrator. In some cases, this record could also become part of the evidence offered later for prosecution purposes, particularly if created during the unfolding of a classic terrorist episode wherein both the crime and the exigent circumstances are obvious.

Predicting totally different outcomes in scenarios such as the Branch Davidian siege or the Ruby Ridge incident solely on the basis of strides made in surveillance technology is risky. More intelligence gathered is preferable to less, however, and therefore responders to terrorist incidents in the 21st century will be prone to rely more and more heavily on advancements in sensory-enhancing devices. Along with this reliance, significant legal debates will probably continue over appropriate levels-of-use restrictions to be placed on the police from case to case in weighing societal security against individual privacy interests. Finally, the current passive versus penetrative technology distinctions relied on by some courts in resolving these issues may direct the eventual paths that technology developed and marketed for U.S. police are allowed to take.

# PART 4

# TERRORISM IN THE 21ST CENTURY

In the opening chapter of Part 4, Moorhead Kennedy warns that terrorism will be a mainstay of the next century if nations fail to recognize some warning signs of things to come. A few of these signals are poor voter turnout, diminishing respect for government, and staggering poverty. Acts of terrorism are likely to occur if "The 21st-Century Conditions Likely to Inspire Terrorism," as the title of Kennedy's Chapter 10 suggests, are not abated.

The future is particularly bleak if we consider that as user-friendly computers become less costly and easier to obtain, cyberspace crime, like terrorism, will also become more frequent and open to all. Because the United States leads the world in developing space age technology, new forms of terrorism can be expected to appear here first. This is the chilling warning of Ralph Eugene Stephen's futuristic Chapter 11, "Cyber-Biotech Terrorism: Going High Tech in the 21st Century."

Back to the future with Chapter 12, "The Internet: A Terrorist Medium for the 21st Century." In this chapter, Kelly R. Damphousse and Brent L. Smith discuss how space age technology has already provided violent protest groups with a new weapon—the Internet. According to Damphousse and Smith, the Internet enables a variety of extremist groups to deliver their messages in ways never before dreamed possible. As a consequence, a very strong possibility exists that acts of terrorism will be committed via cyberspace.

*The Future of Terrorism* concludes by revisiting the question Brian M. Jenkins asked more than two decades ago: Will terrorists go nuclear? Jenkins still thinks not. In Chapter 13, "Will Terrorists Go Nuclear? A Reappraisal," he does, however, caution that the self-imposed constraints against using nuclear weapons are eroding and that weapons-grade nuclear material and nuclear weapons are more accessible then ever before. Although not a significant change that spells an immediate threat, the world, Jenkins concludes, has moved closer to Armageddon.

# 10

# The 21st-Century Conditions Likely to Inspire Terrorism

## MOORHEAD KENNEDY

In 1887, a Russian student group plotted the assassination of Czar Alexander III. Carrying revolvers and bombs, the perpetrators were easily apprehended, and they were brought to trial. As one of them, Alexander Ulyanov, told the court, "[T]error is that form of struggle that has been created by conditions of the nineteenth century" (Lincoln, 1983, p. 172).

"Out of boredom, grief, anguish, apathy, even despair" (Lincoln, 1983, p. 170), the young Russian terrorists of the 1880s were reacting against conditions of the 19th century that may have been oppressive, but not, as perceived by the majority of educated Russians who went along with the system, that oppressive. Linked with orthodoxy and Russification, Czarist autocracy enjoyed widespread support. Many thought this was the only way Mother Russia could be governed.

These students were under no illusions that their act would turn matters around. As Alexander Ulyanov went on to remind the court, "[Terrorism] is the only form of defense to which a minority, strong only in terms of its spiritual strength and in its knowledge of the rightness of its beliefs, can resort against the physical strength of the majority" (Lincoln, 1983, p. 172).

These precursor terrorists were rounded up and hanged or exiled, their actions appearing totally futile. It took military failure in two wars to convince the majority of the corrupt nature of the Czarist system and the need for radical change. Alexander Ulyanov's younger brother, Vladimir Ilyich, who adopted the pseudonym "Lenin," was able to take advantage of the chaos that war, and the failure to reform the system in time, had caused. One wonders: If the "wake-up call" sounded by these young people had been heeded, would Russia and the world not have been better off?

With that in mind, I examine some apparently futile terrorist episodes that have made recent headlines. I ask whether they, too, are not giving us early warning of potentially dangerous "conditions of the 21st century" that we disregard at our peril: These are the bombing of the World Trade Center (WTC) in New York in 1993, the bombing of the Alfred P. Murrah Federal Building in Oklahoma City in 1995, and the takeover and hostage holding in the Japanese ambassador's residence in Lima, Peru, in 1996-1997. If other examples tend to reflect my years of involvement with the Middle East, that does not mean that other valid examples may not also have been selected from Northern Ireland, Sri Lanka, or Pakistan, to name only a few.

## A Caveat

Terrorist actions are never the product of any one motive. For example, even an organization strong only in terms of its spiritual strength and in its knowledge of the rightness of its beliefs needs money to survive. It may resort to terrorist methods to acquire it. Terrorism offers meaning and excitement to rootless, unemployed, and unskilled young people without hope of opportunity in legitimate occupations. Highly labor intensive, hostage holding provides jobs for the unskilled. Terrorism has always been a source of power, a means of ego reinforcement, and an outlet for a propensity to violence. And some hard-line terrorists remain in the business because they know no other way of life.

If some motives or practices of the terrorist do not live up to the nobler of his or her declared political, cultural, or social objectives, that does not mean those objectives are not worth taking seriously. Nevertheless, the existence of these other factors is often cited as a way of disparaging the motives or declared objectives of the terrorist. It is a form of denial that the terrorist just might be giving us something to think about.

For example, I recall that, at the time of the demolition of the U.S. Marine barracks in Beirut in October 1983 by a dynamite-laden truck, a counterterrorism expert in Washington observed, "They say that the driver of the truck was smiling because a trust fund had been set up for his family." A financial guarantee probably had been given. This did not diminish the essential motive for his self-sacrifice, which as his group saw it, was to eliminate one-sided foreign intervention in a Lebanese civil war. But that was not the interpretation this expert wanted to contemplate.

The public is just as reluctant to take terrorist motives seriously. I recall a panel discussion in January 1983 at Brooklyn College, in which I, along with three others held hostage in Iran from 1979 to 1981, tried to air some lessons learned. In the general discussion that followed, a member of the audience berated us for "condoning" the conduct of our captors. Although his exact words were not recorded, they were in the sense of: "What's all this about understanding those bastards? And their motives? Look what they did to you! Put you through mock executions! Lined you up half-naked against the wall! Poked weapons in your necks! You guys ought to be angry! Really angry! What's the matter with all of you?" (Kennedy, 1986).

"If," I replied, "we allow our natural resentment to color our dispassionate view of who these people and what their motives are, then we weaken our chances of understanding the problem." Fellow ex-hostages echoed this rejoinder.

Public disregard for the motives of the terrorist was apparent in the bombing of the WTC, occasioned by Islamic militants, which was widely dismissed as "mindless." After the bombing of the Alfred P. Murrah Federal Building in Oklahoma City, it was widely assumed that because of the involvement of Islamic terrorists with the WTC, Muslims were responsible for this one as well. After all, wasn't the explosive material used in both much the same? As a result of this wrong identification, a long-time resident of Oklahoma City, simply because he was a Muslim from the Middle East, was thrown into jail. Even after persuasive evidence to the contrary had surfaced, a former member of the Carter administration, a most distinguished lawyer, opined that the Middle East must have had a hand in it.

As federal authorities indicted and brought non-Middle Easterners to trial, the public became aware that the two explosions might indeed be the handiwork of representatives of very different subcultures. Oklahoma City was caused by native-born, right-wing sympathizers of military background, Identity Christians who represented views manifested by militias in rural areas. The WTC was brought about by recently immigrated Islamic militants living in urban areas.

Because the subcultures were so different, the motives underlying the two episodes, it was believed, had to be very different. The public failed to realize that the two explosions were not only *chemically*, but also *conceptually*, related. As we will see, they were sending similar messages.

Similarly, when the Japanese ambassador's residence in Lima, Peru, was taken over by the Tupac Amaru Revolutionary Movement (MRTA), Japan and the United States came up with opposite recommendations as to how to deal with the episode. The Japanese urged that the safety of the hostages be given primary consideration; the U.S. Department of State expressed its usual view that no concessions be made to the terrorists. Neither government took into account underlying motives for the takeover. Only as hostages were released and told of the "seminars" on political and social issues they had engaged in with their captors did the world public begin to understand that the takeover was sending an important message about Peruvian society.

What, then, conditions of the 21st century are likely to give rise to terrorist activity, and how have they been foreshadowed by recent events?

## Dangers From Improvement in Communications

"You don't know it," I was informed by "Mailman," one of my Iranian captors, "but we're on prime time!" Terrorism has often been defined as "theater" in which attention is directed to the cause or grievance of the terrorist. In the takeover of the U.S. Embassy in Tehran, Iran, television stations for the first time could provide continuous satellite coverage of a major event in "real time." This led to the view that greater television coverage increased the threat of terrorism. British Prime Minister Margaret Thatcher restricted television coverage of Irish Republican Army (IRA) funerals and events likely to give publicity to terrorists.

Consider, however, the reaction of the American public to the ambassador's residence takeover in Lima. After the first few days, the "theater" in the United States shut down of its own accord. The American public was not that interested in events in Peru, where Americans were not involved, and least of all in its social problems. If terrorism makes poor journalism, television or print media will not abet it.

Rather, the foreshadowing communications event out of Iran was not television coverage of the embassy takeover, but rather the Ayatollah Khomeini's earlier manipulation of the direct-dial telephone system installed by AT&T for the shah. Through it, Khomeini, from his Paris exile, was able to telephone in his sermons for taping and replaying in mosques all over the country. These sermons, in the language of Islam, voiced popular frustrations and offered solutions. A source of support throughout the time of major social upheaval, they helped make revolution inevitable.

The equivalent of Khomeini's telephone and taping is the Internet. Americans without previous connection are able to communicate, anonymously, with others they have never met before. Interests in common can be explored and bonds formed. But we are not talking about widening the membership of Mothers Against Drunk Driving (MADD) or other socially useful commonalities for which there are accepted modes of action, expression, and if necessary, redress. Rather, we are looking at acute social problems at the end of this century, whose victims so far have lacked the means to organize.

Because solutions will not be easy, frustration can grow, and with greater communication come the possibility and acceptability of violent reactions.

Consider, for example, the frustrated and resentful victims of an educational system that has not adequately prepared them for gainful employment. The unemployed, I noted earlier, are a recruitment pool for terrorism. So, too, are the downsized. When a major company in the New York suburbs downsized recently, it paid local gun shops to stay closed. As those left out of our society find ways to communicate and bond, and to the extent there is little hope for amelioration of their situations, terrorism on a wider scale becomes increasingly possible in the next century.

## Dangers From the Weakening of the Authority of the State

### Moral Authority

On June 14, 1985, TWA flight 847 from Athens to Rome was hijacked and flown to Beirut International Airport. During the flight, one hijacker ran up the aisle of the plane, shouting "New Jersey." The reference was to the bombardment of Lebanese villages by the U.S.S. *New Jersey* and other units of the U.S. Navy. The bombardment had caused extensive casualties, fatal and otherwise. Mutilated survivors were then exhibited to the passengers, by then debarked and held hostage. As an act of retaliation, one hostage, an American Navy diver, Robert Dean Stethem, had already been murdered.

Probably as many innocent persons were killed by the U.S. Navy as by these Islamic terrorists. One episode, however, was denominated terrorism; the other episode, the legitimate action of a sovereign state. And correctly so. The difference is that we impute to the sovereign state an ultimate degree of moral authority to which the subnational group cannot aspire. In the pursuit of its broad national interests, which are presumed to be moral, a sovereign state, even when it may be mistaken, is justified in using violence in ways not tolerable in subnational groups.

If every subnational group felt justified in realizing its individual aspirations or in redressing its grievances through violence, anarchy would take the place of national and world order. To the extent the sovereign state loses moral authority, its actions become harder to distinguish from those of the subnational group. "Taking the law into one's own hands," often in the form of terrorism, becomes more and more acceptable.

Both the bombing of the WTC and of the Murrah federal building were, in part, challenges to the moral authority of the United States. The trial of the WTC group brought out their frustration that the United States was more concerned with the security of Israel than with the security of the Palestinians. The perception of a double standard provides a rational for retaliatory terrorist acts; namely, they are not playing by the rules, why should we?

Similarly, the perpetrator of the explosion in Oklahoma City, and his sympathizers, cite the second of two misplaced federal assaults on the Branch Davidian compound near Waco, Texas. The federal government was declared to have forfeited its claim to moral authority by using an unreasonable degree of force that it would not have used in other situations—similarly, with the shoot-out at Ruby Ridge, Idaho, between Randy Weaver and his family and federal agents.

The moral authority of the United States is far more threatened, however, by something deeper than possible mistakes in foreign policy or its agents. To the extent that the government itself is perceived to be a font of moral authority, then, those with unsatisfied aspirations and grievances will maintain the hope that, in time, right will be done. To the extent that its moral authority is diminished, terrorism finds greater justification and practice.

As we approach the next century, lower and lower electoral turnouts, editorials comparing the presidency to a mayoralty, not to mention reports of ethics committees and many similar indications of diminishing respect for government, bode ill for the strength of the moral authority of the United States, and well for the terrorist.

### Problems of Autonomy and Diversity

The bombings in New York and Oklahoma City raised issues of autonomy and diversity that, if left unaddressed, could be a generator of terrorism in the 21st century.

Oklahoma City apparently was caused by militia sympathizers, groups with origins, deep in American history, of populism, vigilantism, and hatred for "the other," in this case minority religious and ethnic groups (e.g., see Stock, 1996). Some militias demand autonomy to the extent that they refuse to recognize political and legal authority above the county level. Other groups of the same subculture demand political autonomy at the level of an independent American state. For example, in 1996, a federal jury in Georgia convicted three members of a militia group, the 112th regiment of Militia-at-Large, Republic of Georgia. The group's demand for autonomy was expressed through a list of potential targets, including bridges, vehicles, power lines, and federal law enforcement officials. Members justify such terrorist behavior as a defense of the moral high ground that the federal government has abandoned.

The Islamic militants who blew up the WTC uphold traditional values in many ways not unlike those of the militias. Moreover, they advocate another form of autonomy, what a leading orientalist has called "the essential difference between the classical Islamic and the modern Western views of the nature of law and authority, and therefore of the function and jurisdiction of the state" (Lewis, 1993, p. 43).

Muslims of strict observance who, largely for economic reasons, have immigrated to the United States do not find here the legal and cultural autonomy that would permit them to function entirely satisfactorily as Muslims. In strict Islamic legal theory, Muslims are either forbidden to reside in countries in which Islamic law is not enforced or are discouraged from doing so. In the United States, however, the law is not a "respecter of persons." There cannot be in the United States, as there is in varying degrees in the Middle East, one law for Muslims, another for Christians, and another for Jews.

However unrealistic their expectations of fuller autonomy may be, the failure to meet these expectations cannot but nurture the feeling, at least among Islamic militants, that they are not being treated equitably. They may argue that, in a diverse United States, concessions are made to demands of other groups for other forms of cultural autonomy—for example, by Hispanic Americans for linguistic autonomy. But why to *this* community, and not to the millions of law-abiding, industrious Muslims living in the United States? Or to other minorities just as decent, hardworking, and proud of their cultural traditions, who may also be disappointed and resentful if not given greater autonomy? How far, realistically, can the process be extended without occasioning more and more grievances?

Similarly, militias entertain a visceral resentment of some minority groups, particularly those benefiting from affirmative action, which the militias do not. If the federal government does not treat them equitably, then, they argue, they would rather govern themselves.

Muslims complain of a refusal to take Islam seriously, leading to ridicule and insult. Remember the *New Yorker* cartoon, *Hey, Mac, which way to Mecca?* Epithets like "camel jockey" and "rag head" are used by those who would never dare to refer in the same way to other ethnic groups.

Related to complaints of unequal treatment are feelings on the part of militias and Islamic militants that they are invisible, powerless, subject to ridicule, and do not count. Feeling powerless, they dramatize their anger in the demolition of symbols of power, economic in New York, political/administrative in Oklahoma City.

Diversity, the official recognition of the uniqueness and dignity of every minority, is a way to defuse these grievances. Like many solutions, however, it can be the root of further problems. For example, to the extent that diversity is viewed as freedom not to have to accommodate to the views of others, not to accept the traditional compromise of majority rule on the basis of common standards, then there is greater excuse to take the law into one's own hands.

Worst yet, giving way too readily to demands for autonomy or putting too much emphasis on diversity can diminish common standards and core allegiances. These are basic feelings that make resorting to terrorism morally unacceptable and that give the state the support it needs in dealing with it. As the 21st century approaches, we may wonder whether we have gone too far the other way.

## Poverty

As I was blindfolded and, hands tied, led down the staircase of the U.S. Embassy in Iran to begin my hostage captivity, my guard whispered in my ear, "Vietnam! Vietnam!" My captors saw themselves as surrogates for the Third World, spokespersons for the poor and the oppressed. Their action would bond the poor and the oppressed to rise against the rich and the powerful. Some carried in the hip pockets of their captured fatigues a paperback book, in English, about their fellow oppressed; it was called *Bury My Heart at Wounded Knee.* Before long, they had allied themselves with a militant Native American group and sent a rallying message to the Penobscot Indians on their island near Orono, Maine.

My captors were precursors to the MRTA in Lima, and not just because in both cases foreign government buildings were involved. Each had its individual grievances and power agenda. The MRTA was more sophisticated in its background and approach, and with a few exceptions, it enjoyed a more sophisticated and potentially more influential audience than my captors. Even though neither terrorist group received the outside vindication and support it hoped for, each saw larger social dimensions to its actions and a message to communicate. Those concerns dramatized by the MRTA may be increasingly crucial in the 21st century and a generator of terrorism.

In selecting the Japanese ambassador's residence, the MRTA evidently had in mind more than the blue-chip hostage pool gathered to celebrate the emperor's birthday. The Japanese are Peru's principal foreign investors; their buildings, like target buildings in New York and Oklahoma City, are symbols of enormous power. For all its undoubted advantages to the receiving state in terms of capital input, backward-and-forward linkages to the local economy, employment, and foreign exchange, investment by richer industrialized countries in poorer countries will also be perceived as a symbol of inequity—or, in other words, the increasingly rich taking advantage of the increasingly poor.

The Japanese ambassador's residence was the ideal stage to make the point, heeded or not, that the bulk of the Peruvian population remains in deep poverty. As the 21st century approaches, groups representing the increasing number of the world's poor, aware through improved communications of how much better off the industrialized countries are, and better able to bond with one another, may well try to raise the consciousness of the world by following the example of the MRTA.

# 11

# Cyber-Biotech Terrorism
## *Going High Tech in the 21st Century*

RALPH EUGENE STEPHENS

As computers become increasingly inexpensive, small, and user-friendly, cyberspace crime, including terrorism, is being "democratized." That is, soon almost anyone will be capable of participating. Beyond this, as biochip computer implants (Stephens, 1992, 1995) emerge, providing an exponential gain in brain power even among the undereducated, new categories of terrorism and terrorists will appear. Possibly the most feared of these future cyberterrorists will be the *brain stalkers:* individuals who hack into biochip implants and harass via intercepting, interacting, demanding, criticizing, humiliating, threatening, and ultimately terrorizing the targeted individual's thoughts and dreams (Stephens, 1995).

Because the United States leads the world in development of the information age and its technology, these new forms of terrorism can be expected to appear here first. As the next century nears, new capacities for using the computer to terrorize are already appearing, and incidents are increasingly being reported. The purpose of this chapter is to examine some of these recently appearing types of terrorism, as well as soon-to-be-expected innovations by domestic terrorists.

## The Changing Face of Terrorism

*Terrorism* is defined broadly as "unlawful" threats or use of violence designed to coerce individuals or groups to modify their behavior, usually to accommodate the terrorists' political or personal agendas (Ward, 1996). Many acts of harassment, however, are not considered acts of terrorism because it is difficult to determine *simple terrorism* (agitating but not felonious acts) from *aggravated terrorism* (acts that clearly cross the line into illegal territory). Classifying acts of terrorism will become even more perplexing as terrorism for entertainment, challenge, and other motivations comes into vogue. Possibly the only determinants of terrorism will be those tactics employed to gain power over others so as to forcibly impose one's agenda on others.

As computers have become the central tool—indeed, the essential catalyst—for the change from an industrial to a high-tech, information-based society in the final quarter of the 20th century, both methods and targets of terrorists have changed. Although traditional hostage holding, armed attacks, bombings, and kidnappings continued, the term *technoterrorism* was coined. In his groundbreaking work *Techno-Crimes: The Computerization of Crime and Terror*, August Bequai (1987) clearly articulated what was becoming obvious:

> The high-tech society is a highly integrated system of diverse technologies. Although complex, our society is also a fragile structure; a disruption in any one of its critical units could cause domino-effect failures in other interdependent-units. . . . Terrorism thrives best in highly industrialized and urban societies: Such an environment offers the terrorist a multitude of targets. (p. 135)

Citing incidents such as power blackouts and computer malfunctions, Bequai (1987) reported that disruptions over an area such as a large city or a few states for more than half a day or so have often resulted in widespread civil disobedience and looting. In the 1996 theatrical release *Trigger Point*, the screenplay provided a scenario in which a total computer/power/electronic blackout over a multistate area leads to fear, armed vigilantism, and borderline chaos.

## A Chronology of Future Terrorism

In a broad sense, the future direction of terrorism has already been charted.[1] Expectations about traditional terrorism to the year 2000 have been examined elsewhere. Here, the focus is on "cyberterrorism," and to facilitate organized examination, the discussion is divided into three eras: (a) late 20th-century expectations, (b) emerging 21st-century cyberterrorism, and (c) concurrent 21st-century cyber-biotech terrorism.

### Late 20th-Century Expectations

Terrorists with traditional motives, such as revenge, and using traditional methods, such as bombs, will find themselves caught up in the computer revolution at the end of this century simply because their targets are computer controlled, computer protected, or both. Increasingly, airports, military bases, banks, power plants, and other crucial institutions in the United States are dependent on computers for daily operations and record keeping. If you attack an airport or an airplane, you are attacking a computer system. This may seem to make the terrorists' work more difficult, but that is not the case. In recent years, the vulnerability and fragility of these systems have been painfully demonstrated by a rash of air traffic control blackouts at major airports, putting thousands of passengers at risk, and airplane crashes traced back to computer glitches. In the 1995 movie *The Net*, a malevolent force is seen reprogramming a flight pattern to eliminate an enemy by crashing his plane into the side of a mountain. As it becomes increasingly difficult to down planes with bombs because of heightened security, it may become decreasingly difficult to accomplish the same purpose by *computer hacking* (systems intrusion by benign but talented computerphiles) and *cracking* (break-ins by malevolent individuals seeking profit, revenge, or terrorism (Stephens, 1995).

The same is true of attacking public buildings or utilities. Security cameras, alarms, locks, and other mechanisms are computer controlled, as are elevators, escalators, heating and cooling systems, and agency operations. Although bombings, such as in the parking garage of the World Trade Center in New York or outside the Alfred P. Murrah Federal Building in Oklahoma City, have proved effective in spreading fear and panic and, above all, in gaining attention, each such success brings new counterterrorist technologies and strategies. Eventually, albeit soon, it will become easier to crack the computers and even program them to blow up the building for you. For example, a slight program modification may cause a boiler to explode or short out a circuit and cause a fire. The catastrophes that dedicated terrorists could create via cracking are limited only by their skill and imagination.

Even for those who continue to believe that bombs or missiles create more fear than a boiler explosion or fire caused by computer cracking, computer technology still can make terrorism easier. Computer networking and computer drones will greatly reduce the personal danger—of injury or death or of getting caught—for the terrorist. Bombs can be planted or placed near targets hours or even days or weeks in advance and detonated from a foreign country by using radio waves and the new Global Positioning System (GPS) of satellites ("Observing Earth From Space," 1995). Similarly, missiles can be placed within a few miles of the target, even in international waters or on nearby foreign soil, and fired remotely from halfway around the world via GPS assistance. Drones (unmanned remotely controlled aircraft often as small as a model airplane) are already being used by government drug enforcement and border patrol agencies for surveillance. Terrorists could use these drones to observe targets, detonate planted explosives, or even deliver bombs in kamikaze fashion.

Possibly the most feared among traditional terrorists has been the religious zealot, who sees terror as a way of accomplishing a "mission for God." Muslim Shiites and other cults have created more concern than others because of their belief that to kill "infidels" is Allah-ordained and that to die themselves during the mission is a ticket to paradise. Finding deterrence of such beliefs difficult, most efforts have centered on infiltrating these groups and learning of plans in time to stop the acts. As difficult as this has been, it will become more difficult as these "fundamentalists" who believe that Western lifestyle and technology threaten the purity of their societies are joined by modern Luddites who believe that high tech, and particularly computers, poses a threat to their jobs and future well-being. So far, it appears the two groups have operated separately, with little evidence, for example, that plans to destroy major landmarks in New York City by religious extremists were coordinated or even connected with a series of letter bombs sent to high-tech administrators and technicians by a terrorist tagged the "Unabomber." Still, the ends sought are common, and the targets, the computers and data systems themselves, are becoming more common. Both groups seem to believe that destroying the technological tools, especially computers, will revert society to the simpler "good old days" they imagine.

Coexisting with these traditional groups are new types of terrorists, some with different motives, different targets, or both. Although greed had motivated some terrorists all along, terrorism for-profit has usually been disguised with some form of political agenda. Ethnic hatred, though motivating the supporters, has often been used by leaders to mask a desire for resources to afford the good life. Kidnappings and hostage holding, as well as bank robberies and extortion, have provided funds for both political and personal desires in many of these groups. Now, technology offers still more, or at least easier access to targets. With the advent of electronic banking, much larger amounts can be stolen via computers than has been possible from bank robberies, and with far less danger or fear of capture. Even if caught, the current penalties that the perpetrators face are less severe than for the armed bank robber.

Beyond profit, some new motives for terrorism will be for fun or entertainment or just challenge. Glorification of violence and terror in the media, from television to computer games, especially the new, very real virtual reality scenarios, has created the environment and value system that somehow allow individuals to see terrorism as an acceptable diversion or avocation. The real pain inflicted may be difficult to recognize (or empathize with) for persons weaned on no-consequences, surreal, media-created violence. This brings us to the second era, one that is only months away.

### Emerging 21st-Century Cyberterrorism

As terrorism for fun and profit emerge as major motives in the next century, a problem of definition and law will also emerge. How much terror equals terrorism? How widespread does the terror have to be to constitute terrorism? Does use of terror with profit as the sole motive equal unlawful terrorism or remain a lesser property crime or white-collar offense (e.g., extortion)? Beyond drawing the line between free speech and harassment on the Internet or in cyberspace, now add drawing the line between harassment via computer and cyberterrorism. Can cyberterrorism involve only one victim, or does it require a group of unacquainted, random victims to qualify as terrorism? In other words, can one person criminally "terrorize" via comments, stalking, and defamation of another person in cyberspace? And how long does such harassment have to go on before it becomes terrorism? Can one person's constant hacking into crucial business and government computers for the "challenge" cross the line into terrorism? What if the person changes data, destroys data, or uses data for profit or to compromise the security or profitability of the industry? If the answers to any of these questions become yes legally, the categories of cyberterrorism in the next century will expand exponentially.

One thing that is known from experience is that the "silent" terrorist is extremely difficult to find (Komarow, 1996; Schulte, 1996). Political terrorists in the past have been quick to claim responsibility (credit, as they see it) for bombings. Look how long it took to establish suspects for the downing of Pan Am flight 103 over Lockerbie, Scotland, because no one claimed credit for the explosion. Moreover, the more terrorists in a group, the more likely someone will talk to an outsider; the "silent," lone terrorist is harder to find, as evidenced by the Unabomber (Howlett, 1996).

Regardless, it is already clear that other new categories of cyber activity likely will be deemed terrorism soon after they appear. For example, the technological interdependence envisioned by Bequai (1987) will emerge more clearly in the first decade of the next century. As telephones, televisions, computers, and fax machines are integrated and networked worldwide via the GPS, this information/communications web will become the lifeblood of society at all levels—neighborhood to world. For the individual or community cut off from this web, it will be as if time were standing still. Cyberterrorists capable of creating such a blackout will have victims at their mercy, unable to communicate with the outside world; it will be back to the Middle Ages, particularly if the cyberspace terrorists also disable all but animal transportation, as modern vehicles and transit systems increasingly are dependent on computers for their mobility. Again, such terrorists could range from well-organized international organizations to the individual teenage "whiz kid," and motives could be as diverse as profit, political ends, entertainment, or challenge. But with massive monetary losses, breakdown in civil authority, vigilantism, chaos, and deaths of the medically dependent at stake, could these things ever be seen as anything less than terrorism at its highest felonious level?

Another major target will be the "cashless society" (Stephens, 1995; Warwick, 1992). As cash and checks disappear and all monetary transactions are reduced to simple electronic transfers of funds, the cyberterrorist will be able to operate at multiple levels—from cracking a few accounts to transfer funds to his or her personal or group's "operating account" to stealing massive amounts or eliminating accounts/balances of targeted enemies to destruction of a nation or even the world's monetary system.

Targeted first in the mid-1990s when electronic returns were introduced, the U.S. tax system will become an even bigger target in the next century as all taxes are paid electronically. Individuals will be motivated to crack this system to lower personal tax liability and to increase refunds; terrorists will be motivated to destroy the system while simultaneously acquiring massive wealth. Destruction of thousands, even millions, of taxpayer records could be accomplished by a variety of methods, such as placing an advanced virus into the systems. Because state and local taxes also will be collected electronically, homegrown terrorists may join the ranks, some motivated by profit, others by political opposition. Inability to secure tax funds could cripple or even destroy governments at all levels.

Other government targets will be benefit programs and record-keeping systems. If money is to be made or a payment or adverse information is to be avoided by cyber manipulation, the common thief of the future, the computer cracker, can be expected to be well motivated and participating. One point at which cracking for profit may turn to terrorism is when, in attempts to cover their electronic tracks, the crackers destroy hundreds or even thousands of records, along with their own, to keep suspicion from falling on themselves or their group. For political terrorists, the destruction of the files becomes an end in itself, creating mass confusion, even chaos.

For terrorists determined to force their political agenda, crippling the military will continue to be a priority. As seen in many documentaries, such as the segment "Highway Robbery" on *60 Minutes* in 1995, military computer systems have been extremely vulnerable. Hackers hired by the Air Force to test its systems infiltrated computers at numerous air bases more than 200 times without being detected. This result does not bode well for the 21st century.

Businesses are also vulnerable, particularly to their most common threat, theft or revenge or both by their employees. Even as employee theft has always resulted in more losses than outsider theft, such as shoplifting, computer theft and terrorism by employees have, to date, been found to be more serious than external threats. From the perspective of terrorism, the greatest vulnerability is to the disgruntled employee—unhappy with his or her job or progress measured by raises or promotions—who has access to the company's computer systems and far more knowledge of their inner workings than even the best crackers. Such a person or group can wreak havoc on every business from the small but computerized mom-and-pop operation to the multinational corporation.

Talented cyberterrorists from the outside can also create massive damage, especially well-organized groups that attack an entire industry, rather than individual factories or companies. For example, industries that are highly computerized and susceptible to terrorism include nuclear energy, natural gas, and petroleum. All deal with highly explosive products, and each controls operating and storage via computer. Here, cracking of one or more facilities could put millions of people at risk, giving terrorists enormous leverage to meet their demands, whether for profit, political advantage, or simply mass recognition.

As the integrated computer systems become commonplace in all homes, and with the advent of "ubiquitous computing" (placing microcomputer chips on walls in all rooms, in cars, on clothes, and so on to keep a complete record of one's activities; "Ubiquitous Computing," 1995), the creation and retrieval of cradle-to-grave dossiers will arrive, providing intelligence information for authorities and stalkers, as well as for the purpose of facilitating efficient, effective, productive lifestyles by individuals. Political terrorists, in particular, will find targets easier to identify and harass, as key words such as *sexual deviants, abortion recipients, ethnicity, religion,* or *party affiliation* will provide complete data on nearly everyone in the population who fits under any category.

Electronic media will be another target of terrorists for two very different purposes. One approach may be a media blackout followed by a campaign of misinformation by terrorists, either by co-opting the airways or by providing an alternative via co-opting many of the paths on the so-called information highway. The second, more surreptitious approach would be to plant self- or group-serving misinformation or propaganda in media to spread terror, enhance the attractiveness of the goals of the individual or group, or both.

Finally, virtual crime will lead to virtual terrorism as the line between cyberspace and outside world realities becomes blurred. Already, authorities believe that *virtual reality* (the creation of special environments that may mimic the outside world but that exist only in cyberspace) has already been used to commit crimes. In a stock fraud case, for instance, all trading and purchases were made via electronic transfer only, and without records of all transactions it is difficult to determine whether all stocks supposedly exchanged actually existed. In the future, a stock or bond may appear on a select group's computer screens and be touted anonymously in cyberspace chat groups only to disappear after thousands of even millions of dollars had been transferred to an account (which also disappears) designated for purchase of the stock. Terrorists could use this type of scheme and others to destroy confidence in financial institutions and governments.

Beyond all that was outlined above, scenes of disasters could be created in cyberspace that would be forced on the public as real-world calamities, spreading fear and terror. Demands may even be made and met before the virtual nature of the event is discerned.

### Concurrent 21st-Century Cyber-Biotech Terrorism

Developing simultaneously with the transformation of information sciences is an equally or possibly even more important revolution in biotechnology. The world, led by the United States, has entered Aldous Huxley's "brave new world" of "participatory evolution" (Stephens, 1992), in which biologists have joined with nature in shaping the future of species on the planet. Genetic engineering is big business, and by the waning years of the 20th century, breakthroughs were already occurring: for example, the insertion of human liver genes into pigs to grow implants (McKeown, 1992); the shaping of human organs on the backs of mice (Associated Press, 1995) to provide implants; and the creation of new microorganisms that would eat frost to protect fruit trees or that would gobble up oil spills (Stephens, 1992). The biotechnologists have literally been changing both life forms and lifestyles on earth.

Like computers, biotechnology offers new targets and new methods to terrorists (Simon, 1994). Some involve biotechnology itself, such as using genetic engineering to create super predators or new lethal microorganisms to threaten, intimidate, or extort. In other cases, the cyberspace and biological advances combine to provide technological advances and new methods for the terrorist.

Possibly the best example will come as computers and human beings are combined to develop bio-logic beings (Bleecker, 1988). Both computers and human beings are hardware systems, with computer software being its programs and human software being the genes, or combined DNA. If computers and their software were made of organic material and used a DNA-mimicking approach to programming, the human body would become compatible with biochip implants (Stephens, 1995). Thus, the computing power of the human brain would increase significantly via these implants. Such biochips could be used to monitor bodily functions and to control and correct their malfunction. The technology to accomplish this historic transformation is already being developed and should be available by the middle of the first decade of the 21st century.

Although humans bask in painlessly acquiring the wisdom of the ages via educational implants and being efficient, effective workers via systems training and data implants, terrorists will have one more method of reaching their target audience—by hacking into the biochips. It is difficult to imagine anything more terrorizing than someone invading one's brain with demands for money or threats to bring excruciating pain or memory loss unless one does as told. Brain stalking surely would quickly become the most serious and most feared form of terrorism.

Terrorists may also be able to disable a significant portion of their enemies by cracking their enemies' medical biochips, such as creating heart palpitations or kidney shutdowns in federal antiterrorist agents. The term *virus* would take on new, or revert to original, meanings as organic viruses would threaten both an individual's health and information storage and processing capabilities.

"Loops" may be inserted in organic brain biochips by terrorists to take advantage of the power of subliminal conditioning. Via unnoticed messages such as "Listen to the Liberation message and follow the Liberators" or "Transfer funds to the Liberators" or "Your life depends on devotion to the Liberators," an individual could unwittingly become a pawn of the terrorist group.

Cyber-biotech terrorism may also be used to enhance traditional terrorist methods, such as threatening to destroy or poison a community, city, state, or nation. In the past, contaminating vast water systems or airspace has been difficult, given the bulk associated with sufficient toxic substances to do the job. Thanks to nanotechnology ("Technology," 1994) and genetic engineering, developments include biotoxins and microorganisms so small that several million cannot be seen with the naked eye. This means a small amount, possibly a speck on a microdot, could be lethal to a population of millions. Because laboratories and storage areas of genetic engineering firms are highly computerized, cracking could result in diverted shipments or even release directly into the target environment.

Virtual crime, too, would take on new meaning, as the virtual world designed to instill terror and secure demands would seem even more real and frightening if it were injected into biochip brain implants of thousands or even millions simultaneously. As noted earlier, the targets and methods are limited only by the imagination.

## Closing Thoughts on Counterterrorism

Technology is both amoral and a proverbial two-edged sword. Both computer and biological technological advances hold promise of solving many of the world's problems: ignorance, diseases, low productivity, pain, drudgery, and boredom. But technology clearly, as illustrated above, also provides a plethora of new approaches to those who would use terror to seek power and advantage over others. *Counterterrorism,* to date, has involved using traditional methods to infiltrate terrorist groups and to develop technological safeguards, such as encryption, limited access, sophisticated user identification, locks, alarms, and vaults, against terrorism.

But a word of warning is in order. Attacking high-tech crime with high-tech crime-fighting innovations is, in the long run, a no-win approach. Although securing crucial data and limiting access to the extent possible are necessary as temporary protections, a long-range strategy based on such a plan will be doomed. Motivated terrorists will not be deterred or stopped, but a fascist society will be created. The level of secrecy of data and spying on the populace necessary to accomplish even a semblance of safety from terrorists in society will replace one source of terror with another (Powell, 1996). Few who lived through the Nazi or other totalitarian regimes would welcome the change.

Prevention, a proactive approach with the best chance of success, must go beyond high-tech spying and widespread searching without warning in cyberspace if the public is to be protected and served by authorities. Real prevention begins with inculcating values and desires in the population for an open and safe society in which individuals would consider the use of terror for any reason to be unethical and thus unacceptable, for themselves as well as for everyone else. Although on the surface this may seem to be utopian, look at how society got to the point discussed above. Individual, societal, and media messages glamorizing and even promoting violence as a legitimate tool to achieve desired ends have created the current environment. The same forces can be turned to make violence unacceptable. This reversal alone will not be enough. It must be accompanied by a positive approach by parents, institutions, and community—that is, rewarding and thus reinforcing positive traits and actions, especially among children, in a systematic and consistent fashion. Only then will both the message that terror is unacceptable and the populace, including many who otherwise would be susceptible to using terror, be in congruence. Cognitive dissonance would be eliminated.

Brian Jenkins (1996), who directed a major think tank's research on terrorism for nearly two decades, has said:

> Our most effective defense against terrorism will *not* come from
> more surveillance, concrete barriers, metal detectors or new laws,
> but from our own virtues: courage, continued dedication to our
> ideals, of a free society, realism in our acceptance of risk, stoicism,
> intelligence and the skepticism that comes with it, the avoidance
> of extremism, the humanity and sense of community too fleeting-
> ly expressed when we mourn our dead—a true patriotism. (p. 6G)

Beyond this, society must counter one of the major motives emerging
for terrorism; *the quest for attention*. To date, the message has been
clear to the millions of people who are lonely and starved for simple
acknowledgment that they exist, that they are alive and a part of
society: Terrorism makes a statement; terrorists get center stage.
Infamy may be gained, but as experimental psychologist B. F. Skinner (1974) documented, any attention is better than no attention.

The good news is that attention-seeking terrorists will not be
silent. They will be quick to take responsibility to bask in the
limelight. The bad news is that the media can be expected to give
immediate and seemingly unlimited attention to terrorism and terrorists, and the arrest and even conviction of these offenders will
reinforce, rather than deter, terroristic methods by the copycats
searching desperately for recognition.

There are no shortcuts. Parents, neighbors, and the entire community or "village" must be involved in child rearing—all giving
attention and praise to all children for positive, kind, cooperative
behavior. At the same time, the best way to extinguish behavior that
will later lead to terrorism will be to turn a blind eye toward it and
avoid giving the child any reinforcement for such activities. To work,
the message and the approach must be delivered consistently, a
difficult task in a multicultural society of "free" Americans.

## Note

1. Unless cited, material in this section comes from Stephens (1992, 1995).

# The Internet
## *A Terrorist Medium for the 21st Century*

KELLY R. DAMPHOUSSE
BRENT L. SMITH

This chapter investigates the use of the Internet by two types of violent protest groups: (a) those that hate certain types of *people* (e.g., blacks, Jews, women) and (b) those that oppose certain types of *policies* (e.g., affirmative action, abortion rights, immigration). Although the ultimate focus of each may differ, the two certainly overlap some in terms of behavior, strategy, membership, and etiology (Lofland, 1996). The term *protest group* is used to refer to both potential and active terrorist groups. It would be incorrect, for example, to refer to a group of militia members as terrorists until they have actually performed some act of terrorism. At the same time, these protest groups are still interesting to study because of their marked potential for (a) engaging in terrorist acts or (b) providing for others the incentive to engage in violence.

How the members of these groups communicate with each other and with outsiders (potential members, financial supporters, targets) has been a topic of interest in the past. New technology, such as the Internet, however, has allowed protest groups to communicate with greater ease. This chapter traces how communication by protest groups has changed in the past two decades. The analysis begins by reviewing common practices used before the advent of the Internet. Then it describes how the Internet came about and the history of how protest groups have made use of the technology. After that, it discusses how the new technology not only allows for an increased capacity to communicate but also makes possible the threat of "cyberterrorism," using the World Wide Web as a tool of terror. Finally, the chapter addresses one unintended consequence of protest group use of the Internet: the establishment of citizen counterterrorism activity on the Internet.

## Previous Communication Practices

Protest groups in general, and terrorist groups in particular, engage in behaviors designed to send messages to outsiders. Violent behavior, for example, has been considered an attempt by terrorist groups to call attention to some problem that needs to be fixed (Herman, 1982; Rubenstein, 1987). It has been suggested that terrorism could not exist without communication (Schmid & Graaf, 1982). Acts of terror by protest groups can be considered indirect efforts at communication that use the news media to inform the public about the motives of the group in an effort to give "violent voice to the voiceless, and to awaken their sleeping brethren to the necessity of mass action" (Rubenstein, 1989, p. 323).

Less extreme, though more direct, measures have also been taken by protest groups to get their message out. In general, this tactic is referred to as *propaganda* (Wright, 1990). Propaganda is used by protest groups to inform the general public or other more specific groups about some problem in an effort to make them "feel the urgency, the necessity of some action, its unique characteristics, . . . [and] what to do" (Ellul, 1969, p. 208). Traditionally, protest groups have used the printed word—via leaflets, fliers, posters, and newsletters—to inform others about their cause (Wright, 1990). More recently, protest groups have used faxes to communicate with each other and with selected outsiders, such as the media and academics. Two problems with the use of these media are the relatively high cost and the limited scope of coverage. There is little "bang for the buck" when much of the material is discarded by uninterested members of the public.

Protest groups experimented with the use of shortwave radio for a time and still continue to do so, to a lesser extent, but access to a larger audience was still restricted. The next advance that allowed greater access to the general public was made possible by the increased popularity of nationally syndicated talk radio programs. Talk radio first allowed members of protest groups to discuss their concerns with a host and, presumably, a national audience. Conservative talk radio shows that allowed, as well as fostered, the discussion of topics that angered groups of individuals blossomed in the late 1980s. Still, access to a wide audience by the protest groups was somewhat limited, as was the information that could be provided. Even worse, the information was also limited in that it was in verbal format that was both easily discarded or forgotten. Although members of protest groups were able to communicate readily with each other and with a limited sympathetic audience, they were still unable to get their message to the "uncommitted audience" (Wright, 1990).

## The Information Revolution

The advent of the World Wide Web (WWW) in the mid 1990s provided protest groups with access to a communication arena that was in printed format, relatively inexpensive, and accessible to almost anyone in the world. To the extent that antigovernment groups were among the first to use the Internet for propaganda, the information revolution coincided with the conservative revolution in an ironic twist. The Internet was developed in the late 1960s by the federal government (U.S. Department of Defense) to allow for the sharing of computer files between research scientists located around the country. The irony was that the project initially developed by the federal government was now being used by protest groups to encourage the government's downfall.

Protest groups were not latecomers to the computer age. In fact, discussion lists (listservs), bulletin board systems (BBSes), and news groups (e.g., alt.activism.militia, alt.society.anarchy) had been actively used by protest groups in the decade before the WWW came into existence. *Listservs* make use of the Internet's e-mail system as a means of communication. Usually, a moderator operates a "site" where members of the "list" can send e-mail messages. Everyone who has subscribed to the list receives the message onto their computer as an e-mail message and has opportunity to respond. In *news groups*, messages (articles) are posted to servers. With few limitations, anyone who has access to the news group can read the messages. These slow-motion communication processes are now being replaced by real-time applications called multi-user dungeons (MUDs) and Internet relay chat (IRC), which allow groups of individuals to communicate instantly with each other by way of their computers.

These early computer links were important for the planning and transmission of information between group members. But this medium was accessible only to a limited audience, mostly people who were active computer users and interested in the topic. The advent of the WWW changed the importance of the Internet for protest groups. For the first time, activists had access to people from all walks of life who were potential members, supporters, and contributors to their cause. Unfortunately for the protest groups, potential enemies also had access to the information they made public.

How protest groups and their opponents use the WWW is discussed in the following sections. But before detailing the activities of protesters on the WWW, it is necessary to provide some background regarding how the WWW makes communication via the computer more accessible to a larger group of people.

## How the WWW Works

As described above, the WWW is based on the Internet system established in the late 1960s. Before the WWW, knowledge of several software programs was required to perform different tasks, such as sharing files and sending e-mail. Compatibility problems emerged because of the diversity of programs used to share information. The creation of the WWW solved this problem through the use of *hyper-text markup language (html)*. *Hypertext* is a system that allows different parts of a document, even those housed in a different computer, to be accessed by the click of a mouse button. The link between any two computers is also simplified because the "language" is readable by all computers.

This system was made even more accessible in 1993 when *browsers* were developed that allowed computer users to interact with other computers through a graphical interface. With the Mosaic browser, and subsequently others like Netscape and Microsoft Explorer, users were able to access the picture-based pages created by other users on their servers. Increasingly, the graphical interface of the "home pages" are being supplemented with sound and video. Excerpts of speeches and videos, for example, can be easily accessed by users. Individuals with little computer acumen are able to create home pages that can be viewed by anyone in the world with access to the Internet. With the decreased cost of personal computers, increased access onto the Internet via companies like Compuserve and America Online, increased modem speed, and increased knowledge, activity on the Web has grown dramatically. From 1993, when there were virtually no home pages, to the beginning of 1997, the growth of the Web has virtually exploded. There are now nearly five million home pages.

On these home pages, the host/creator can present information to an audience that can download a copy to their own computers or print for future use. Finding a home page can be relatively simple. Companies such as Alta Vista and Yahoo have created *search engines* that serve as databases containing the addresses of all the home pages on the Web. The engines continuously search the Web for new sites and updates to old sites and then catalogue each site by category. Search engines allow users to use *key word searches* to find pages pertaining to certain topics. For example, a search using the term *terrorism* would return a list of all the home pages that use the term. Typical searches last anywhere from a few seconds to half a minute. Simply clicking on one of the links provided by the search engine sends the user to the appropriate page.

Once the home page is accessed, the user is able to click on buttons, icons, and underlined text (links) that take the user to other areas of the same site or to other sites. For example, a typical white supremacist home page may link the user to other white supremacists, with links to music groups that hold similar views, and to a collection of news items the host has been gathering that reflect a similar political or social agenda. Following these links, along with the search process described above, represents the act of "surfing the Web" and provides much of the accidental access to individual home pages.

## Method of Study

The data presented below were compiled during a 2-year research project (1995-1996) designed to examine how protest groups use the Internet for communication purposes. The initial project began by the researchers conducting WWW searches via Yahoo for the virtual presence of specific known terrorist groups such as the Ku Klux Klan (KKK) and the Armed Forces of National Liberation (FALN, after its Spanish name).

It is not enough to search for *terrorism* because protest groups do not always have the word *terrorism* in their home pages, so the search must be more creative. For example, a recent search on *terrorism* yielded 68 links, most of which pertained to news stories about terrorists. A search on Yahoo for *Aryan,* however, yielded nine pages all directly related to Aryan Nations groups. More than 3,700 pages with the word *Aryan* were found on Alta Vista. Other locations were found by conducting searches for militia groups and by following links from one site to another. For example, one site maintained by a white supremacist group may have links provided to several other locations (home pages) that share the same interests. Many of these links were followed to the new location. Each location that was located was "bookmarked" for ease of later access and then visited monthly during the 2-year period. In this way, it was possible to track the way these violent protest groups use the Internet and the WWW.

## The Internet as a Tool for Protest Groups

The Internet, especially the WWW, can be used by protest groups in five ways. First, the inexpensive and potentially broad access to millions of people allows protest groups to present propaganda explaining their position to people who are passive and uncommitted or just "dropping by." In this case, the expected audience is the potential new members, those who have not yet "seen the truth." Second, the Internet provides information to like-minded people about specific topics of concern. The Internet allows people who might never have met otherwise to communicate with each other about topics that anger them. Third, the Internet allows angry protest groups to level written attacks on the objects of their anger. Thus, persons who are targets of a protest group's written venom may be subjected to these diatribes. Fourth, protest groups can use the Internet to request financial assistance from the general public. Fifth, and most ominous, the Internet can be used to *perform* acts of terrorism. The potential threat of cyberterrorism has been causing increased concern (Collin, 1996). Each of these potential uses is described in the sections that follow.

### Propaganda Machines

The WWW offers an outstanding opportunity for protest groups to proselytize potential members because so many people have access to the information. Most sites that were examined for this research had sections that described why the host was angry. In these sections, the host appealed, through the use of vivid imagery, to the reader's sensitivity. Most sites suggested that America was worse off now than it had been in the past because of some problem (e.g., immigration, gay and minority rights, excessive taxation and government control). Anecdotal evidence was often provided. Like the moral entrepreneurs of other moral panics (Victor, 1993), these hosts often appealed to the readers' emotions through the use of atrocity stories. For example, one site suggested that the events in the Waco "holocaust" were part of a continuing pattern of attacks by federal law enforcement agencies against the citizenry. To further alarm its audience, the host provided links to the autopsy reports of the Waco burn victims. These files showed the coroner files and photographs of the people who were killed in the fiery end of the siege. Other pages offered similarly vivid stories:

> As I was preparing to mail this double issue of "The Watchman"
> an event took place in the Chicago area which demands comment.

> Three black animals butchered a White woman and her young White children, one by torture and then cut her open to remove the half-breed baby she was pregnant with. A seventeen month old mulatto male was also spared. It seems that they were using her as an incubator to breed a light-skinned child, and decided to eliminate her, having no further need for her reproductive ability. The one who removed the little bastard was a negress nurse who used her medical training to carry out her part in the crime. I do not know all of the circumstances surrounding the event but it is becoming more apparent with every day that passes that unless the White Race rises up against their tormentors in a consuming fury, we will instead be consumed by them. I do not hate these people as individuals but only a fool would believe that we will ever live together in peace. Events like this, as well as Waco, the Randy Weaver massacre and Oklahoma City portend a darkening future for America and it is becoming increasingly clear that unless heroic measures are taken without delay, there will be no future for us or our children.
> (http://www2.stormfront.org/watchman/index.html [1996, November 24])

At the same time, protest group propaganda on the WWW often tries to show the readers they have been deceived into a complacency (false consciousness) that threatens to destroy them. The following quote, which appeared on the home page called "The Patriot's Soapbox," demonstrates this line of reasoning:

> If there is one thing I want to accomplish by publishing these thoughts on the Internet, it is to stimulate you American slaves out there to WAKE UP and become sovereign Americans again. While you were slumbering, watching television, drinking beer, being amused, your "servants" captured and enslaved you, and became your "masters." You could be free, but you are entangled in a web of deceit: lies, fictions and frauds committed by your friendly public servants and their attorneys.
> (http://www.geocities.com/CapitolHill/1781 [1997, February 10])

The takeover of the Japanese ambassador's residence in Lima, Peru, by rebels from the Tupac Amaru Revolutionary Movement (MRTA) at the end of 1996 is a further example of how terrorist groups use the WWW to get their messages out to the people of the world. During the crisis, Tupac Amaru militants who were participants in the hostage taking provided interviews and statements to the outside world via their European home page in three languages (http://burn.ucsd.edu/ats/mrta.htm). They also provided a video clip showing the terrorists preparing for their mission.

### Communication Devices

One fear about the growth of the Internet is that it allows many people who would never have met to be able to communicate with each other. Thus, a person in Idaho who hates African Americans can create a home page to exhibit this hatred. A person living in Florida can visit this home page and read the material placed there. Further, if the Florida reader is impressed with the page, the reader might add the Idaho address to a list of hot links. This action would allow people who visit the Florida page to find and access the Idaho page easily. The importance of the Web for this capacity is exhibited in the following quote:

> For those of you who are surfing the net, you can access the CAUSE web page at http://www.cheta.net/cause. The net is the most powerful free speech forum that has ever existed. Support all efforts to keep it uncensored. Wild claims of your children being carted away by internet pedophiles, etc. are meant to frighten the unaware. The powers that be are terrified by the internet because they are no longer in control of the information that you can receive. Through the internet one can set up a web page and state his opinion to the world, literally. Everyone in the world who is interested in that subject can then access that page and read that opinion for themselves. How unbelievable! We no longer have to wait to be told what someone or some group is saying. We can now get it straight from the horse's mouth. Well, expect the world control freaks to move to crush this situation. (http://207.15.176.3:80/cause [1997, February 10])

The greatest potential for communication is that people who are interested in a topic and see something that is potentially of interest to other fellow believers can almost instantly make that information available. The information and the interpretation are then made available to all.

Some protest groups use the Internet as a method of communicating with the group as a whole. For example, the Republic of

Texas—a secessionist group whose aim is to reclaim Texas from the federal government and overturn the de facto (state) government—holds its meetings all over Texas. Because all members cannot attend every meeting, the minutes of the meetings are published on the home page. At the same time, the group publishes all its press releases and its interpretations of previous events. Although most information housed here appears to be more for storage and public access, this information distribution can also be conducted for emergency purposes. When the group's "ambassador" was arrested by federal agents, for example, an urgent alert was placed on the Web, asking citizens to call local, state, and federal law enforcement agencies demanding his release. (http://www.rapidramp.com/Users/marine/rmtaken.htm [1996, May 5]).

Further efforts at the coalescing of like-minded individuals and groups have evolved into a Web page with a more social than political agenda. The Aryan Dating Page allows men and women who are white and heterosexual to meet over the Web. Pictures of available and interested men and women, as well as their personal information, are also made available by Alpha Headquarters, an Aryan rights group (http://www.alpha.org/lifestyles/lifestyles.html [1997, February 10]). In addition, one can access Resistance Records, a recording company that produces music suitable for those with pro-Aryan attitudes. Its home page advertises that the company is "Forging a new destiny for White Power music: For Blood, Soil, Honor, Faith & Folk" (http://www.resistance.com/founder.html [1997, February 10]).

### Virtual Graffiti

As we have shown, the nature of Web use is such that happening upon some home page is usually not a planned event. In fact, one problem with performing research on the Web is that, in the act of following links from one page to another, the researcher can get distracted by interesting side links. Thus, a user can end up far removed from where he or she had ever intended to go. This feature of the Web works to the advantage of protest groups who want to inflict harm on others through the written word or artwork. Thus, an

African American may have happened upon the Alpha, or Aryan, home page in December 1996 and seen the following messages scrolling at the bottom of the screen:

> African American, what a joke, why not just call them what they are? NIGGERS!
> America for Whites, Africa for blacks, ship those apes back to those trees, send them niggers back!
> Ring that bell, jump for joy, White mans day is here, no more nigger civil rights, led by queers!
> Who needs Niggers?

In a similar vein, the Alpha home page and other Aryan-type pages proclaim allegiance to a sacred 14-word code of honor that is portrayed prominently on most of the pages: "We Must Secure the Existence of Our People and a Future for White Children!" T-shirts, posters, and bumper stickers showing the 14 words in different formats are readily available over the Web.

But race is not the only feature that Aryans attack on the Web. One page, "White Aryan Resistance Hate Page (WAR)," exhibits cartoons and a joke book attacking gays ("Life isn't easy for the modern gay activist. . . . For one thing, there's all those heavy protest signs to carry around.") and Jews ("What's the difference between a Jew and a Pizza? . . . "Pizzas don't scream when you put them in the oven."). The use of stereotypical humor is a common phenomenon appearing on many of these sites.

### Support Activities

One of the most common protest group activities on the Web is the attempt to garner funds from the audience. The pleas used in these sections are mainly addressed to fellow believers and stress the lack of good equipment and funding. Often, the funding request is associated with a desire to be a better service to the user:

> Many people have told us how they can not access our web site much of the time, this is due to lack of funding. Our web site is run on an old and slow machine which allows only two people at any time to be on the site. The site is now receiving between 50

and 100 users per day with not a second of idle time. That 50-100 per day can be improved to hundreds of white people per day world wide accessing great writings of white leaders and learning more about the movement for White Power. We must upgrade and improve our equipment a.s.a.p. Every white man or woman who can not access our site may not return to try again becoming a lost soul. (http://www.alpha.org [1997, February 10])

There is such great potential for ALPHA with the proper financial foundation. Our opposition at the ADL and NAACP receive millions of dollars in donations form their members and supporters, yet the supporters of our cause fail to see just how important financial contributions are to a growing organization. Keep in mind that ALPHA has no clout when applying for a loan at the local bank, yet the ADL has a working budget of millions of dollars to spread lies. (http://www.alpha.org [1996, November 10])

ALPHA needs help from all our brothers who use and enjoy our web site. For the past 50 years groups of Aryan men and women throughout the world have been working for the cause of White Power, and now it is YOUR turn to assist us. Your financial donations can help the white youth of the earth make sense out of what has happened to their world. ALPHA, although not registered as such, is a non-profit organization. Every cent received from people goes right into the movement. (http://www.alpha.org [1997, February 10])

At other times, efforts at fund-raising display the personal hardships endured by the host that are the result of efforts to be a good citizen.

Your prayers and financial support are urgently needed at this time. I am currently under tremendous attack and the threat of criminal prosecution. In the last six months I have lost my disability allowance, had many of my belongings stolen by the feds and am being driven from my home of 18 years. I have six children and staggering legal bills. Without a miracle, I am going under, and if the feds have their way, to prison. I have given my life to this struggle on faith, without regard to the consequences to my self or even my family. Our future is in God's hands and they are attached to your forearms. We are unable to cash checks without using a bank account that could be seized at any time by the feds. Postal Money Orders made out to Wendy Watkins are best and

they protect your privacy as well. Please help us to survive
and continue the struggle for His Kingdom at the Watchman.
(http://www2.stormfront.org/watchman [1996, August 10])

Even international terrorist groups, such as Peru's Shining Path
(Sendero Luminoso), have Web sites where supporters seek to export
the revolutionary message ("Welcome to a REAL revolution in
cyberspace!") while the groups seek financial support by hawking
revolutionary products like T-shirts, posters, and videos
(http://www.csrp.org/index.html [1997, February 10]).

### The Web as a Weapon

The possibility that the Web will be used to conduct acts of
terrorism has increased dramatically since its inception. Indeed,
because corporations that are the victims of computer crime are wont
to deal with virtual invasions discretely, it is likely that much more
cyberterrorism is occurring than is currently known. Protest groups
using the WWW to perform acts of terrorism pose four possible
threats. First, protest groups can access other home pages and either
deface them or change them to provide alternative information.
Already, several examples of this have occurred. Perhaps the most
infamous recent incident was the defacing of the home page of the
Central Intelligence Agency (CIA): On September 18, 1996, the home
page of the CIA was vandalized by a Swedish protest group called
Power Through Resistance. The group changed the title of the page
to "Central Stupidity Agency" and added several links to nongovernment home pages, like Playboy. Although no sensitive
material was available to the attackers, the fact that individuals on
another continent were able to sabotage this computer link is
evidence of the potential for remote activity. Earlier, hackers had
renamed the Department of Justice home page the "Department of
Injustice."

Second, protest groups can impair, or at least threaten to impair, vital government or corporate communication processes. It is
not difficult, for example, to imagine a protest group "hacking" its
way into the computer system that controls the power supply to an
area and then threatening to cut off power unless some demand is
carried out. In fact, such a problem has been occurring in Japan,

where groups attacked the commuter train computer system (Devost, Houghton, & Pollard, 1996). The threat is even greater if one considers the impact such a threat would have on the operation of a nuclear facility. The relative ease of impairment of other computers is evidenced by the large growth in computer *viruses*, which infect computers with programs designed to destroy software or data, in the past several years.

Third, protest groups could directly access financial institutions and perform account transfers. The extent to which this has already occurred is not clear. Fourth, governments are increasingly concerned that information housed on their computers may be accessed by unauthorized individuals. In 1994, a British youth was arrested for suspicion in a case in which a military base in New York was impaired for more than a month (Wilson, 1996). Two potential problems exist here. First, intelligence information may be gained more easily by opposition groups. Second, and perhaps more deadly, false or illegitimate commands could be delivered to military forces, ordering them to unwittingly perform some terrorist act.

The problems associated with virtual attacks perpetuated through the Internet have created a new industry of software protection referred to as *firewalls*. These programs are designed to allow only legitimate users access to the information housed on corporate or agency computers (Alpert, 1996). In general, firewalls are designed to inspect each attempt to access a computer network. Those users who attempt to get into the network without authorization are rejected.

### Summary

The World Wide Web is being used by protest groups in the United States, as well as throughout the world, to deliver their message in ways never dreamed possible before 1980. Access to the Web has allowed protest groups to attempt to proselytize more individuals than ever before. They have also become better able to communicate with each other for political and social ends. And they are in a better position to attract funding from people with whom they would not otherwise have contact. The most serious threat, however, appears to be the potential of actual terrorist acts committed via the Web. The presence of protest groups on the Web has spawned a new aspect of terrorism/counterterrorism previously never imagined—the explosion of citizen counterterrorists.

## Citizen Counterterrorists

Counterterrorist efforts of the past have traditionally been composed of two types of organizations. First, government agencies, the military, and special task forces have been charged with the mandate of gathering intelligence about potential terrorist groups. Second, some social/civic groups have created formal organizations whose function is to publicize the operations of protest-type groups. The Klanwatch project of the Southern Poverty Law Center and the Anti-Defamation League, for example, focus on making available information about the KKK and anti-Semitic activities. In fact, these two organizations have continued these activities in cyberspace, operating home pages that describe activities of protest groups. Also available at these home pages are opportunities to purchase literature describing the history of the militia groups and other protest groups.

What is unique about the advent of the WWW on the Internet, however, is the proliferation of home pages spawned by private citizens who have dedicated portions of their home pages to documenting links to both pro- and antiterrorism pages. A common example of civilian counterterrorism on the WWW is the "Police Officer's Internet Directory" home page, hosted by a Boston police officer. This page has little independent commentary but many links to pro- and antiprotest groups (e.g., hate groups, terrorists, radicals). The commentary supplied by the host is limited to suggesting that the 17 sites provided on the page are offensive and may be unpleasant to view.

One of the most progressive of these counterterrorism pages is called "The Militia Watchdog," which grew out of a Usenet FAQ (frequently asked questions). In this location, the host (a writer who is an expert on the history of the militia in America) tracks news about protest groups and provides links to, and commentary about, the home pages of various protest groups. The page provides Patriot profiles (thick descriptions of contemporary militia groups), essays (e.g., description of gun show activities), collection of news articles about terrorists (e.g., the *Militia Follies*), and special reports (e.g., election 1996 coverage). Interest in the home page is exhibited by statistics provided by the host that suggest the number of accesses to the page by visitors, or *hits*, per month grew from around 4,000 in January 1996 to almost 9,000 by May 1996. In fact, the various pages on this site had been accessed more than 100,000 times in the 5-month time period. During the Freemen standoff in Montana, more than 2,000 hits were made on the Freemen page at this Web site.

Perhaps the most interesting development along these lines is the formation of counter-counterterrorism on the Web. At least two home pages have been created that challenge the information provided on the "Militia Watchdog" and other similar pages:

> [The author of the Militia Watchdog] is feeding the paranoia of the mass population, fueled by the news media, that the patriots and militias are somehow planning to commit terrorist acts. [He] and his traitorous counterparts in the government in the media have yet to prove there to be a link between the militias and the Oklahoma City Bombing. Having recently re-viewed footage of the initial 2 hours following the bombing in Oklahoma City, simple things I noticed REFUTE the claims to a 4800 pound truck bomb full of cow manure! Rather, the basic evidence supports an INTERNAL blast blowing out from INSIDE the building. (http://www.execpc.com/warning/dogpound.html [1996, November 10])

Clearly, the use of the WWW by protest groups and those who oppose them is a new phenomenon that bears continued observation. The impact of citizen counterterrorists on the propaganda and fundraising efforts of the protest groups is uncertain at this time. The fact that counter-counterterrorism home pages have begun to spring up is evidence that the effect is beginning to be noticed.

## Conclusion

The creation of the Internet and the WWW has been referred to as the beginning of the information revolution. How fitting, then, that the political revolutionaries of our time are among the first to make the most creative use of it. It is interesting that the term *leaderless resistance* may take on a new meaning in this age of generating information and then making it available to the world. Serious implications await discussion concerning the liability of those whose home pages—filled with anger, hate, and protest—become the catalyst for some violent action by an unknown actor. The Oklahoma City bombing, for example, has been compared with activities described in William Pierce's *The Turner Diaries* (Macdonald, 1978), which is now also available on the Web (www.geocities.com/Athens/Acropolis/1406 [1996, November 10]).

In essence, individuals who operate home pages perform essentially one-way communication with other people. The information provided on the WWW is a special case. Much like leaflets of old, the information is distributed to individuals only indirectly; that is, propaganda about the excesses of government or some other threat are distributed rather anonymously so that the reader and the writer may never meet. The author of the information in the home page can rightfully claim that he or she did not intend for the reader to take any specific action. Information provided via a home page may be used to stimulate or legitimate terroristic activity. It is certain that the Internet in general, and the WWW in particular, will come to play an important role in our understanding of protest groups and how they function in our society.

# 13

# Will Terrorists Go Nuclear?
## *A Reappraisal*

### BRIAN M. JENKINS

Cities across the globe have been hollowed by the blinding blasts, their centers instantly incinerated. Many more metropolises have been threatened with destruction. The immediate casualties run into the millions, and the resulting contamination will continue to kill for years. The attacks have also had enormous political consequences, provoking regional wars as they were intended to do, but a global nuclear exchange has been narrowly averted. The carnage, bad as it is, would have been much worse were it not for the heroic efforts of a handful of dedicated secret agents, and sometimes maverick ex-agents, who struggled against great odds, often alone, armed with little more than their own determination (and often an ability to seduce beautiful women), racing against countdowns to thwart the diabolical schemes of mad scientists, power-mad potentates, masters of vast underworld empires, crazed cultists, die-hard communists, neo-Nazis, and insubordinate generals bent upon revenge, extortion, world domination, and war. Nuclear terrorism, if not a fact of today's news, is certainly an accepted "reality" of its fictional parallel, an apparent source of endless inspiration for novelists and screenwriters, a mirror of society's deepest anxieties.

Will terrorists go nuclear? is a question almost invariably asked in any discussion about terrorism. Sometimes the phrasing differs—How long will it be before terrorists acquire nuclear weapons?—implying that it is not a matter of *if*, only *when* terrorists cross the nuclear threshold. Has not the use of nerve gas by terrorists only recently moved from fiction to fact? Is it only a matter of time before terrorists escalate from truck bombs to nuclear weapons?

## Revisiting the World of 1975

The concern described above is undoubtedly real and goes beyond what we might read on beaches and airplanes. Sober scientists, serious members of the academic and research communities who devote themselves to the analysis of terrorism, and the heads of intelligence services all discuss the possibility that terrorists in the future may acquire and use weapons of mass destruction, not excluding stolen or clandestinely fabricated explosive nuclear devices.

The concern is not a new one, although for reasons we will come to in a moment, it has become more urgent. The threat of nuclear terrorism began to attract serious analytic attention in the late 1960s with the emergence of contemporary terrorism. Interest grew in the early 1970s as analysts sought to understand and thereby counter the growing threat of terrorism and to anticipate and prepare for what terrorists might do next. This was a period of tactical innovation as political extremists quickly expanded their repertoire to include not only assassinations and bombings—the traditional tactics of terrorism—but also airline hijackings and the sabotage of aircraft, bloody assaults on airports, dramatic seizures of hostages at embassies, the kidnapping of diplomats to win freedom for imprisoned comrades, and later the kidnapping of executives of multinational corporations to obtain tens of millions of dollars in ransom to fund further campaigns of violence. If nuclear terrorism seemed perhaps far-fetched, the headlines of the moment, had they been predicted just 5 years before, would have been dismissed as the stuff of novels.

In 1975, I wrote my first essay on the topic "Will Terrorists Go Nuclear?" What did I answer then, and how would I answer the same question today? The 1975 monograph, which was written for the California Seminar on Arms Control and Foreign Policy and presented at a conference on the Prospects for Proliferation held, appropriately, at Los Alamos, New Mexico, offered observations and very tentative conclusions that I was careful to label as "hunches." The paper defined nuclear terrorism to include a broad spectrum of potential actions ranging from a well-publicized nuclear hoax in which terrorists threatened to detonate a nuclear device in a populated area, bolstering their credibility with a detailed diagram of the weapon and possibly a small sample of fissile material, to the detonation of a stolen or homemade nuclear bomb. Between these two extremes are other scenarios, including the sabotage or seizure of a nuclear facility, the theft of a nuclear weapon, and the deliberate dispersal of radioactive material. My intention in introducing a range of actions was twofold: (a) In focusing on the higher end of the spectrum—a nuclear explosion—we should not ignore the possibility of lesser actions; and (b) because the mere mention of the words *nuclear* and *terrorism* in close proximity were likely to produce great alarm, terrorists could achieve their traditional tactical goals of publicity, fear, and possibly leverage without having the resources or running the risks of building a bomb; therefore, lesser acts were more likely.

In the essay, I recognized an equally broad spectrum of potential adversaries, including ordinary criminals, extortionists, terrorists, authentic lunatics, hostile employees, and even foes of nuclear power. Obviously, not all the potential actions would appeal to all the potential adversaries, but that now takes us into the realm of motives, an issue we will return to in a moment.

In the essay, I suggested that, given increasing public attention to the possibility of nuclear terrorism, it was unlikely that terrorists would not at least have thought about it as a serious option or momentary fantasy. I also suggested that opportunities for terrorists to carry out some type of nuclear action would increase as a result of the rapid growth of a civilian nuclear industry, the increasing traffic in nuclear material and radioactive waste material, and the spread of nuclear technology and know-how.

According to a television documentary broadcast at the time, a nuclear bomb could be designed by any bright graduate student at

MIT, but designing a weapon differed from building a weapon. Nuclear experts debated how easily a nuclear bomb could actually be built by an individual or group outside government. Those with knowledge of nuclear weapons design argued that, with a basic understanding of the principles, it could be done; that is, a small group of perhaps six or seven individuals with the right mix of scientific knowledge and skills and, of course, access to the requisite material could, in a few months, fabricate at least a crude nuclear device. Its detonation would be uncertain, and its yield would be low—perhaps in the tenths of a kiloton range—but it could be done. Those with actual experience in building nuclear weapons countered that knowledge of mathematical formulas and principles of weapons design by itself was insufficient. Building a nuclear weapon, they asserted, was a complex and dangerous undertaking. The debate continues today. Twenty years ago and today, both sides agree, however, that the biggest obstacle to nuclear terrorism is the acquisition of the necessary fissile material to make a nuclear device.

In my 1975 essay, I indicated dissatisfaction with the studies of the potential terrorist threat that had been written, for the most part, by scientists and engineers knowledgeable about nuclear programs but not always knowledgeable about terrorists or other criminal adversaries. These studies generally favored one of two technical approaches. The first assessed the vulnerabilities in security systems and projected scenarios to exploit them. This approach was similar to that used in studying the potentialities and consequences of nuclear accidents and in assessing the vulnerabilities of the United States to various scenarios of a nuclear attack launched by the Soviet Union. The second approach was to assign certain physical and technical capabilities to a hypothetical adversary that was then set against the existing security system. Both approaches were useful in designing and testing the viability of security systems, and as a result, tremendous progress was made during the 1970s and 1980s in improving security at nuclear facilities. Neither approach, however, told us much about why any adversaries would carry out a particular action in the nuclear domain and what they would hope to achieve by doing so. My interest focused on the motives of the adversaries, their objectives, and their possible modes of action. Looking at it from their point of view, why would terrorists go nuclear?

This was fascinating but treacherous territory for analysis. Fortunately, in 1975 we did not—we still don't—have a large number of cases of nuclear terrorism to examine. Some nuclear hoaxes, most of which were easily dismissed as puerile concoctions, a handful of incidents involving contamination with radioactive material, and low-level sabotage of nuclear facilities represented the range of our practical experience. As of 1975, there had been no actual attempts by terrorists—insofar as we know—to overtly seize a nuclear weapon or nuclear material to assemble and detonate a nuclear bomb. Therefore, we were—and still are—compelled to make breathtaking inferential leaps, projecting the observations and conclusions we can make regarding terrorism and terrorists into a new environment.

> This type of forecasting is hazardous. The resultant predictions are highly conjectural, tentative, and quite possibly dead wrong. The possibility that some madman would somehow acquire and use weapons of mass destruction is by no means a new concern, but it has not happened yet and it is interesting to ask why. On the other hand, it is difficult to recall any predictions made ten years ago [in 1965] that airline hijacking would suddenly become a major problem of international proportions requiring enormous expenditures for airport security and the rigorous searches of baggage and person that have become so customary. (Jenkins, 1975, p. 7)

I repeat this salvo of cautionary notes here because it still applies. In assessing the threat of nuclear terrorism, we maneuver on the terrain of uncertainty and conjecture.

Caveats in full display, I offered my hunches. The primary attraction to terrorists in going nuclear, I thought, was not that it would enable them to cause mass casualties, but rather that almost any action in the nuclear domain would automatically generate fear in the mind of the public. Drawing attention to themselves and their causes and creating alarm—which had been typical objectives of terrorists—could be achieved by undertaking less sophisticated actions at the lower end of the spectrum. As for scenarios involving the deliberate dispersal of toxic radioactive material, these did not appear to fit the pattern of terrorist actions carried out thus far.

Moving up the scale on improvised nuclear devices, I thought some smaller groups with nihilistic aims and little popular support might be willing to use weapons of mass destruction to take the lives of thousands but probably would lack the resources to do so. Larger terrorist groups that were more likely to have the resources to undertake more serious nuclear actions were also more likely to be constrained "by fears of polluting their cause, of alienating their constituency, and of provoking reprisals" (Jenkins, 1975, p. 8).

The *theory of self-imposed constraints* even on the part of those we labeled terrorists was a novel one, and because it became the focus of subsequent debate, it may merit further elaboration here. The idea derives from the observation that terrorists, without resorting to exotic weapons of mass destruction, have always had the capacity to kill more people than they have killed. In 1975, terrorism was primarily symbolic violence. Fewer than 20% of terrorist incidents involved any fatalities, and most of these involved only one fatality. Incidents in which terrorists tried to kill a lot of people—defining "a lot" as scores or hundreds—were extremely rare.

Long-running guerrilla wars and terrorist campaigns have caused thousands of deaths, but I am not talking about the accumulated casualties of protracted armed conflict nor the systematic slaughter that is sometimes an attribute of state terror. That terrorists had not resorted to large-scale murder could be partially explained by the fact that it was hard to do—and it *is* hard to kill a lot of people at one time. The historical evidence indicates an upper limit in the worst explosions, fires, and terrorist bombings of something in the low hundreds of fatalities. Genocide and massacres involve thousands of individual murders, not a single act. But difficulty could not be the entire explanation. It was not that terrorists were trying to kill in quantity but failing in their attempts; they clearly were *not* trying to do so, and often were *trying not* to do so, and that suggested the existence of self-imposed constraints.

As I have written many times, terrorists want a lot of people watching, not a lot of people dead. *Terrorism* is violence calculated to publicize the terrorists' cause, to inspire fear, to create an atmosphere of alarm that, in turn, causes people to exaggerate the strength and importance of the terrorist movement. Because most terrorist groups are small and militarily weak, the violence they carry out must be deliberately shocking, but simply killing a lot of people is not the objective of terrorism. Mass casualties may not serve the terrorists' goals and could be counterproductive.

Wanton murder could tarnish a group's image, imperil the group's cohesion, alienate its perceived constituents, and provoke crackdowns that would have popular support. Obviously, not all such constraints apply equally to all groups, nor are they immutable. We will return to how these constraints have changed.

Terrorists theoretically could view nuclear weapons, not as instruments of mass destruction, but as means of irresistible coercion. Instead of taking hostages, terrorists could hold cities for ransom. But the utility of nuclear weapons in this context was not entirely convincing. Although nuclear action would theoretically enable terrorists to escalate their demands, there were limits to what terrorists, even those with nuclear weapons, could expect to achieve. They still could not demand impossible things—for example, that a government liquidate itself.

The concern in 1975 could not be confined to terrorists, extortionists, or lunatics. Unlike other possible targets of terrorist attack, nuclear programs possibly had an additional set of potential adversaries found among those who oppose nuclear programs. Such adversaries might contemplate sabotage, the occupation or seizure of nuclear facilities, or actions designed to demonstrate to the public that existing security measures were inadequate, but actions that could endanger human lives or the environment, I thought, were not likely to appeal to groups whose primary concern was the threat that nuclear programs posed to human life and the environment.

Fissile nuclear material would seem to be a highly marketable commodity, raising the possibility of a profitable black market traffic; therefore, criminals at the service of far less ambitious causes than changing the world order could pose a threat to nuclear programs. One had to be cautious, however, not to overestimate the attractiveness of trafficking in fissile material to the criminal underworld, especially to organized crime, which conceivably would be able to muster the resources, but which historically had tended to be "a conservative, service-oriented industry." Nuclear blackmail or nuclear black-marketing could bring tremendous heat on the organization and provoke crackdowns that could interrupt the flow of large, steady profits from more acceptable crimes.

Blowing up the world or threatening to do so may appeal to the truly deranged found in mental institutions or at loose in society— ambitious versions of the Mad Bomber of Manhattan, who carried on his campaign in the 1940s and 1950s; the Alphabet Bomber, who launched his bombing campaign in the 1970s; or the Unabomber, who was to emerge later, but terrorist actions masterminded by an individual with serious mental impairments were likely to be those that could be carried out single-handedly. A hoax or scheme involving radioactive contamination may be within the capabilities of the madman—there was at least one such case in 1974—but probably not the acquisition of weapons-grade nuclear material and the fabrication of a nuclear bomb.

In other words, there seemed to be an inverse correlation (to apply a mathematical term to a highly conjectural analysis) between capability and constraint. At one end were the "mad bombers" who might be willing to employ weapons of mass destruction but lacked the capacity to carry out nuclear terrorism, at least those actions at the higher end of the spectrum. At the other end were a handful of large, well-organized groups that theoretically might be able to mobilize the financial, scientific, and other resources to carry out a complex and sophisticated operation involving a nuclear device but whose political calculations would discourage them from doing so. In the middle were groups lacking constituencies and not necessarily constrained by fears of alienating world opinion. "An essential ingredient of such a group's philosophy would permit the negation of human values, allowing widespread and indiscriminate murder" (Jenkins, 1975, p. 22). That ingredient, I wrote, might be some claim of divine inspiration—the mandate of God or adherence to a racist ideology that would permit genocide. As we shall see, causes incorporating large components of ethnic hatreds and religious fanaticism have largely replaced political ideology as the engines driving today's armed conflicts and terrorist campaigns.

In rereading this essay more than 23 years after it was written and more than 4 years after the bombing of the World Trade Center, I was discomforted to discover that I had made two unrecalled references to New York's World Trade Center as a potential target of large-scale terrorism. It was, I wrote, "a favorite scenario" of those who warned of the potential consequences of nuclear terrorism, which 10 pages later was expanded to "In an extreme scenario, the detonation of a nuclear bomb at the base of the World Trade Center in New York City would cause tremendous casualties and potentially widespread contamination" (Jenkins, 1975, pp. 6, 16). In 1993, terrorists attempted to cause widespread casualties by detonating

1,500 pounds of conventional explosives—less than a 100th of a kiloton in nuclear weapons terms—beneath the World Trade Center. They also reportedly laced their bomb with cyanide in an unsuccessful attempt to increase casualties by lethal contamination. "Only" six people were killed; it could easily have been much worse, as we have seen in other truck bombs.

Clearly, the World Trade Center bombing must be regarded as an attempt to cause massive destruction with mass casualties—certainly hundreds, conceivably thousands, even tens of thousands, had the terrorists succeeded in their ambitions. Such incidents are instructive. We will return to them later.

In sum, I did not, in 1975, see nuclear terrorism as the inevitable consequence of what appeared at the time to be a growing phenomenon—the spread of nuclear technology and the growing number of nuclear facilities throughout the world—for this was before the scare at Three Mile Island and the catastrophe at Chernobyl dampened enthusiasm for nuclear power. The growing traffic in fissile material would theoretically increase the opportunities for some type of nuclear action by terrorists. Whether terrorists would try to exploit these opportunities, we simply did not know.

Some actions, however, seemed more likely than others. Few terrorists seemed interested in simply killing thousands or tens of thousands of people, and extortion based on a nuclear threat ignored some of the operational difficulties involved in establishing credibility, calibrating the demands, credibly guaranteeing that the threat would be permanently removed if the demands were met, and collecting the payment or enforcing the demand once the threat was removed. Nuclear hoaxes, sabotage of nuclear facilities, and contamination with radioactive material seemed more likely scenarios, and even here the perpetrators might just as likely include the mentally deranged, ordinary criminals, and antinuclear extremists as terrorist groups.

## Two Decades After

The world has changed dramatically in the more than 20 years since I wrote "Will Terrorists Go Nuclear?" The collapse of the Soviet Union ended the Cold War and greatly reduced the threat of global nuclear war, which had kept the planet on the edge of destruction for nearly half a century. Communist rule crumbled in the former Soviet Union, Eastern Europe, and the Balkans. East Germany united with West Germany, but centrifugal forces triumphed elsewhere; 27 independent states emerged from the ruins. Fortunately for the world, this momentous political upheaval involving the rapid disintegration of a huge land empire, military withdrawals, an attempted coup, a brief political rebellion put down with military force, and a bloody war of secession in the Caucasus all occurred without international confrontation, civil war, military coup, or the brandishing of nuclear weapons as pessimistic political analysts had forecast. The fall of communism was fast and remarkably peaceful. Still, it would not be surprising to read in some future memoirs of as yet unrevealed close calls involving the security of nuclear weapons.

With the end of the Cold War, the United States and Russia embarked on an ambitious program of nuclear disarmament. But as the threat of war between the nuclear superpowers diminished (it has not disappeared), concerns about nuclear proliferation and nuclear terrorism increased. "The chilling reality," the director of the Central Intelligence Agency told the U.S. Senate, "is that nuclear materials and technologies are more accessible now than at any time in history." This accessibility has fundamentally altered the situation. Although we know of no diversion or theft of nuclear weapons or of fissile material in quantities sufficient to construct a nuclear weapon, confidence in the safeguards and security measures protecting the former Soviet nuclear arsenal has seriously eroded. Acquisition of nuclear material, once perceived as the principal obstacle to nuclear terrorism, probably has become easier. It is difficult to say *how* much easier.

Not everybody agrees. Writing in a recent issue of *Bulletin of the Atomic Scientists*, William M. Arkin (1997), a contributing editor to the journal, listed the arguments against the assertion that the fall of the Soviet Union has made nuclear terrorism more likely:

> The number of weapons that are operational today is less than half of the number just ten years ago. Only a handful of warheads are being produced worldwide [contrasted with a 5,000 annual production rate a decade ago]. . . . Fewer than a dozen nuclear storage sites remain outside the homelands of the nuclear powers. (p. 37)

And terrorism was far more prevalent in the 1970s than today.

In terms of the number of international terrorist incidents, that may be true, but the world is hardly a more peaceful place. The end of the Cold War enabled the settlement of some armed conflicts, but civil wars continued in Africa, Asia, and Latin America, and new wars broke out in the republics of the former Soviet Union and the former Yugoslavia. Terrorist campaigns continued and, in some ways, became bloodier.

The last vestiges of direct colonial rule were almost entirely erased from Africa. Years of protest, armed struggle, and external pressure finally ended apartheid in South Africa, which made a peaceful transition to black majority rule.

After years of bloody terrorist attacks and reprisals and a new Palestinian uprising, the *Intifada*, Israel decided finally to come to terms with the Palestinians as a political entity with some claim to the territories occupied by Israel in the 1967 war and began to negotiate. This did not end terrorism emanating from the Middle East, but along with the end of Soviet support for Arab hard-liners and continued U.S. pressure on Israel to negotiate, it did sideline the major Palestinian terrorist organizations. The new terrorist threat came from Islamic extremists inspired and sponsored principally by the Islamic Republic that came to power in Iran in 1979.

Three major wars were fought in the region: (a) a lengthy contest between Iran and Iraq, (b) an ultimately successful war of resistance against Soviet occupation in Afghanistan, and (c) a brief, lopsided contest between a U.S.-led Western alliance and Iraq when that country invaded Kuwait. Islamic extremists came to be seen as the principal international terrorist threat.

The collapse of the Soviet Union, the impoverishment of its once mighty scientific establishment, rampant corruption, and the growth of organized crime in Russia have fueled fears that its vast nuclear arsenal may become accessible through theft or diversion to nations seeking to develop their own nuclear weapons capability, as well as to terrorists. Russian authorities, while admitting problems of corruption and crime, have asserted that nuclear weapons and weapons-grade material remain secure and that no successful thefts of fissile material have occurred. Reports indicate, however, that large quantities of conventional weapons and commercially valuable strategic metals have been sold illegally and smuggled out of the country. Corrupt military and civilian officials and criminal gangs have participated in these operations.

It is also true that the past several years have seen a significant increase in incidents in which stolen nuclear material from Russia is being offered for sale. Several of these incidents have involved highly enriched uranium or plutonium, which could be used in a nuclear explosive device. In all these cases, the quantities of weapons-grade material have been far less than that needed for a bomb, and the impetus for the sale seems to have come from the sting operations of police in Western Europe.

Numerous scams—offers to sell weapons-grade material that turns out to be depleted uranium or other nonfissile substances— have also occurred. Many of these scams have involved so-called red mercury, an ingredient said to have been developed by Soviet scientists that would facilitate the construction of simple and tiny nuclear weapons even without fissile material. Every investigation thus far has shown red mercury, as advertised, to be nonexistent, but the substance continues to fascinate novelists and journalists and occasionally to take in gullible buyers. I also have one report of a near sale of a nuclear weapon by a junior officer in the Soviet Army to a Western environmentalist group that wanted to demonstrate that nuclear weapons were inadequately protected. The planned purchase fell through when security arrangements were suddenly changed at the time of the attempted communist coup in 1991. Collectively, these developments have raised the specter of a black market in fissile material and its consequence—nuclear weapons in the hands of terrorists.

The most thorough review of the existence or potential for a nuclear black market was carried out by the Nuclear Black Market Task Force, one of the study groups that make up the Global Organized Crime Project (1996) managed by the Center for Strategic and International Studies in Washington, D.C. In its 1996 report, the task force concluded that the probability of theft of a nuclear weapon or a bomb quantity of weapons-grade materials from the former Soviet Union is growing. The task force described the nuclear black market as "inchoate at present" but noted that interested buyers exist. It described the suppliers thus far identified in sting operations as "unsophisticated" and lacking connections on the demand side, but task force members worried about the potential involvement of organized crime.

Ironically, nuclear disarmament agreements exacerbate the problem. As Russia dismantles its nuclear weapons, it will increase its inventory by 6 tons of plutonium and 30 tons of weapons-grade uranium each year for the next 10 years—a tempting target for diversion or theft. At the same time, the weapon-decommissioning process transfers the material from easily inventoried weapons under more effective military control to less easily monitored stockpiles under comparatively less secure civilian supervision.

Some analysts assert that despite the travails of Russia's civilian economy and the weaknesses of its fighting forces so apparent during the war in Chechnya, the country's defense-industrial complex remains relatively intact, although actual production has declined. Although it may sound perverse, until the government of Russia can establish a more stable political system and a better functioning economy, one is tempted to hope that its nuclear weapons and weapons production programs remain under the firm control of Soviet-style leaders.

Would-be buyers, beside undercover police officers, exist in countries that are known to have active nuclear weapons development programs and have offered money for nuclear weapons or material. Terrorist buyers also theoretically exist but are harder to identify. The Nuclear Black Market Task Force concluded:

> [T]raditional terrorist groups are more likely to use a conventional explosive or other means to disperse stolen radioactive materials than to improvise a nuclear explosive device using stolen weapons-usable materials. By contrast, anarcho-terrorists (such as the Aum Shinrikyo) or a technically sophisticated extortionist group might be less daunted by technical difficulties or political (sponsor) disincentives. (Global Organized Crime Project, 1996, p. 4)

The market has not yet been made, in that I know of no occasion where real sellers have transferred weapons-grade nuclear material to real buyers. Nor, despite the involvement of organized crime in the sale of weapons and strategic metals for which there is a ready market, is there any evidence that Russian gangs have entered the nuclear arena. The Nuclear Black Market Task Force admitted that it could not "point to the involvement in nuclear materials trafficking of large organized crime groups with established structures and international connections" and that "there is no consensus among authorities about whether international crime groups will engage in nuclear smuggling" (Global Organized Crime Project, 1996, p. 17).

We must be careful that the term *black market* does not dictate an inappropriate model for investigation. A nuclear black market would be unlikely to resemble other black markets, such as those for conventional weapons, drugs, or contraband smuggled to avoid customs duties where there are numerous buyers and sellers. The risks of trafficking in nuclear material are much higher and the opportunities for sale far more limited. A nuclear black market would have fewer buyers, among them intelligence operatives and undercover police pretending to be buyers. And there would be fewer sellers and, as now, many scams. Both buyer and seller must beware. Acquisition of nuclear material through clandestine channels will more likely take the form of commissioned thefts—single operations, rather than a market of many transactions; there would be lengthy negotiations and mutual testing among conspirators, requiring numerous contacts before any material is actually transferred.

This is good news and bad news for intelligence services. The likelihood of few participants and few transactions will make it difficult to infiltrate the market at the middle, and the need for testing as both sellers and buyers confirm each others' bona fides will make it easy to slide into the role of provocateur, which is what the German authorities who set up the successful stings that have netted small quantities of plutonium and highly enriched uranium stand accused of. Buying small samples to get a lead on a major source of supply means risking large sums of money for tiny amounts of material, and it may produce nothing further than a financial windfall for a petty smuggler or the arrest of a minor figure in a sting. Stings are still useful, however, because they disrupt the market and delay transactions. The good news is that the paucity of participants and the cautious probing likely to accompany transactions will slow the completion of any deal, offering the authorities time to close in if they have any knowledge of the deal. An alternative intelligence strategy would be to shift focus from the middlemen in the market to the ultimate sources and potential end users.

## The New Nuclear Players

Several new nuclear weapons states have emerged in the last 20 years. Israel, long suspected of developing nuclear weapons, is now routinely counted as an undeclared nuclear weapons power. Observers now believe that Pakistan also has a small nuclear arsenal; it, too, has not publicly admitted the fact. South Africa developed nuclear weapons and tested one in the Indian Ocean; however, its leaders claim that all its nuclear weapons have been dismantled and its nuclear ambitions shelved.

Proliferation as a result of fragmentation occurred when the Soviet Union broke into independent states, leaving four of them with nuclear weapons; however, diplomatic persuasion plus economic inducements persuaded Belarus, Ukraine, and Kazakhstan to turn their inherited weapons over to Russian control.

A handful of nations, mainly in the Middle East and North Africa, are believed to harbor nuclear ambitions, including the usual suspects identified by the West as state sponsors of terrorism. Close examination of documents acquired by United Nations inspectors and reports by defectors since the Gulf War indicate that Iraq was closer to developing a nuclear weapon than intelligence analysts originally had estimated. Although economically and militarily crippled by the war and continuing sanctions and closely watched by the international community, Saddam Hussein seems determined to continue his special weapons programs.

Intelligence analysts also believe Iran to have an active nuclear weapons development program. The Iranians reportedly have offered huge sums to gain access to Pakistan's know-how and have tried to acquire nuclear material in the former Soviet Union, an effort that was blocked, in one case, by a preemptive U.S. purchase.

Syria, though behind Iran, also appears on the list of would-be proliferators, as does Libya. Libyan leader Moammar Gadhafi has taken a more direct route, reportedly offering cash for a nuclear warhead. Algeria is also mentioned occasionally as a country seeking to develop nuclear weapons.

On the other side of the world, intelligence analysts sounded the alarm that North Korea was on its way to building nuclear weapons. Blunt warnings and intense diplomacy, coupled with generous bribes to help North Korea solve its severe economic crisis, have persuaded North Korea's leadership to change course for the time being. Timely intelligence and pressure from the United States also persuaded Taiwan to suspend its nuclear weapons program.

The emergence of three undeclared nuclear weapons states (India, Israel, Pakistan) over a period of 30 years indicates cracks but not a collapse of the nonproliferation regime. Clearly, the landscape is messier. Intelligence warnings, military action, preemptive purchase, strong-arm diplomacy, and generous offers of economic aid prevented a doubling of the population of countries with nuclear weapons and averted some potential nuclear confrontations in Asia. These cases demonstrate that nuclear weapons remain attractive to a handful of countries, that clandestine efforts to develop or acquire nuclear weapons will continue, and therefore that continued intelligence efforts are required.

Nuclear proliferation may increase the likelihood of nuclear terrorism in several ways. First, efforts to clandestinely acquire fissile material and the associated weapons technology create a market that, by its very nature, would also be clandestine and thus vulnerable to double-cross and diversion. Second, the identity of the potential proliferators causes concern. Several of these countries are ruled by ambitious tyrants or revolutionary regimes. Although the longevity of their current leaders in office far surpasses that of contemporary leaders in democratic countries, succession, when it does occur, could be violent, thus increasing the chances of a breakdown in control and unauthorized use of a nuclear weapon by a rogue commander or political faction. Third, chaos resulting from a violent internal struggle could also increase the opportunities for theft of nuclear material or weapons. (France, faced with the revolt of its generals during the war in Algeria in the early 1960s, had concerns about the security of its nuclear weapons at its Algerian test site.) One would not like to see nuclear weapons in places like the former Yugoslavia or Albania.

Fourth, state-sponsored nuclear terrorism is another concern. According to this scenario, a state provides terrorists with a nuclear weapon that they then use, or threaten to use, against an opposing state, allowing the patron to thereby avoid direct responsibility and the risk of retaliation. Because the idea is a popular one, it merits some discussion. The risks to the sponsoring state would be enormous. Any nuclear detonation, even one claimed by terrorists, would very likely arouse suspicions of state involvement. Although it is true that state sponsors of terrorism have demonstrated their willingness to secretly carry out terrorist actions that are clearly acts of war, including the sabotage of commercial aircraft (Syria, North Korea, and Libya) and the assassination of foreign political leaders (North Korea, Iraq, and Sudan), a nuclear explosion would fall into a different category. The hunt for the author, as well as the perpetrator, of the attack would be intense, and pressure to retaliate could become irresistible even though evidence may be incomplete. This prospective hunt raises the danger of retaliating against the wrong party. (Had the United States retaliated immediately in the wake of the bombing of Pan Am 103, Syria would likely have been the target instead of Libya, which further investigation ultimately identified as the culprit.)

This danger, in turn, suggests that innocent governments likely to be considered suspects on the basis of motive would have a strong incentive to cooperate with the victim if only to ensure that they were not erroneously targeted for retaliation; it provides a powerful incentive to cooperate before an incident occurs: A loose nuke is a direct and an indirect danger to everyone.

The sponsoring state may try to maintain further distance by using additional cutouts between itself and its terrorist agents, but as the history of covert operations shows, additional cutouts mean loss of control. Most states don't operate this way. When Syria unsuccessfully sought to sabotage an El Al airliner in 1986, when North Korea tried to assassinate the entire South Korean cabinet in 1983 and blow up a South Korean airliner in 1987, and when Libya decided to blow up a U.S. airliner in 1988, they used government agents, not terrorist surrogates; terrorists are unreliable actors.

This use suggests that state-sponsored nuclear terrorism, as it is popularly perceived, may not be attractive. Still, it is possible to think of scenarios in which it might work. A nuclear explosion in

Baghdad or Tehran may not bring immediate retaliation. Several interpretations would be possible: an accident, an internal power struggle, or a foreign-sponsored attack for which any of several suspects might be responsible. The major powers would intensify their intelligence collection efforts but probably not enter the fray.

## Thirty Years of Terrorism: What Have We Learned?

History does not dictate the future. Nonetheless, 30 years of terrorism should tell us something about the tactics, the strategies, the decision making, and the mind-set of terrorists. It tells us that although terrorists have become more bloody-minded, there is no inexorable trend in the direction of nuclear terrorism. It suggests difficulties and disincentives, which may explain why terrorists have not done what some analysts have for years been telling us they would do. Caution is in order here. Because something has *not* happened, does not mean it *will* not happen, but nuclear terrorism, if it does occur, will not be the end point of a long-term trend. It will rather represent a dramatic departure from terrorists' well-established modus operandi.

The use of terrorist tactics has persisted into the 1990s as a form of political expression and sometimes as an instrument of state policy. The tactics themselves have changed very little since the late 1960s and early 1970s, which in retrospect can be seen as a period of innovation as terrorists revived old tactics such as assassinations and bombings and adopted new ones such as airline hijackings and political kidnappings. By the mid-1970s, however, the tactical repertoire of terrorism was set. After defining a new mode of armed conflict, terrorists seemed content to repeat the old tactics—bombings, assassinations, armed assaults mostly on undefended targets, and various forms of taking hostages. They made only incremental adjustments or added new twists, rather than invent new tactics, although they did abandon some tactics that increased security made more difficult or that government response made more dangerous.

This apparent conservatism reflects the fact that, with unlimited targets, terrorists do not need to innovate. They can solve virtually any tactical problem they encounter simply by switching their sights to another, more vulnerable target. For perhaps the same reason, terrorism remains a low-tech activity. So long as the tactics remain the same, little need exists for new weapons or technologically ambitious endeavors.

Most technological innovations have occurred in the construction and concealment of bombs. As the most common terrorist tactic, bombings comprise more than half of all terrorist attacks and provide thousands of opportunities for innovation. At the same time, countermeasures in the form of explosive detection procedures and systems and technology to render safe any bombs that are located have kept pressure on the bomb makers and the bombers. This type of contest encourages innovation. From a population of thousands of terrorists, a few ingenious gadgeteers have emerged.

But the fact that bombings continue to comprise the majority of all terrorist attacks tells us something fundamental about how terrorists approach their activity. Bombings are easy to do, especially if there is no requirement to penetrate security. Escape is easy: The bomber does not have to be there when the bomb explodes. And no matter where the bomb goes off, because we do not know its intended target, it is a success *if* it goes off. Ease of execution, low risk, and high probability of success are the terrorists' operational goals. Terrorists avoid technically demanding operations, uncertainty, and risk.

Some changes have occurred. Organizationally, terrorism has become more fluid. Terrorist campaigns still require organization, but we find fewer identifiable groups and more examples of actions by ad hoc conspiracies that form within galaxies of like-minded extremists. There are fewer terrorist "fronts," "armies," "brigades," and other organizational pretensions that lend themselves to wiring diagrams and battle analysis.

The long war in Afghanistan and the more recent fighting in Bosnia have created a global community of Islamic warriors that connect in different combinations in different locales. Inspired by a common paranoid view of the world and connected via the Internet, anti-federal government extremists in the United States preach "leaderless resistance." Alienated, often emotionally disturbed, loners also remain a problem. Such adversaries are increasingly preoccupied with punishment or pure destruction instead of recognition of a cause or advancement of a political program, which brings us to motives.

Motives have also changed. In the 1970s and 1980s, those using terrorist tactics mainly sought ideological goals. In the 1990s, armed conflict and terrorist attacks are increasingly motivated by ethnic hatreds and religious fanaticism, and this has affected the quality of terrorist violence.

The constraints set forth in my essay 20 years ago continue to apply: Most incidents of terrorism remain acts of symbolic violence; simply killing a lot of people is not the objective. Most terrorists may still see wanton killing as counterproductive, but the constraints, which did not apply equally to all groups and never were thought to be immutable, seem to be eroding. Ethnic hatreds lend themselves to genocidal strategies, massacres, and other atrocities. And the constraints imposed by a reluctance to tarnish a political cause or by conventional morality do not apply to those who believe they act for God, however defined.

In addition, there is a built-in requirement for escalation. Terrorist tactics depend on drama. But as terrorism over the years has become banal, it requires human sacrifice, lest it not be noticed at all. The proportion of terrorist incidents with fatalities is growing, albeit slowly—a subtle indicator. More dramatically, large-scale indiscriminate violence has become today's terrorist reality.

The principal manifestation of this trend is the car or truck bomb—hundreds or thousands of pounds of explosives delivered to the target or the vicinity on wheels, detonated at night or with warning to cause massive destruction, or detonated without warning in daylight hours to cause heavy casualties—the needed "body count" in words attributed to the convicted perpetrator of the Oklahoma City bombing that killed 168 persons. Although the truck bomb represents an escalation in terrorist violence, the tactic remains technologically crude. The issue in a car bomb is quantity, not quality. Sabotage of commercial aircraft with small, powerful explosive devices designed to avoid current detection systems and cruder devices detonated on crowded train coaches or subway stations are other examples of large-scale indiscriminate attacks.

Even with this apparent willingness to escalate, terrorism still does not yet constitute a major threat to human life. Compared with conventional war or common crime, terrorism kills few. The very worst terrorist incidents involve 200 to 300 deaths. Of more than 10,000 incidents of international terrorism since 1968, fewer than a dozen involve more than 100 fatalities. These are incidents involving car bombs or airline sabotage.

My observation 22 years ago that it is simply hard to kill a lot of people at one time remains true, but it also reinforces the view that most terrorists are after something other than casualties. Terrorists could escalate by coordinating multiple large-scale attacks, but these seldom succeed. Sikh extremists tried to do this when they planted bombs on several airliners in a brief time span in 1985. Only one went off, bringing the airplane down and killing all 329 persons onboard. Another went off at the airport in Tokyo. Following the World Trade Center bombing, Islamic extremists planned to blow up several targets in New York, but their plot was discovered and foiled. Another Islamic extremist in the Philippines (and a participant in the World Trade Center bombing) planned to blow up 12 airliners in a single attack. Had he succeeded, thousands would have died.

Even terrorist offensives or surges of activity have quickly declined to sporadic, low-level attacks. A sustained campaign of significant acts of terrorism requires organization, resources, logistics, and above all, the ability to maintain secrecy. This is increasingly difficult as the carnage mounts and the group comes under intense external pressure from law enforcement, probably operating under fewer constraints. The group may also be under growing internal pressure as individual doubts and reasons to defect increase. To survive, such a group would have to had time to prepare for protracted clandestine operations without attracting attention to these preparations and to maintain absolute obedience among its followers. Few groups have these capabilities. These difficulties are significantly reduced by state sponsorship, which can provide terrorists with resources and a secure base, but as already discussed, state-sponsored nuclear terrorism raises other difficulties.

I know of no inexorable progression from truck bombs to weapons of mass destruction; however, the use of nerve gas by Japan's Aum Shinrikyo sect underlines the possibility that, in the future, terrorists may move toward chemical, biological, or even nuclear weapons. The nerve gas attack in Tokyo shocked the world, but it was not unanticipated. A 1985 survey of intelligence analysts (Jenkins, 1985), security officials, and researchers focusing on terrorism showed that 69% of respondents considered it likely that terrorists would use chemical or biological weapons before the end of the century. Most respondents thought it unlikely that terrorists would use nuclear weapons.

With scores of novels based on the premise of nuclear terrorism, with speculation about nuclear terrorism featured on the covers of popular science magazines, on television, and in tabloids, surely it must have crossed the mind of those prepared to use terrorist tactics. It did. A former German terrorist, writing in the 1970s about his experience underground, remarked that, with a nuclear weapon, terrorists could make the chancellor of Germany dance atop his desk on national television. It was more adolescent fantasy than indication of serious intention. The fictional nuclear destruction of U.S. cities (which are attacked because large concentrations of blacks and Jews live in them) appears in William Pierce's *The Turner Diaries* (Macdonald, 1978), a violent, racist novel about a future war against the U.S. government, widely read by right-wing extremists in the United States and a possible inspiration for the bombing of the Alfred P. Murrah Federal Building in Oklahoma City—more fantasy. I have heard a report of a 1991 letter faxed to one of Russia's nuclear research centers, purportedly from the Islamic Jihad, offering to buy a nuclear weapon.[1] That a Middle Eastern terrorist group would openly fax an inquiry to purchase a nuclear weapon raises questions about its authenticity.

In the midst of the war in Bosnia, the leader of Bosnia's Serbs threatened to use atomic weapons, a threat that was taken seriously by Croatian scientists, who claimed that Yugoslavia had been working on developing its own nuclear weapons since the 1950s. Although no one believed the Serbs capable of constructing a nuclear weapon, Croatians feared they might be able to acquire one from Russia. In Japan, one of the Aum sect's scientists wondered about the availability and cost of procuring a Russian nuclear weapon—a less fantastical threat because the group acquired and used chemical weapons. The authors of these few mentions I know about underline where the greatest threat comes from, at least as it concerns motive. Apart from the aforementioned ex-German terrorist, we have Islamic extremists, white supremacists, one side in a bloody ethnic war, and a religious cult—skin, tongue, and God's will.

In a handful—but only a handful—of incidents, the intent to cause death and destruction on a catastrophic scale is so patent—the bombing of the World Trade Center, for example—that the terrorists would have used a nuclear weapon had they possessed one. And yet, insofar as I know, no terrorist group has actually attempted to buy or steal a nuclear weapon or the nuclear material necessary to make one. Nor do interrogation reports, insofar as I know, provide any evidence of serious plans to do so.

During the past 20 years, we have seen more than 100 nuclear threats, all hoaxes, most the product of pranksters or persons who clearly have a mental disturbance. We have seen several low-level attacks aimed at sabotaging nuclear power facilities—more often indirectly by attacking the related infrastructure—power lines, and railroads and carried out mostly by extremist foes of nuclear energy. And we have one incident of deliberate radioactive contamination when Chechen rebels planted radioactive material in a public park in Moscow. (Although other attempts have been made to use radioactive material in attempted homicides, this was the first one directly linked to political cause.)

Nuclear weapons, as other weapons of mass destruction, could appeal to certain groups that have used terrorist tactics; however, their use would represent, not the culmination of any discernible trend, but rather a leap beyond anything thus far seen in the annals of modern terrorism. The unique combination of capability and mind-set prerequisite to nuclear terrorism may be more easily found outside the galaxy of currently active terrorist organizations. Ethnic conflicts and violence inspired by religion appear to offer the most fertile ground.

Although the "city held hostage" scenario provides the most suspense for the novelist and writer of screenplays, the use of a nuclear bomb as a doomsday device, an instrument of punishment— of mass destruction without warning or demands—seems more consistent with the motives and mind-set of the type of group most likely to engage in nuclear terrorism. The ability to brandish a nuclear weapon as a deterrent may be attractive to a particular ethnic group fearing extinction but is a less likely scenario. The use of a nuclear weapon for the purpose of coercion, or "compellance" in strategic parlance, though theoretically attractive to the extortionist, would pose major operational problems for a terrorist group and is the least likely scenario.

Some inquires have been made into the potential for nuclear terrorism. The Rand Corporation continued its research and produced several reports on the possible motives and capabilities of would-be nongovernment nuclear adversaries (Bass et al., 1980). In 1985, Paul Leventhal and Yonah Alexander convened an International Task Force on the Prevention of Nuclear Terrorism. The group's report contains two excellent papers by Jerrold M. Post (1987) and Konrad Kellen (1987) that address the issue of motives. A recent study by Graham Allison (1996) revisited the issue in 1996; Allison concluded that the fall of the Soviet Union has removed the principal obstacle to nuclear terrorism—the acquisition of fissile material.

## Conclusions

It is possible to conjure up scenarios of state-sponsored nuclear terrorism, but as is the case with nuclear terrorism by nongovernment groups, these would represent a dramatic departure from anything seen thus far in the realm of state-sponsored terrorism. This brief survey of terrorist trends during the past two decades leaves us with the following conclusions: Terrorism has continued, but terrorist operations continue to be tactically conservative and technically crude. The fact that, despite nearly three decades of intense worldwide terrorist activity and 25 years of warnings, *nuclear terrorism*, defined as the use or credible threatened use of a nuclear explosive device, has not occurred suggests that nuclear terrorism is neither attractive nor as easy as it is often imagined. In addition to the technical difficulties involved in acquiring or fabricating a nuclear bomb, it appears that terrorists still make other calculations of a moral or political nature that dissuade them from going nuclear. In other words, as suggested in my earlier thesis, terrorist violence still appears to be limited by self-imposed constraints although these seem to be gradually eroding.

That is one of two changes that stand out. The willingness of terrorists to engage in acts of mass destruction has increased. Self-imposed constraints still exist, but they seem to be eroding as the motives that drive armed conflict change. One group of religious fanatics in Japan has already crossed the threshold into chemical warfare. Another group of religious fanatics tried unsuccessfully to do so in the attack on the World Trade Center. Belligerents in ethnic conflicts have used radiological weapons and threatened to use nuclear weapons. These few incidents do not make a trend. Nuclear terrorism, if it does occur, will not reflect a trend. It would still be an exceptional event, a radical departure, which is much harder to predict.

The second change concerns capabilities. Weapons-grade nuclear material, if not nuclear weapons, is more accessible today than it was 10 or 20 years ago. Because difficulty in obtaining nuclear material was seen as the principal obstacle to nuclear terrorism, this change is perhaps the most significant development. As yet, no black market exists where nuclear material can routinely be purchased. The theft or diversion of weapons-grade material in a quantity sufficient for a weapon would be unprecedented.

Other factors have not changed significantly. It is not easier or more difficult for a group outside a government weapons program to design or build a nuclear device, although some would argue that the emigration of Soviet nuclear weapons designers and builders may make the knowledge and practical experience more accessible to a well-paying terrorist group. It is not easier or more difficult to maintain the secrecy of such a project or to deliver a device clandestinely.

The change in terrorist mind-set and the increased accessibility of nuclear material oblige me to conclude that nuclear terrorism, though not inevitable, has increased in likelihood, whether by 20% or by twentyfold, and would depend entirely on numerical values assigned 20 years ago and today. I concluded my 1975 essay with the observation that "at some point in the future, the opportunity and capacity for serious nuclear terrorism could reach those willing to take advantage of it." As we approach the 21st century, we are closer.

## Note

1. The letter was cited by Renselaer Lee, president of Global Advisory Services, Inc., and is mentioned in Global Organized Crime Project (1996, p. 15).

# References

Adams, J. (1986). *The financing of terror: How the groups that are terrorizing the world get the money to do it*. New York: Simon & Schuster.

Aho, J. A. (1990). *The politics of righteousness: Idaho Christian patriotism*. Seattle: University of Washington Press.

Allison, G. T., et al. (1996). *Avoiding nuclear anarchy: Containing the threat of loose Russian nuclear weapons and fissile material*. Cambridge: MIT Press.

Alpert, B. (1996, November 25). On fire: Fear of hackers should keep the computer firewall market smokin'. *Barons, 76*, 15-17.

Andradé, D. (1997a). Stingers: The terrorist SAM threat. *Counterterrorism & Security Report, 5*, 3-4.

Andradé, D. (1997b). Toe-to-toe with terrorists: The high-level debate over fighting international terrorism. *Counterterrorism & Security Report, 5*, 1, 4.

Annin, P., & Morganthau, T. (1996, February 19). Blowing smoke. *Newsweek*, pp. 29-31.

Anti-Defamation League (ADL). (1993). *Young Nazi killers*. New York: Author.

Anti-Defamation League (ADL). (1994). *Armed and dangerous*. New York: Author.

Anti-Defamation League (ADL). (1997a). *Danger: Extremism—The major vehicles and voices on America's far-Right fringe*. New York: Author.

Anti-Defamation League (ADL). (1997b). *Vigilante justice: Militias and "common law courts" wage war against the government*. New York: Author.

*Antigovernment terrorism in the United States: The nature and extent of the threat and possible legislative response: Subcommittee on Crime of the House Judiciary Committee*, 104th Cong., 1st Sess. (1995). [Testimony of Brian Levin]

*Appearance before the Senate Subcommittee on anti-terrorism: Senate Judiciary Committee*, 104th Cong., 1st Sess. (1995). [Testimony of John Trochmann]

Arizona v. Hicks, 480 U.S. 321 (1987).

Arkin, W. M. (1997). The bomb has many friends. *Bulletin of the Atomic Scientists, 63*, 36-39.

*Army of God manual*. (1997). (Available from the Center for Hate and Extremism, Richard Stockton College, Jim Leeds Road, Pomona, NJ 08240)

Aronowitz, A. A. (1994a). A comparative study of hate crime: Legislative, judicial, and social responses in Germany and the United States. *European Journal on Criminal Policy and Research, 2*, 39-64.

Aronowitz, A. A. (1994b). Germany's xenophobic violence: Criminal justice and social responses. In M. S. Hamm (Ed.), *Hate crime: International perspectives on causes and control* (pp. 37-70). Cincinnati, OH: ACJS/Anderson.

Associated Press (AP). (1995, October 26). Mice being used to grow human tissue. *The (Columbia, SC) State*, p. A9.

Associated Press (AP). (1996, October 31). Top FBI official pleads guilty, admits destroying Ruby Ridge report. New York.

Associated Press (AP). (1997a, March 24). Reward offered for capture of two brothers. Wilmington, OH.

Associated Press (AP). (1997b, May 10). Police arrest 5 reputed militia members and seize hundreds of weapons. Los Angeles, CA.

Back, L., Keith, M., & Solomos, J. (1995, December). *The new modalities of racist culture: Technology, race, and neo-Fascism in a digital age.* Paper presented at the conference on Brotherhoods of Nations and Race: The Emergence of a Violent Euro-American Racist Subcultures, New Orleans.

Ball, R., & Curry, G. D. (1995, March). *Preliminary findings from National Report on Juvenile Hate/Bias Crime.* Paper presented at the annual meeting of the Academy of Criminal Justice Sciences, Boston.

Barkun, M. (1994a). Millenarian groups and law enforcement agencies: The lessons of Waco. *Terrorism and Political Violence, 6,* 75-95.

Barkun, M. (1994b). *Religion and the racist Right: The origins of the Christian Identity movement.* Chapel Hill: University of North Carolina Press.

Baron, S. W. (1989). The Canadian west coast punk subculture: A field study. *Canadian Journal of Sociology, 14,* 289-316.

Bass, G., et al. (1980, February). *Motivations and possible actions of potential criminal adversaries of U.S. nuclear programs* (Paper No. R-2554-SL). Santa Monica, CA: RAND.

Baxter, R. R. (1974). A skeptical look at the concept of terrorism. *Akron Law Review, 7,* 380-387.

Beam, L. (1992, February). *The seditionist: Leaderless resistance.* Idaho: Author.

Bequi, A. (1987). *Techno-crimes: The computerization of crime and terrorism.* Lexington, MA: Lexington.

Berk, R. A. (1994). Foreword. In M. S. Hamm (Ed.), *Hate crime: International perspectives on causes and control* (pp. v-ix). Cincinnati, OH: ACJS/Anderson.

Bleecker, S. E. (1988, May/June). The bio-logic age: The merging of man and machine. *Futurist, 22,* 60.

Blumstein, A., Cohen, J., Roth, J. A., & Vister, C. A. (Eds.). (1986). *Criminal careers and "career criminals."* Washington, DC: National Academy Press.

Boettcher, M. (Reporter). (1997, January 31). *NBC News Nightside.* New York: National Broadcasting Company.

Bowling, B. (1994). Racial harassment in east London. In M. S. Hamm (Ed.), *Hate crime: International perspectives on causes and control* (pp. 1-36). Cincinnati, OH: ACJS/Anderson.

Bullard, S. (Ed.). (1989). *Hate violence and white supremacy: A decade review.* Montgomery, AL: Southern Poverty Law Center.

Bullard, S. (Ed.). (1991). *Special report: The Ku Klux Klan—A history of racism and violence* (4th ed.). Montgomery, AL: Southern Poverty Law Center.

Cable News Network (CNN). (Producer). (1994). *Terror nation? U.S. creation?* [Videotape]. (Show #373, Available from Journal Graphics)

Chalmers, D. M. (1981). *Hooded Americanism.* New York: Franklin Watts.

Christopher, W. (1994, October 24). [Speech at Georgetown University, Washington, DC]

Chronis, P., & Pankratz, H. (1997, May 3). Three in home raid face charges, illegal arsenal found, documents say. *Denver Post,* p. A1.

Civil Disobedience Act of April 1968, 82 Stat. 90, 18 U.S.C. §§ 231-233 (1968).

Cline, R. S., & Alexander, Y. (1984). *Terrorism: The Soviet connection.* New York: Crane, Russak.

Clutterbuck, R. (1980). *Guerrillas and terrorists.* Columbus: Ohio State University Press.

Coates, J. (1987). *Armed and dangerous: The rise of the survivalist Right.* New York: Noonday.

Collin, B. (1996, September). *The future of cyberterrorism: Where the physical and virtual worlds converge.* Paper presented at 11th Annual International Symposium on Criminal Justice Issues. Available: http://www.acsp.uic.edu/OICJ/CONFS (1996, September 9)

Corcoran, J. (1990). *Bitter harvest: Gordon Kahl and the Posse Comitatus: Murder in the heartland.* New York: Penguin.

Criminal acts of a terrorist character. (1985). U.N. Doc. A/40/53.

Declaration on measures to eliminate terrorism. (1995). U.N. Doc. A/49/49.

Dees, M., with Corcoran, J. (1996). *Gathering storm: America's militia threat.* New York: HarperCollins.

Devost, M., Houghton, B., & Pollard, N. (1996). Information terrorism: Can you trust your toaster? *Terrorism Research Center* [On-line]. Available: http://www.terrorism.com/terrorism/itpaper.html (1997, February 10)

Dorman v. United States, 435 F. 2d. 385 (D.C. Cir. 1970).

Ellis, W. W. (1990). *Bias crime.* Washington, DC: National Research Council.

Ellul, J. (1969). *Propaganda: The formation of men's attitudes.* New York: Knopf.

Emerson, S. A. (Producer). (1994). *Jihad in America* [Videotape]. (Available from PBS Video)

Emerson, S. A. (1995). Political Islam promotes terrorism. In P. A. Winters (Ed.), *Islam: Opposing views* (pp. 157-163). San Diego: Greenhaven.

Emerson, S. A., & Del Sesto, C. (1991). *Terrorist: The inside story of the highest-ranking Iraqi terrorist ever to defect to the West.* New York: Villard.

Esposito, J. L. (1992). *The Islamic threat: Myth or reality?* New York: Oxford University Press.

*Existence of radical Islamic groups: Hearing before the Senate Foreign Relations Subcommittee on the Near East,* 104th Cong., 2d Sess. (1996). [Testimony of Seif Ashmawi]

Ezekiel, R. S. (1995). *The racist mind: Portraits of American Neo-Nazis and Klansmen.* New York: Viking.

*False patriots: The threat of antigovernment extremists.* (1996). Montgomery, AL: Southern Poverty Law Center.

Fangen, K. (1995, December). *Living out our ethnic instincts: Ideological beliefs among racist activists in Norway.* Paper presented at the conference on Brotherhoods of Nations and Race: The Emergence of a Violent Euro-American Racist Subcultures, New Orleans, LA.

Federal Bureau of Investigation (FBI). (1990). *Uniform crime reports.* Washington, DC: Government Printing Office.

Federal Bureau of Investigation (FBI). (1991a). *Hate crime statistics, 1990: A resource book.* Washington, DC: U.S. Department of Justice.

Federal Bureau of Investigation (FBI). (1991b). *Terrorism in the United States: 1990.* Washington, DC: Government Printing Office.

Federal Bureau of Investigation (FBI). (1992). *Hate crime statistics, 1991: A resource book.* Washington, DC: U.S. Department of Justice.

Federal Bureau of Investigation (FBI). (1993). *Hate crime statistics, 1992: A resource book.* Washington, DC: U.S. Department of Justice.

Federal Bureau of Investigation (FBI). (1994). *Terrorism in the United States: 1993.* Washington, DC: U.S. Department of Justice.

Federal Bureau of Investigation (FBI). (1995). *Terrorism in the United States: 1994.* Washington, DC: U.S. Department of Justice.

Federal rules. (1995). *Federal criminal code and rules.* St. Paul, MN: West.

Fernandez, R. (1987). *Los Macheteros: The Wells Fargo robbery and the violent struggle for Puerto Rican independence.* Upper Saddle River, NJ: Prentice Hall.

Ferracuti, F. (1990). Ideology and repentance: Terrorism in Italy. In W. Reich (Ed.), *Origins of terrorism* (pp. 59-64). New York: Cambridge University Press.

Finn, P., & McNeil, T. (1988). *Bias crime and the criminal justice response.* Washington, DC: U.S. Department of Justice.

Fleming, P., Stohl, M., & Schmid, A. (1988). The theoretical utility of typologies of terrorism: Lessons and opportunities. In M. Stohl (Ed.), *The politics of terrorism* (3rd ed., pp. 153-195). New York: Marcel Dekker.

Frazier, L. (1995, August) *Surveillance through walls and other opaque materials.* Paper presented at the Annual Conference of Applied Sensory Technology Engineers in Las Vegas, NV.

Gerth, J., & Miller, J. (1996, August 14). Funds to terrorists traced to Persian Gulf businessmen. *New York Times,* p. A1.

Gertz, B. (1996, April 28). FBI sees Islamic militants as greatest threat. *Washington Times,* p. A3.7.

Gibbs, J. P. (1989). Conceptualization of terrorism. *American Sociological Review, 54,* 329-340.

Gibson, J. W. (1994). *Warrior dreams: Violence and manhood in post-Vietnam America.* New York: Hill & Wang.

Global Organized Crime Project. (1996). *The nuclear black market.* Washington, DC: Center for Strategic and International Studies.

Golan, G. (1990). *Gorbachev's "new thinking" on terrorism.* New York: Praeger.

Goren, R. (1984). *The Soviet Union and terrorism.* Sydney, Australia: Allen and Unwin.

Greason, D. (1994). *I was a teenage fascist.* Victoria, Australia: McPhee Gribble.

Group weighed cyanide assault, witness testifies. (1988, February 23). *Birmingham News,* p. 6b.

Guillen, A. (1973). *Philosophy of the urban guerrilla* (D. Hodges, Trans.). New York: William Morrow.

Guilty plea in Ruby Ridge probe. (1996, October 31). *Chicago Tribune,* p. A1.

Hale, L. T. (1995). *United States v. Ford:* The Eleventh Circuit permits unrestricted police use of thermal surveillance on private property without a warrant. *Georgia Law Review, 29,* 819-826.

Halpern, T., & Levin, B. (1996). *The limits of dissent: The constitutional status of armed civilian militias.* Amherst, MA: Aletheia.

Hamm, M. S. (1993). *American Skinheads: The criminology and control of hate crime.* New York: Praeger.

Hamm, M. S. (1994a). Conceptualizing hate crime in a global context. In M. S. Hamm (Ed.), *Hate crime: International perspectives on causes and control* (pp. 173-194). Cincinnati, OH: ACJS/Anderson.

Hamm, M. S. (1994b). A modified social control theory of terrorism: An empirical and ethnographical assessment of American neo-Nazi Skinheads. In M. S. Hamm (Ed.), *Hate crime: International perspectives on causes and control* (pp. 71-90). Cincinnati, OH: ACJS/Anderson.

Hamm, M. S. (1994c). Review essay on Jack Levin and Jack McDevitt's hate crimes: The rising tide of bigotry and bloodshed. *Journal of Criminal Justice, 22,* 71-74.

Hamm, M. S. (1994d). Review essay on Michael Schmidt's *The New Reich:* Violent extremism in unified Germany and beyond. *Criminologist, 19,* 20-23.

Hamm, M. S. (1995). Hammer of the gods revisited: Neo-Nazi Skinheads, domestic terrorism, and the rise of the new protest music. In J. Ferrell & C. R. Saunders (Eds.), *Cultural criminology* (pp. 190-212). Boston: Northeastern University Press.

Hamm, M. S. (1997). *Apocalypse in Oklahoma: Waco and Ruby Ridge revenged.* Boston: Northeastern University Press.

Hanson, S. (1996, May). A rule of their own. *American Lawyer,* 52-56.

Harrison, E. (1997, March 14). Unsolved blasts unnerve Atlantans, baffle the FBI. *Los Angeles Times,* p. A1.

Hasselbach, I., & Reiss, T. (1996). *Führer-Ex: Memoirs of a former neo-Nazi.* New York: Random House.

Hedges, C. (1996, January 24). Fearing attack, U.S. is tightening security. *New York Times,* pp. A1, A6.

Heitmeyer, W. (1993). Hostility and violence toward foreigners in Germany. In T. Björgo & R. Witte (Eds.), *Racist violence in Europe* (pp. 17-28). New York: St. Martin's.

Herman, E. (1982). *The real terror network: Terrorism in fact and propaganda.* Boston: South End.

Hoffman, B. (1988). *The contrasting ethical foundations of terrorism in the 1980s.* Santa Monica, CA: RAND.

Homans, G. (1974). *Social behavior: Its elementary forms* (Rev. ed.). Orlando, FL: Harcourt Brace.

Howlett, D. (1996, April 4). Recluse matches FBI's profile. *USA Today,* p. A7.

Hutman, B. (1996, March 9). Attack with car kills 1, injures 22. *Jerusalem Post,* p. 1.

Illinois v. Gates, 442 U.S. 213 (1983).

*An indictment of the ATF and FBI.* (1997). (Available from the Center for Hate and Extremism, Richard Stockton College, Jim Leeds Road, Pomona, NJ 08240)

International convention against the taking of hostages. (1979). U.N. Doc. A/34/786.

*International crime: Hearings before the Foreign Operations Subcommittee of the Senate Appropriations Committee,* 104th Cong., 2d Sess. (1996). [Testimony of Louis Freeh]

Its greatest operation, Hamas takes credit for the bombing of an Israeli bus in the center of Tel-Aviv. (1994, October 27). *Al-Zaitanouh,* p. 1.

Jenkins, B. M. (1975). Will terrorists go nuclear? *California Seminar on Arms Control and Foreign Policy Discussion* (Paper No. 64). Santa Monica, CA: RAND.

Jenkins, B. M. (1980). *Terrorism in the United States.* Santa Monica, CA: RAND.

Jenkins, B. M. (Ed.). (1985). Terrorism in the year 2000. *TVI Report, 6,* S13-S15.

Jenkins, B. M. (1996, August 4). Striking home: The terrorist threat on America's doorstep. *San Diego Union Tribune,* pp. 1G, 6G.

Jensen, E. (1993). International Nazi cooperation: A terrorist-oriented network. In T. Björgo & R. Witte (Eds.), *Racist violence in Europe* (pp. 80-95). New York: St. Martin's.

Jim Crow Laws. (1975). *In family encyclopedia of American history* (pp. 578-579). Pleasantville, NY: Reader's Digest.

Kaplan, J. (1995). Right-wing violence in North America. *Terrorism and Political Violence, 7,* 44-95.

Katz v. United States., 389 U.S. 347 (1967).

Kellen, K. (1987). The potential for nuclear terrorism: A discussion. In P. Leventhal & Y. Alexander (Eds.), *Preventing nuclear terrorism: The report and papers of the International Task Force on Prevention of Nuclear Terrorism* (pp. 104-122). Lexington, MA: D. C. Heath.

Kellen, K. (1990). Ideology and rebellion: Terrorism in West Germany. In W. Reich (Ed.), *Origins of terrorism* (pp. 43-64). New York: Cambridge University Press.

Kellett, A. (1995). Terrorism in Canada: 1960-1992. In J. I. Ross (Ed.), *Violence in Canada: Sociopolitical perspectives* (pp. 286-315). New York: Oxford University Press.

Kelly, R. J., & Rieber, R. (1992). Collateral damage on the home front: The gulf in America. *Journal of Social Distress and the Homeless, 1,* 95-106.

Kennedy, M. (1986). *The Ayatollah in the cathedral: Reflections of a hostage.* New York: Hill & Wang.

Klanwatch. (1990). *The Ku Klux Klan: A history of racism and violence.* Montgomery, AL: Southern Poverty Law Center.

Komarow, S. (1996, August 5). "Silent" terrorists even more deadly. *USA Today,* p. A11.

Kühnel, W. (1995a). *Hostility toward foreigners in the form of violence by youth from various social environments in West and East Germany.* Berlin, Germany: Humboldt University, Department of Social Sciences.

Kühnel, W. (1995b, December). *The mobilization of violent and xenophobic networks and subcultures: Opportunities and limitations for the emergence of a right-wing social movement in Germany.* Paper presented at the conference on Brotherhoods of Nations and Race: The Emergence of a Violent Euro-American Racist Subcultures, New Orleans, LA.

Ku Klux Klan. (1975). *In family encyclopedia of American history* (pp. 618-619). Pleasantville, NY: Reader's Digest.

Kupperman, R., & Kamen, J. (1989). *Final warning: Averting disaster in the new age of terrorism.* Garden City, NY: Doubleday.

Kushner, H. W. (1994). The new Middle-Eastern terrorist. *IALEIA Journal, 8,* 41-46.

Kushner, H. W. (1996). Suicide bombers: Business as usual. *Studies in Conflict and Terrorism, 19,* 329-337.

Laird, F. (1994). Infrared temperature measurement and imaging sensors. *Journal of Applied Sensing Technology, 11,* 8.

Laqueur, W. (1977). *Terrorism: A study of national and international political violence.* Boston: Little, Brown.

Laqueur, W. (1987). *The age of terrorism.* Boston: Little, Brown.

Lauk, K. J. (1994). Germany at the crossroads: On the efficiency of the German economy. *Daedalus, 123,* 57-84.

Levin, B. (1993). A dream deferred: The social and legal implications of hate crime in the 1990s. *Journal of Intergroup Relations, 20,* 22-23.

Levin, J., & McDevitt, J. (1993). *Hate crimes: The rising tide of bigotry and bloodshed.* New York: Plenum.

Levitas, D. (1996, October). *Posse Comitatus.* Lecture presented at the annual meeting of the Northwest Coalition Against Malicious Harassment, Spokane, WA.

Lewis, B. (1993). *Islam and the West.* New York: Oxford University Press.

Lincoln, W. B. (1983). *In war's dark shadow: The Russians before the great war.* New York: Simon & Schuster.

Lofland, J. (1996). *Social movements organizations: Guide to research on insurgent realities.* Hawthorne, NY: Aldine de Gruyter.

Lööw, H. (1993). The cult of violence: The Swedish racist counterculture. In T. Björgo & R. Witte (Eds.), *Racist violence in Europe* (pp. 62-79). New York: St. Martin's.

Lööw, H. (1995a). Racist violence and criminal behavior in Sweden: Myths and reality. *Terrorism and Political Violence, 7,* 119-161.

Lööw, H. (1995b, December). *White power rock 'n' roll: A growing industry.* Paper presented at the conference on Brotherhoods of Nations and Race: The Emergence of a Violent Euro-American Racist Subcultures, New Orleans, LA.

Lyall, S. (1997, January 14). London and U.N. mail bombs hurt 2 at Arabic newspaper. *New York Times,* pp. A1, A6.

Lynching. (1975). *In family encyclopedia of American history* (pp. 668-669). Pleasantville, NY: Reader's Digest.

Macdonald, A. (1978). *The Turner diaries.* Hillsboro, WV: National Vanguard Books.

Marighella, C. (1971). *For the liberation of Brazil* (J. Butt & R. Sheed, Trans.). Harmondsworth, UK: Pelican.

Marks, R. (1995). *America under attack.* New York: Carlyle.

Marx, K. (1956). *Karl Marx: Selected writings in sociology and social psychology* (T. B. Bottomore, Trans.). New York: McGraw-Hill.

Marx, K., & Engels, F. (1970). *The German ideology* (C. J. Arthur, Ed. & Trans.). New York: International Publishers.

Mascolo, E. (1992). The emergency doctrine exception to the warrant requirement under the Fourth Amendment. *Buffalo Law Review, 22,* 419-426.

McKeown, L. (1992, July 14). Pigs might become organ donors. *The (Columbia, SC) State,* pp. D1, D6.

Mijares, T., & Perkins, D. (1995). Police liability issues: Tactical units and the use of specialized equipment. *Police Liability Review, 7,* 1-10.

Miller, J. (1994, November/December). Faces of fundamentalism. *Foreign Affairs, 73,* 123-142.

Miller, J. (1996). *God has 99 names.* New York: Simon & Schuster.

Moore, S. (1994). Does heat emanate beyond the threshold? Home infrared emissions, remote sensing, and the Fourth Amendment threshold. *Chicago-Kent Law Review, 70,* 803-859.

Morlin, B., & Walter, J. (1997, January 26). Olympic bomb probe looks at NW trio. *Spokesman-Review,* pp. A1, A15.

My restless aspiration is to murder. (1997, February 26). *New York Times,* p. B3.

National Governors Association. (1978). *Domestic terrorism.* Washington, DC: Author.

Nelson, M. M., & Stout, H. (1996, July 31). U.S. and allies agree on antiterrorism measures. *Wall Street Journal,* p. A3.

Nullification doctrines. (1975). *In family encyclopedia of American history* (p. 13). Pleasantville, NY: Reader's Digest.

Observing earth from space. (1995, May/June). *Futurist, 29,* 7.

Office of the Attorney General. (1983). *Attorney General's guidelines on domestic security/terrorism investigations.* Washington, DC: U.S. Department of Justice.

Olson, N. (1997). Citizen militias defend liberty. In C. Cozic (Ed.), *The militia movement* (pp. 10-18). San Diego: Greenhaven.

*Omnibus Counterterrorism Act of 1995: Hearings before the House Judiciary Committee,* 104th Cong., 1st Sess. (1995). [Testimony of William Studeman]

Parks, S. (1997, May 1). Klan leader labeled informant; suspects in robbery-bombing plot say he talked to FBI. *Dallas Morning News,* p. 24A.

Perez de Cuellar, J. (1990). Report presented to the 44th General Assembly: August 1989. *U.N. Chronicle, 27,* 41-44.

Person v. Miller, 854 F.2d 656 (4th Cir. 1988).

Pochurek, L. (1994). From battlefield to the home front: Infrared surveillance and the war on drugs place privacy under siege. *St. Thomas Law Review, 7*, 137-167.

Post, J. M. (1987). Prospects for nuclear terrorism: Psychological motivations and constraints. In P. Leventhal & Y. Alexander (Eds.), *Preventing nuclear terrorism: The report and papers of the International Task Force on Prevention of Nuclear Terrorism* (pp. 91-103). Lexington, MA: D. C. Heath.

Poveda, T. (1990). *Lawlessness and reform: The FBI in transition.* Pacific Grove, CA: Brooks/Cole.

Powell, M. (1996, April 2). Orwellian snooping. *USA Today,* p. A13.

Presser v. Illinois, 116 U.S. 252 (1886).

Prichard, F. N., & Starr, J. M. (1994). Skinheads in New Orleans: An inside view. *Humanity & Society, 18,* 19-36.

Regan, L. (1993). *Public enemies.* London: Andre Deutsch.

Reno, J. (1995). Keynote address: 1994 ASC meeting in Miami, Florida. *Criminologist, 20,* 1-9.

Report of the Eighth U.N. Congress on the Prevention of Crime and the Treatment of Offenders. (1990). A/CONF.144/28.

Ridgeway, J. (1995). *Blood in the face.* New York: Thunder's Mouth.

Rosga, A. (1996, February). *Good cop/bad cop: Refashioning law enforcement as the thin blue line between bigotry and tolerance.* Paper presented to the Criminal Justice Department, Indiana University, Bloomington.

Ross, J. I. (1994). Hate crime in Canada: Growing pains with new legislation. In M. S. Hamm (Ed.), *Hate crime: International perspectives on causes and control* (pp. 151-172). Cincinnati, OH: ACJS/Anderson.

Rubenstein, R. (1987). *Alchemists of revolution: Terrorism in the modern world.* New York: Basic Books.

Rubenstein, R. (1989). Rebellion in America: The fire next time. In T. R. Gurr (Ed.), *Violence in America: Protest, rebellion, and reform* (pp. 307-328). Newbury Park, CA: Sage.

Russell, C., & Miller, B. (1977). Profile of a terrorist. *Terrorism: An International Journal, 1,* 17-34.

Said, E. (1981). *The politics of dispossession.* New York: Pantheon.

Said, E. (1993). *Culture and imperialism.* New York: Knopf.

Schmid, A., & Graaf, J. (1982). *Violence as communication: Insurgent terrorism and the Western news media.* Beverly Hills, CA: Sage.

Schmid, A. P. (1983). *Political terrorism.* Amsterdam: North-Holland.

Schmidt, M. (1993). *The new Reich: Violent extremism in unified Germany and beyond.* New York: Pantheon.

Shulte, B. (1996, July 3). Terrorism hard to track, harder to prevent, experts say. *The (Columbia, SC) State,* p. A5.

Schwartz, A. M. (Ed.). (1996). *Danger: Extremism—The major vehicles and voices on America's far Right fringe.* New York: Anti-Defamation League.

Seiff, M. (1996, July 31). Experts questioning tough talk on curbing terrorism. *Washington Times,* p. A15.

Shumer, C. (1996, March 13). [Comments of Seif Ashmawi at press conference of Congressman Charles Shumer, U.S. Capitol, Washington, DC]

Simon, J. D. (1994). *Terrorists and the potential use of biological weapons: A discussion of possibilities.* Santa Monica, CA: RAND.

Skinner, B. F. (1974). *About behaviorism.* New York: Knopf.

Slobodzian, J. A. (1997, January 31). Supremacist charged in robbery plot. *Philadelphia Inquirer*, pp. A1, A10.

Slobodzian, J. A., & Fazlollah, M. (1997, February 19). Aryan leader pleads guilty. *Philadelphia Inquirer*, pp. A1, A10.

Slover, P. (1997, May 6). Authorities kill fugitive separatists; group's jailed leader asks second man to surrender. *Dallas Morning News*, p. 1A.

Smith, B. L. (1985). Antiterrorism legislation in the United States: Problems and implications. *Terrorism: An International Journal, 7*, 213-231.

Smith, B. L. (1988). State antiterrorism legislation in the United States: A review of statutory utilization. *Conflict Quarterly, 8*, 29-47.

Smith, B. L. (1994). *Terrorism in America: Pipe bombs and pipe dreams*. Albany: State University of New York Press.

Smith, B. L. (1995). *Violent antigovernment groups in America: Testimony before the U.S. House of Representatives Judiciary Subcommittee on Crime, November 2, 1995*. Washington, DC: Government Printing Office.

Smith, B. L., & Damphousse, K. (1996). Punishing political offenders: The effect of political motive on federal sentencing decisions. *Criminology, 34*, 289-321.

Smith, B. L., & Morgan, K. (1994). Terrorists right and left: Empirical issues in profiling American terrorists. *Studies in Conflict and Terrorism, 17*, 39-57.

Smith, B. L., & Orvis, G. (1994). America's response to terrorism: An empirical analysis of federal intervention strategies during the 1980s. *Justice Quarterly, 10*, 661-681.

Southern Poverty Law Center (SPLC). (1993, December). *Klanwatch intelligence report* (Issue No. 71). Montgomery, AL: Author.

Southern Poverty Law Center (SPLC). (1994, February). *Klanwatch intelligence report* (Issue No. 72). Montgomery, AL: Author.

Southern Poverty Law Center (SPLC). (1995a, March). *Klanwatch intelligence report* (Issue No. 77). Montgomery, AL: Author.

Southern Poverty Law Center (SPLC). (1995b, August). *Klanwatch intelligence report* (Issue No. 79). Montgomery, AL: Author.

Southern Poverty Law Center (SPLC). (1995c, October). *Klanwatch intelligence report* (Issue No. 80). Montgomery, AL: Author.

Southern Poverty Law Center (SPLC). (1996, February). *Klanwatch intelligence report* (Issue No. 81). Montgomery, AL: Author.

State v. Cramer, 851 P. 2d 147 (Ariz. Ct. App., 1992).

State v. Mckee, 510 N.W. 2d 807 (Wis. Ct. App. 1993).

State v. Young, 867 P. 2d 593 (Wash. Sup. Ct., 1994).

Stephens, G. (1992, November/December). Crime and the biotech revolution. *Futurist, 26*, 38-42.

Stephens, G. (1995, September/October). Crime in cyberspace: The digital underworld. *Futurist, 29*, 24-28.

Stern, K. S. (1996). *A force upon the plain: The American militia movement and the politics of hate*. New York: Simon & Schuster.

Stern, K. S. (1997). *The McVeigh trial*. New York: American Jewish Committee.

Stock, C. M. (1996). *Rural radicals, righteous rage in the American grain*. Ithaca, NY: Cornell University Press.

Sudan: Terrorist haven. (1997). *Counterterrorism & Security Report, 5*, 1, 9.

Suga, M. (1995). *State v. Young* and the new test for privacy in Washington. *Washington Law Review, 70*, 907-927.

Sykes, G. M. (1978). *Criminology*. Orlando, FL: Harcourt Brace.

Taylor, M., & Ryan, H. (1988). Fanaticism, political suicide, and terrorism. *Terrorism,* *11,* 91-111.

Technology: Micro machines. (1994, January/February). *Futurist, 28,* 50.

Thomas, P., & Hall, C. W. (1995, July 28). Palestinian with local ties is detained as suspected Hamas leader. *Washington Post,* p. A31.

Tittle, C. (1994). The theoretical bases for inequality in formal social control. In G. S. Bridges & M. Myers (Eds.), *Inequality, crime, and social control* (pp. 21-52). Boulder, CO: Westview.

Toameh, K. A. (1993, March 11). Intifada on a shoestring. *Jerusalem Post,* pp. 24-26.

Turk, A. (1982). *Political criminality: The defiance and defense of authority.* Beverly Hills, CA: Sage.

Ubiquitous computing. (1995, February). *Popular Science,* p. 48.

U.S. Department of Justice. (1993). *Terrorism in the United States.* Washington, DC: Federal Bureau of Investigation.

U.S. Department of Justice. (1995). *Sourcebook of criminal justice statistics.* Washington, DC: Author.

U.S. Department of State. (1992). *Patterns of global terrorism: 1991.* Washington, DC: Author.

U.S. Department of State. (1993). *Patterns of global terrorism: 1992.* Washington, DC: Author.

U.S. Department of State. (1994). *Patterns of global terrorism: 1993.* Washington, DC: Author.

U.S. Department of State. (1996). *Combating terrorism: Fact sheet No. 1. The Paris ministerial.* Washington, DC: Author.

U.S. Sentencing Commission. (1991). *United States Sentencing Commission: Annual report, 1990.* Washington, DC: Government Printing Office.

United States v. Cusumano, 67 F. 3d 1497 (10th Cir. 1995); affirmed on rehearing 83 F. 3d 1247 (10th Cir. 1996).

United States v. Domitrovich, 852 F. Supp. 1460 (E.D. Wash. 1994).

United States v. Field, 855 F. Supp. 1518 (W.D. Wis. 1994).

United States v. Ishmael, 843 F. Supp. 205 (E.D. Tex. 1994).

United States v. Karo, 468 U.S. 705 (1984).

United States v. Melucci, 888 F. 2d 200 (1st Cir. 1989).

United States v. Penny-Feeny, 773 F. Supp. 220 (1991).

United States v. Pierce, 959 F. 2d 1297 (5th Cir. 1992).

United States v. Pinson, 24 F. 3d 1056 (1994).

United States v. Porco, 842 F. Supp. 1393 (D.Wyo. 1994).

United States v. Sanginette, 859 F. 2d 1501 (6th Cir. 1988).

United States v. Shye, 492 F. 2d 886 (6th Cir. 1974).

Vetter, H., & Perlstein, G. R. (1991). *Perspectives on terrorism.* Pacific Grove, CA: Brooks/Cole.

Victor, J. (1993). *Satanic panic: The creation of a contemporary legend.* Chicago: Open Court.

Vietnamese Fishermen's Association v. Knights of the Ku Klux Klan, 543 F. Supp. 198 (S.D. Tex. 1982).

Wallace, W. (1997, May 7). Others sought in explosion case: Police probe militia ties to cache found in Yuba City. *San Francisco Chronicle,* p. A18.

Walter, J. (1995). *Every knee shall bow: The truth and tragedy of Ruby Ridge and the Randy Weaver family.* New York: HarperCollins.

Ward, R. (1996). Terrorism. In *Encyclopedia of the future* (Vol. 2, pp. 928-930). New York: Macmillan.

Warden v. Hayden, 294 U.S. 294 (1967).

Wardlaw, G. (1989). *Political terrorism.* New York: Cambridge University Press.

Warwick, P. (1992, November/December). The cash-free society. *Futurist, 26,* 19-22.

Weber, M. (1976). *The Protestant ethic and the spirit of capitalism.* New York: Scribner.

Whiskey rebels. (1975). In *Family encyclopedia of American history* (p. 1223). Pleasantville, NY: Reader's Digest.

White, J. (1991). *Terrorism: An introduction.* Pacific Grove, CA: Brooks/Cole.

Whitney, C. R. (1996, July 31). Major powers announce steps to counter global terrorism. *New York Times,* p. B6.

Wilkinson, P. (1987). Support mechanisms for international terrorism. In R. Slater & M. Stohl (Eds.), *Current perspectives on international terrorism.* New York: St. Martin's.

Wilkinson, P., & Rapoport, D. G. (1989). Editorial manifesto. *Terrorism and Political Violence, 1,* 5-6.

Willems, H. (1995). Development, patterns, and causes of violence against foreigners in Germany: Social and biographical characteristics of perpetrators and the process of escalation. *Terrorism and Political Violence, 7,* 162-181.

Williams, H. [News wire service]. (1995, June 17). G7, Russia seek new era of global cooperation, but problems remain. *Agence France-Presse.*

Wilson, D. (1996). 40 million potential spies. *CNN Interactive News.* Available: http://www.cnn.com (1996, May 23)

Wilson, M. G. (1995). The prewarrant use of thermal imagery: Has this technological advance in the war against drugs come at the expense of Fourth Amendment protections against unreasonable searches? *Kentucky Law Journal, 83,* 891-914.

Witte, R. (1994). Comparing state responses to racist violence in Europe: A model for international comparative analysis. In M. S. Hamm (Ed.), *Hate crime: International perspectives on causes and control* (pp. 91-104). Cincinnati, OH: ACJS/Anderson.

Witte, R. (1995). *Racist violence and the state: A comparative European analysis.* The Netherlands: University of Utrecht.

Wolfgang, M., Figlio, R., Tracy, P., & Singer, S. (1985). *The national survey of crime severity.* Washington, DC: Government Printing Office.

Wright, J. (1990). *Terrorist propaganda: The red army faction and the provisional IRA, 1968-86.* New York: St. Martin's.

Zabel, M. L. (1995). A high-tech assault on the "castle": Warrantless thermal surveillance of private residences and the Fourth Amendment. *Northwestern University Law Review, 90,* 267-303.

# Index

# About the Editor

**Harvey W. Kushner** received a BA degree in political science from Queens College and MA and PhD degrees in political science from New York University. He currently is Professor and Chair of the Department of Criminal Justice and Security Administration at Long Island University, Brookville, New York.

An internationally recognized expert on terrorism, antigovernment violence, and extremism, in recent years Professor Kushner has conducted workshops on the mind-set of the terrorist for a variety of state and federal agencies, including the Federal Aviation Administration, Federal Bureau of Investigation, U.S. Federal Probation Department, and the U.S. Drug Enforcement Administration. He has also conducted similar seminars and training for such organizations as Crime Stoppers International, the New York State Crime Prevention Coalition, the Eastern Armed Robbery Conference, and the Southern States Correctional Association.

Professor Kushner's opinions and criticisms are much sought after by the media. His commentary has appeared in the Associated Press, Cable News Network (CNN), Canadian Broadcasting Corporation (CBC), and *Time, Newsweek,* and other magazines and newspapers worldwide. Advocacy groups, as well as victims of terrorism, also rely on his expertise.

Professor Kushner's writings on terrorism have appeared in academic, professional, and trade publications such as *Studies in Conflict and Terrorism, Counterterrorism & Security International,* and *Security Management.* His forthcoming books are *Terrorism in America, Hate in America,* and *The Militia Movement: Past, Present, and Future.*

# About the Contributors

**Kelly R. Damphousse** is Assistant Professor, Department of Sociology, University of Oklahoma, Norman. He has conducted research on domestic extremist and terrorist groups that tests theoretical models explaining differential sentencing outcomes. In addition, he has researched collective behavior as it relates to domestic terrorism and the "satanic panic." His latest research involves documenting the use of the Internet for both extremist groups and counterterrorism operations. His writings include articles in a variety of academic and professional journals, including *Criminology, Deviant Behavior,* and *Crime and Delinquency,* as well as a number of book chapters.

**Steven Emerson** is an internationally recognized expert on Middle Eastern terrorism and militant Islamic fundamentalist networks. He has previously served as a correspondent for CNN and a senior editor for *U.S. News and World Report.* Before entering journalism, he served as a professional staff member of the U.S. Senate Foreign Relations Committee. The producer of the PBS documentary *Jihad in America,* which exposed the secret Islamic terrorist movements operating on U.S. soil, he is producing a new documentary series and completing a book detailing his 3-year investigations into radical Islamic activities. A regular contributor to national newspapers and magazines such as the *New York Times, Washington Post, Wall Street Journal,* and *The New Republic,* he is also author or coauthor of four books on the Middle East and international terrorism, including *The Fall of Pan Am 103: Inside the Lockerbie Investigation* (1990) and *Terrorist: The Inside Story of the Highest-Ranking Iraqi Terrorist Ever to Defect to the West* (1991).

**Mark S. Hamm** is Professor in the Department of Criminology, Indiana State University, Terre Haute. Considered one of the nation's leading experts on Skinheads and hate crime, his pro seminar entitled "Satanic Cults and Hate Groups" is recognized by the American Sociological Association as a model bias-motivated crime curriculum. Such diverse groups as the Dutch Ministry of Justice, U.S. Immigration and Naturalization Service, Baltimore Police Department, and the Klanwatch Project of the Southern Poverty Law Center have sought his counsel on matters related to Skinheads, hate crime, and terrorism. Among his numerous books, articles, technical reports, and reviews are *American Skinheads: The Criminology and Control of Hate Crime* (1993), *Hate Crime: International Perspectives on Cases and Control* (1994), and *Apocalypse in Oklahoma: Waco and Ruby Ridge Revenged* (1997).

**Brian M. Jenkins** is Deputy Chairman, Kroll Associates, Los Angeles, California. One of the world's leading authorities on international terrorism, from 1986 to 1989 he was Chairman of RAND Corporation's Political Science Department and from 1972 to 1989 directed RAND's research on political violence and international crime. He serves as a consultant to numerous government agencies and major corporations. A former Captain in the Green Berets, he served in the Dominican Republic and later in Vietnam, where he was decorated on several occasions for valor in combat. He returned to Vietnam as a member of a special planning unit and was honored with the Department of the Army's highest award for his work there. In August 1996, he was appointed a member of the White House Commission on Aviation Safety and Security. He has contributed chapters to many books, has published numerous reports, papers, and articles, and is the author of *International Terrorism: A New Mode of Conflict* (1974) and the editor and coauthor of *Terrorism and Personal Protection* (1985).

**Douglas A. Kash,** an Attorney in Washington, D.C., has lectured extensively on the legal aspects of abducting, extraditing, and prosecuting terrorists. As a Strategic Assessments Analyst in Arlington, Virginia, he developed and managed projects on terrorism and related international security affairs, as well as lectured to the U.S. State Department's Bureau of Consular Affairs. He is a member of the American Bar Association's Standing Committee on Law and National Security and an Adjunct Professor of criminal justice at Northern Virginia Community College, Annandale. His publications on prosecuting, abducting, and assassinating terrorists have appeared in magazines, journals, and law reviews. He currently serves as the Legal Editor for *Counterterrorism and Security Magazine.*

**Robert J. Kelly** is Broeklundian Professor of Social Science and Criminal Justice, Brooklyn College, Brooklyn, New York. He has served as a Consultant for the U.S. Departments of Treasury and Justice; the intelligence division of the New Jersey State Police; the Pennsylvania Crime Commission; the Royal Ulster Constabulary in Belfast, Northern Ireland; and the Anti-Mafia Commission of the Italian Parliament. A Past President of the International Association for the Study of Organized Crime, his research interests include the study of organized crime and terrorism. Among his many publications are *Organized Crime: A Global Perspective* (1986) and the *Handbook of Organized Crime in the United States* (1994).

**Moorhead Kennedy** is Chairman, Moorhead Kennedy Group, New York. A graduate of Princeton University, the Harvard Law School, where he specialized in Islamic Law, and the National War College, his honorary doctorates include the University of Pittsburgh and Middlebury College. He entered the U.S. Foreign Service and worked in Yemen, Greece, Lebanon, Chile, and Iran, specializing in economic and commercial affairs. As a State Department official, he established the Office of Investment Affairs to deal with expropriations and other hostile reactions to U.S. overseas investment. His second assignment took him to Iran, where on November 4, 1979, the U.S. Embassy was taken over by militant students. Held hostage for 444 days, he was awarded the Medal for Valor by the U.S. Department of State and the Gold Medal of the National Institute of Social Sciences. He is the author of *The Ayatollah in the Cathedral: Reflections of a Hostage* (1987) and the coauthor of *Think About Terrorism: The New Warfare* (1988).

**Brian Levin** is Director of the Center on Hate and Extremism and Associate Professor of Criminal Justice, Richard Stockton College, Pomona, New Jersey. A former 3rd-generation New York City police officer, he was the Associate Director for Legal Affairs at the Southern

Poverty Law Center's Klanwatch Project/Militia Task Force in Montgomery, Alabama. While at Stanford University Law School, he was awarded the Block Civil Liberties Award for his research on hate crime. His work on bias crime was used by the House Judiciary Committee in the enactment of the first piece of federal hate crime legislation. As a nationally recognized expert on hate crime, extremism, and domestic terrorism, he has testified before Congress and various state legislatures, as well as authored or coauthored several U.S. Supreme Court *amici curiae* briefs. His training materials on, and criminal profiles of, hate offenders and terrorists are used by state and federal agencies. He is coauthor of *The Limits of Dissent: The Constitutional Status of Armed Civilian Militias* (1996) and *Hate in America* (in press).

**Tomas C. Mijares** is Associate Professor, Department of Criminal Justice, Southwest Texas State University, San Marcos. A retiree from the Detroit Police Department, he has extensive law enforcement training in special weapons and tactics, hostage negotiations, and other antiterrorism techniques. He has served as a counterterrorist consultant to domestic and foreign law enforcement agencies and has published in professional and academic journals on matters relating to terrorism and the tactical use of sensory-enhancing equipment and tactics.

**Wayman C. Mullins** is Chair and Professor, Department of Criminal Justice, Southwest Texas State University, San Marcos. He has served as a consultant on hostage negotiations to domestic and foreign law enforcement agencies and has written extensively on hostage negotiations, as well as international and domestic terrorism. His work on hostage negotiations, cited throughout the literature, includes *Terrorist Organizations in the United States* (1988) and *A Sourcebook on Domestic and International Terrorism* (1997).

**David B. Perkins** is Assistant Professor, Department of Criminal Justice, Southwest Texas State University, San Marcos. He has more than 20 years of experience as a Criminal Defense Attorney, 3 years of service as a Municipal Prosecutor, and for the last 18 years has been a Magistrate in New Braunfels, Texas. His research interests involve constitutional law and Fourteenth Amendment issues as they relate to surveillance technology. His latest publications focus on police liability issues related to tactical units and specialized equipment.

**Brent L. Smith** is Chair and Professor, Department of Justice Sciences, University of Alabama at Birmingham. A respected authority on domestic terrorist groups, he has offered testimony to Congressional subcommittees and governmental fact-finding inquiries on domestic terrorism. His current research interest is focused on terrorism and governmental response. His published works on terrorism have appeared in academic journals, including *Criminology, Justice Quarterly, Terrorism: An International Journal,* and *Studies in Conflict and Terrorism,* and his book is titled *Terrorism in America: Pipe Bombs and Pipe Dreams* (1994).

**Ralph Eugene Stephens** is Professor, College of Criminal Justice, University of South Carolina, Columbia. With many years of experience as a teaching, writing, and consulting futurist, he also has appeared before a variety of agencies and organizations, such as the FBI Academy, the Canadian Police Academy, the American Bar Association, the National Institute of Justice, the U.S. Congress Office of Technology Assessment, and the U.S. Departments of Labor and Energy to discuss the shape of things to come. His futuristic methods and findings have been published in numerous magazines, journals, and books. This Pulitzer Prize nominee is the editor of the *Police Futurist* and a contributing editor of *The Futurist.*